The New Nomadic Age

The New Nomadic Age:
Archaeologies of Forced and Undocumented Migration

Edited by Yannis Hamilakis

SHEFFIELD UK   BRISTOL CT

Published by Equinox Publishing Ltd.

UK: Office 415, The Workstation, 15 Paternoster Row, Sheffield, South Yorkshire S1 2BX
USA: ISD, 70 Enterprise Drive, Bristol, CT 06010
www.equinoxpub.com

Introduction and chapters 1 to 16 first published in Volume 3.2 of the *Journal of Contemporary Archaeology* (minor revisions made).

British Library Cataloguing-in-Publication Data

A catalogue record for this book is available from the British Library.

ISBN-13 978 1 78179 711 2   (paperback)
         978 1 78179 712 9   (ePDF)

Library of Congress Cataloging-in-Publication Data

Names: Hamilakis, Yannis, 1966- editor.
Title: The new nomadic age : archaeologies of forced and undocumented
  migration / edited by Yannis Hamilakis.
Other titles: Journal of contemporary archaeology.
Description: Sheffield, UK ; Bristol, CT : Equinox Publishing Ltd, 2018. |
  "First published in Volume 3.2 of the Journal of Contemporary
  Archaeology." | Includes bibliographical references and index. |
  Identifiers: LCCN 2018007803 (print) | LCCN 2018029170 (ebook) | ISBN
  9781781797129 (ePDF) | ISBN 9781781797112 | ISBN
  9781781797112 q(paperback) | ISBN 9781781797129 q(ePDF)
Subjects: LCSH: Forced migration. | Refugees. | Social archaeology.
Classification: LCC HV640 (ebook) | LCC HV640 .N47 2018 (print) | DDC
  304.8--dc23
LC record available at https://lccn.loc.gov/2018007803

Typeset by ISB Typesetting, Sheffield, UK
Printed and bound by Lightning Source Inc. (La Vergne, TN), Lighting Source UK Ltd. (Milton Keynes), Lightning Source AU Pty. (Scoresby, Victoria)

Contents

List of Figures

List of Tables

The New Nomadic Age: Preface

Yannis Hamilakis

It can be said that we are currently living in a new nomadic age, an age of global movement and migration. This observation is not meant to designate yet another "evolutionary" stage, a move that would elicit objections not only for its arbitrary nature but also because of the associations of "backwardness" the term may evoke: nomads are still seen by many as preceding "civilized", settled life. Rather, the term is used here because of its potency in a volume situated within the field of archaeology: the chapters that follow show how undocumented border crossing and migration in general are material, embodied, and sensorial phenomena first and foremost, structured by and structuring a distinct temporality. As such, they do and must concern archaeology, as the discipline or the craft that engages with materiality and with time.

Official data on global migration show that between 1990 and 2017 more than 100 million people were added to the category that the United Nations defines as "international migrant stock", referring to the segment of a country's permanent population that is foreign-born. In relative terms, and taking into account world population growth overall, this is a modest increase, from 2.9% to 3.4%. Yet such statistics underplay the significance of the phenomenon, not only because they do not accurately report undocumented border crossing, but because they flatten a highly diverse picture. They obscure the dramatic impact of global mobility and migration for certain countries, regions, routes, and entry points, especially from the Global South to the Global North, and they fail to reflect on the extent to which global mobility – and especially undocumented border crossing – is also a media event that has entered public consciousness in the Global North. Furthermore, they conceal the fact that migration is an affective, embodied, and sensorial experience of becoming, a process of place making, self making, and world making, which cannot be understood by statistics alone. And as is discussed in the introduction to this book and in several of the chapters, global mobility is a process that will intensify in the coming decades, due to warfare and permanent low-intensity conflict, structural inequalities and poverty, and climate change.

The choice of title thus signals the great extent to which migration, including undocumented migration, shapes our world, our cities, our material and embodied daily lives, in ways that are rarely acknowledged. It not just people who move, but things too. The contributors to this volume thus turn their attention to the things and artefacts which move with people – the objects that cross borders and accumulate in borderlands and entry points. They also investigate how forced and undocumented migration produce new materialities, resulting in new assemblages, new edifices, and new architectural and material complexes that demand to be taken seriously.

But the mention of nomads and of nomadic age serves an additional role. It evokes nomadism as a mode of becoming, as a way of making, unmaking, and remaking subjectivities, as a state of thinking and practice. The nomadic figure of the migrant today constitutes a novel social and political subject that places into doubt the certainties and fixities of western modernity, including the colonial and national order. It invites societies in the Global North to reflect on their own identity. It shows that what we have called a "migration crisis" is, in fact, a reception crisis in the Global North, a crisis that points to broader and deeper identity crises, and a crisis with the national-cum-colonial genealogical charter of these societies. Finally, the nomadic figure challenges both scholars and various publics to rethink their own modes of imagining, their categories and conceptual tools, and their ethical and political stances. As the Deleuzian and Spinozean philosopher Rosi Braidotti has pointed out time and again (and also emphasized by one of our commentators after the main chapters), our nomadic times require new, nomadic ethics (e.g. Braidotti 2006).

These are immense challenges, of course, and well beyond the remit and scope of any one discipline, let alone of a single volume. But the implicit message of this book is that given the material, sensorial, and temporal dimensions of the phenomenon, contemporary archaeology can make a significant contribution to its understanding. The chapters that follow explore the diverse intellectual, methodological, ethical, and political frameworks for an archaeology of forced and undocumented migration in the present. Matters of historical depth, theory, method, ethics, and politics, as well as heritage value and public representation, are investigated and analysed, adopting a variety of perspectives. The book contains both short reflections and more substantive treatments and case studies from around the world, from the Mexico–USA border to the Mediterranean, the Indian subcontinent, and Australia, and it utilizes a diversity of narrative formats, including several photographic essays.

Most of the chapters in this book were first published in 2016 as part of a forum in the *Journal of Contemporary Archaeology* (3 [2]). As such, they maintain their urgent, debating, and exploratory character, which is essential in a field that is in the process of being constituted. In addition to the printed content, the on line-only chapters from that journal forum are also included here. Furthermore, three new and previously unpublished chapters (Chapters 17 to 19) are included. They serve here as commentaries to the volume but also as reflections on the challenges ahead and the prospects of the diverse archaeologies of undocumented migration. Their authors come from different fields, from contemporary archaeology to the historical archaeology of South America and to socio-cultural anthropology, and their insights point toward the open, cross-disciplinary, and cross-cultural nature of this endeavour.

I am grateful to all the contributors for their dedication to this project and their patience. I am also grateful to Rodney Harrison, who oversaw the publication of the initial journal issue, and supported the endeavour in many ways (including in serving as one of the commentators to this volume), and to the staff at Equinox for working tirelessly to facilitate the production of both the journal issue and this book. Any editor royalties from this book will be donated to migrant solidarity initiatives.

Reference

Braidotti, R. 2006. *Transpositions: On Nomadic Ethics*. Cambridge: Polity.

Introduction

Archaeologies of Forced and Undocumented Migration

Yannis Hamilakis

"Chips!" ordered the boy on the other side of the metal fence, pushing a two-euro coin through one of the holes. He looked about nine or ten. He may have thought I was working for one of the mobile canteens parked nearby, little family enterprises that have mushroomed here recently. But I doubt it. After all, he had clearly seen me getting out of a car with two friends a few minutes before, when he was playing football with two dozen other kids on a sloping cement surface not fit for any sport. It's more likely that this boy, locked up in the Moria migrant detention centre in Lesvos, was teaching me a lesson in dignity: "I am not begging for anything. You are outside, I am inside; I am asking you to cross a road and buy me a packet of chips."

Undocumented Migration: From Humanitarianism and Criminalization to Social Movement

The above opening field notes were scripted in April 2016 (Hamilakis 2016), during my first visit to Lesvos, the Greek border island with a long history of forced migration and displacement (cf. Hirschon 2007). Border crossers had been a constant presence on the island for many years now, but it was during the summer and autumn of 2015 that the island found itself at the epicentre of global attention, a world stage for the border-crossing spectacle (Kirtsoglou and Tsimouris 2016; Papataxiarchis 2016a, 2016b; cf. Andersson 2014): more than 500,000 people crossed from Turkey, migrants and war refugees from Syria, Afghanistan, Iraq, as well as many other Asian and African countries, to an island with 85,000 permanent inhabitants. At the same time, celebrity after celebrity paraded on this stage, enacting the rituals of global humanitarianism (cf. Fassin 2012). Along with them, and often backstage, many anonymous people from the island and from many different parts of the world – some of them working with NGOs, others not – laboured endlessly, day and night, to provide support and express solidarity. In April 2016, the Pope concluded his visit to the island by taking a dozen migrants with him to Rome, a chosen few who were fast-tracked to the Promised Land.

The year 2015 may have been the year that this mass border-crossing spectacle acquired global visibility and attention, yet we tend to forget that in the modern era undocumented migration has been around since formal travel documents and migration control procedures were introduced, roughly after the First World War. Much of that earlier migration, however, happened across borders in Asia and Africa, and was thus, save for a few exceptions, out of sight for most western eyes and away from western media. In recent years, certain border regions have acquired prominence and visibility in the west: particular examples here are the Mexico–USA border and the extended borderlands between the European Union (EU) and African and Asian countries that range from the Canary Islands to the Greek–Turkish border.

The recent war in Syria and the subsequent mass out-migration has not only heightened public attention on the matter; it has also again brought to the surface the distinction between refugees, meaning those who flee war and persecution and are thus forced to migrate in order to find a safe haven, and migrants, who are assumed to have left voluntarily for economic reasons. The former category was enshrined in international law in the post-war years: the rights of the refugee were safeguarded through a series of protocols following the 1951 United Nations Refugee Convention, and guaranteed by then newly founded bodies such as the International Refugee Organization (1947), and eventually the United Nations High Commission on Refugees (1950). However, given the historical contingencies of today – when warfare as a continuous, often low-intensity affair is widespread, when economic necessity and deprivation are closely entangled with military interventions and displacement due to invasion and colonization, and when we are faced with the immediate prospect of mass migrations due to climate change – it is debatable whether the distinction between refugee and migrant is still valid and appropriate. Also, it has been shown (e.g. Scalettaris 2007) that it is not helpful for research (and I would add, activism and advocacy) to use analytical categories (such as that of the refugee) that were devised as a part of policy and regulation procedures. In the contemporary moment, the distinction between migrant and refugee serves primarily as a device which promotes racist and xenophobic agendas: the refugee is deemed in need of protection, whereas the undocumented migrant, a mostly propertyless, willing transgressor, becomes automatically and *de facto* a criminal (Neocleous and Kastrinou 2016, 7). As such, s/he is seen as someone who is justly subjected to detention, punishment, and eventual deportation. Solidarity movements, however, have often used the label of the refugee instrumentally, but successfully, to denote migrants in general, and thus to attract support.

This is not the only problematic term in the contemporary discussion on migration. For example, while in this chapter and in this volume as a whole we employ the rubric of "forced migration" for convenience, as it resonates with many public discourses, it will be clear in the discussion which follows that the term does not accurately portray contemporary migration. It has been shown time and again that human mobility across and within national boundaries is motivated by both voluntary and involuntary factors, external pressures as well as human will and initiative. Necessity and conscious action are intertwined, and the agency and initiative of the migrant are paramount. The term "undocumented" has been adopted by solidarity movements and researchers for use instead of the problematic and inevitably xenophobic terms "illegal" or "irregular", although the word also emanates from the optic and procedural logic of the state: it refers to those people whose mobility has not been registered by state apparatuses, although that mobility is often being documented through other processes, such as ethnographic research and activism, for example. Moreover, once undocumented border crossers are subjected to state migration procedures they are fast transformed from undocumented to over-documented, especially in preparation for detention and deportation; hence migrants' ambivalence towards documents, as discussed below.

In public discourses, the current phenomenon has been called a "migration crisis", although some would prefer to call it a "reception crisis" (Christopoulos 2016) on the part of the rich countries of the Global North. This critique highlights that the number of migrants who attempt to enter the EU, the USA, or other developed countries such as Australia is at present relatively small (or in some cases even tiny) compared to the numbers that much smaller and poorer countries, in the Middle East for example (Lebanon, Jordan), have had to accommodate for many years.

The two dominant tropes that seem to have shaped the responses of this migration/reception crisis are that of victimization-humanitarianism on the one hand, and of criminalization-securitization and militarization on the other. The former points to the real tragedies of forced exile, especially in situations of warfare, and the persecution of the migrant, as well as the many fatalities in the undocumented border-crossing attempts, whether in the Sonoran Desert, the Sahara, or the Mediterranean. But in attempting to raise public awareness and mobilize humanitarian assistance, the advocates of this trope often portray migrants primarily as helpless individuals deprived of agency. Such terms of suffering – which have been co-opted by states and other authority structures (Vaughan-Williams 2015) – "invoke trauma rather than recognizing violence", and inevitably "mobilize compassion rather than justice" (Fassin 2012, 8; cf. Rozakou 2012).

The latter trope, advocated primarily by state apparatuses as well as conservative media, organizations, and groups, see the vast majority of migrants as criminals who not only violate the sovereignty of the state and its boundaries but who also threaten the financial and social stability of the West by "stealing" jobs, exploiting public services, spreading diseases, and polluting the national body. The racism of this argument is self-evident. What is less evident is its groundless financial logic, which obscures the reality that in most cases and in the long run the country that receives migrants benefits demographically, financially, and culturally to an enormous extent, for example by reducing old-age dependency (United Nations 2016).

"Photo, photo!" another boy insisted when he saw my mobile phone. Several more gathered around him and posed, smiling and making the victory sign. I hadn't planned to take photos of people, and I hesitated. But this was different. These children were asking to enter into what the artist and cultural theorist Ariella Azoulay has called "the civil contract of photography" (Azoulay 2008): they were offering themselves up as a photographic subject, while my side of the contract was to disseminate the photo to the outside world. They wished to become visible, to be seen, but to be seen smiling, assertive, courageous. They were claiming their agency, understanding only too well the globalizing power of images. (Figure I.1)

The political philosopher Giorgio Agamben in his 1995 article "We Refugees" elaborates on a discussion which was begun by Hannah Arendt in her 1943 essay of the same title (Arendt 1994 [1943]) about Jewish exiles from Nazi Germany. Agamben's thought, however, is haunted by modern migrants to the EU and to the West in general. Both Arendt and Agamben attempt

Figure I.1. Through the metal fence at the Moria detention camp, Lesvos, Greece (photograph by author, April 2016).

to rescue migrants and refugees from the state of victimhood, and emphasize instead their positive and even revolutionary role, as figures who throw into disarray the status quo of the nation-state. Migrants embody, they argue, a new kind of citizen who demands above all to be accepted as a distinctive human being, rather than as a member of a national body or as someone who exists because s/he is inscribed by birth and descent into a national community. These perspectives accord with comments by Edward Said (talking, however, primarily about intellectuals) on the exilic condition as a privileged state of autonomy, as a space of freedom, despite the pain and angst that comes with exile (Said 1996).

These insights seem to find support in recent empirical, ethnographic, and other research. Undocumented migration is a specific strand of the global migration phenomenon, counting 244 million in 2015, and up by c. 30% since 2000 (United Nations 2016). Further, a recent wave of important ethnographies (e.g. Khosravi 2010; Andersson 2014) as well as other writings on the matter have demonstrated that global undocumented migration today must be seen as a social movement, rather than as a phenomenon of crisis. Of course, as a social movement it has distinctive characteristics and differs from the conventional social movements of the past, but it is still a movement that makes colonialism present, that brings the Global South centre stage. It is also a movement that enacts the conscious decision of millions of primarily poor people, mostly from the Global South, to take their future into their hands – or better, onto their feet. These are people who assert their right to flee, to reject the global allocation of roles determined by the world elites, to refuse simply to become cheap and dispensable labour in the sweatshops of developing countries in order to supply cheap commodities for the Global North. In a world which constantly proclaims, through its media and its elites, its globalized nature, these people want to take such proclamations seriously, to experience the "time-space compression" (Harvey 1989), to enact global connectivity. Hence their efforts to keep trying, to attempt to cross increasingly reinforced and militarized borders, until they succeed. In this process, they accumulate enormous border-crossing knowledge which is shared *en route*, creating global migratory commons (Papadopoulos and Tsianos 2013).

Migrants may hold placards saying "we are human", asking us thus to stare at our ontological mirrors, but it is animal metaphors that are very often used to describe the status of the migrant: from *pollos* (chicken) for Mexican border crossers, to *gosfand* (sheep) for Iranians (Khosravi 2010, 27). This animalization can be taken to designate the border crossers as "sacrificial creatures for the border ritual" (Khosravi 2010, 27). They also produce a distinctive zoo-political discourse whereby border crossers from the Global South entering the "First World" are deliberately designated as closer to animality and are thus detained in zoo-like facilities for further inspection and recording; after all, it was an Austrian Minister who, in 2012, declared that the Greek–Turkish border "is open like a barn door" (Vaughan-Williams 2015, 4). But what about cases where migrants themselves choose to temporarily adopt the persona of the non-human animal, testing the boundaries of the human and of humanly tolerable hardship, in order to achieve their goal? Cases where migrants hide in dog kennels to avoid detection in the Spanish enclave of Ceuta, on the Africa–EU border (Andersson 2014, 169), or in which they crawl into the smallest possible spaces under cars and lorries, where one would have thought that only small animals could fit, in their attempts to cross national borders? And is it not that state of being *en el camino*, *en route* for months, years, for the rest of their lives, a process of continuous becoming (cf. Deleuze 2004), of continuous identity negotiation (cf. Agier 2002), of endless transformation? Of willingly enacting the becoming-animal or the becoming-other human, beyond conventional definitions?

There is always a danger of projecting our own political fantasies onto other people or romanticizing the migrant experience: the almost daily fatalities in the Mediterranean or the Sonoran Desert must operate as our reality check. Migrants may potentially constitute a powerful political force that can threaten the edifice of nationalism in the transit or destination countries but they do not necessarily leave behind conservative, essentialist, and primordialist views themselves, as the history of nationalism in the nineteenth and twentieth centuries demonstrates (cf. Anderson 1991, 1994; Hamilakis 2007). Migrant and refugee camps can foment both radical, emancipatory, and revolutionary as well as conservative and reactionary movements.

Also, while Agamben (1998) and others, especially through the concept of migrants as "bare lives", seem to emphasize citizen rights (Papastergiadis 2006), that category may not be relevant for many migrants today, as some invent their own versions of being as they go along. In that sense, while the protection that national citizenship can offer is, under certain conditions, desirable, this malleable state of "bare life" can be at times preferable, a situation that can allow a flexible and on-going process of becoming. In addition, it is clear that undocumented migration today is a highly diverse phenomenon. The families fleeing war in Syria may have very different aspirations and dreams from the men from sub-Saharan Africa who regularly charge at the metal fences in the Spanish enclaves of Ceuta and Melilla in Morocco (Andersson 2014, 156). Yet despite these warnings and reservations, it is beyond doubt that undocumented migrants today exercise social and political agency, an agency that harbours great transformative potential for themselves and for others, for the places they migrate through and to, as well as the places that they leave behind. As such, rather than charity or humanitarian aid, it is understanding, support, and critical solidarity that we should offer.

It is also abundantly clear that the production of legality and illegality associated with migration is a major global business, a network of apparatuses and processes that do not so much aim at keeping migrants out but rather at regulating their movement, at managing the timing and the duration of crossing, and at determining the conditions of their entry and stay in the host countries (cf. Papadopoulos *et al.* 2008). The neoliberal economic incentives for keeping millions of people (11 million in the USA alone) undocumented and in limbo are obvious. Less explored, however, are the financial gains in expanding and exporting the border, in outsourcing the regulation of migrant movement. Examples here include the 2006–2008 agreements between Spain (and the EU) and a number of West African countries which were tasked with stopping people from embarking on a border crossing (Andersson 2014), and the 2016 agreement between EU and Turkey, in which the latter was asked to block the movement of Syrian and other refugees and migrants into the EU. Equally unexplored is the financial edifice that sustains the growing number of major NGOs in the humanitarian sector, or the media industries that thrive on the spectacularization of migration, on the creation of global stages of border crossing (Andersson 2014, 137–173). And finally, and more pertinently in the context of this book, there is the booming academic and contemporary art "industry" on migration which, with several exceptions, appears to act both opportunistically and exploitatively in commodifying border-crossing stories and images, and even fatalities and tragedies. Andersson (2014, online appendix) notes that in addition to the biopolitics of migration there is also a bio-economics of border crossing. To take his argument further, is there also perhaps a danger of producing an academic "disaster capitalism" (Klein 2007) centred on migration? A cottage industry that gains academic capital by focusing mostly on the "crisis" aspects and on the tragedies of border crossing, disregarding its agentic and transformative power, seemingly of less sensational value?

I went back to Lesvos in late July 2016, and again in January 2017. The situation on the island had changed drastically since April. Local people were complaining that, despite all the publicity and the many celebrities that had paraded on the island, tourism was significantly down, and it is migration that they blamed. Solidarity camps, especially the visible ones close to the city, had been dismantled by the authorities, which insisted that the "management" of the "refugee issue" should be left to the state, the municipal authorities, and the recognized and approved NGOs. But it was clear that not everything was under their control. The dismantled solidarity camps were re-emerging elsewhere, following every eviction. Several migrants were clearly refusing to be part of official structures, and were living clandestinely in squats, abandoned buildings, even in archaeological monuments and sites. Outside the Moria detention centre, the long lines of parked cars spoke of the inflated humanitarian/illegality industry; at the same time, the traces of burning and the holes in the metal fence, despite the façade of high security and militarization, spoke of the regular migrant revolts, some of which had been started by the detained children. On the 19th of September, 2016, a major migrant uprising broke out in Moria, following attempts to stage an organized protest. That day, a 21-year-old Ethiopian woman from the Oromo tribe who was detained there – let's call her Adanach – happened to be away from the camp, as she was ill and at hospital. When she returned, she discovered that all her things, including her papers, had been burnt. But there was something else she was more upset about, as reported at the time:

> *My shoes burned in Moria. Before my shoes burned, I used to run. You know, I used to run when I was in school. I was number one in my school […] Training shoes are very expensive in my country. My family used to buy them for me so I keep them with me always. Even when I left everything behind, I kept the running shoes with me. Then, that day I got sick, I went to hospital from Moria so I didn't wear the sport shoes. I left them in Moria and Moria burned. I cried about my shoes. I told my friend who had stayed in Moria that day: "Why didn't you save my shoes?"*
>
> (quoted by *Infomile* 2016)

According to news reports, the uprising that led to the fire started when someone shouted "Freedom!"

Why an Archaeology of Contemporary, Undocumented Migration?

One way or another, undocumented migration is a key matter of concern for societies today. And while the topic is at the centre of attention and study in a wide range of scholarly fields, the materiality of the phenomenon and its sensorial and mnemonic dimensions are barely understood and analysed. Anthropological archaeologists and other material culture specialists, including specialists on museum and commemorative practices, can contribute immensely to a new understanding of the phenomenon. Forced and undocumented migration is primarily a material and sensorial experience (cf. Dudley 2011; Andersson 2014, 153–154). It is about mobility, movement through space; it is a kinaesthetic experience through various landscapes and seascapes. Archaeologists have been studying landscapes and seascapes for many years and have analysed how interaction with human and anthropogenic space shapes human experience. In the study of migration, they have often shown how landscape can become a crucial material agent in the process of border crossing. De León (2015), for example, has shown how, as part of the "The Prevention through Deterrence" policy on the Mexico–USA border, migrants were pushed away from the city entry points and towards the unforgiving desert, thus resulting in a very high mortality rate. The desert was drafted as key ally in that policy, and the deaths were naturalized. But what makes De León's contribution both insightful and gripping, and highly affective, is his archaeological sensibility, his sensorial attention to the textures of the border-crossing experience and its entanglement with the landscape. Such mobilization of the landscape in the service of border control and migrant movement regulation is not, of course, unique to the Mexico–USA border. The EU authorities and its constituent nation-states have followed a similar policy, especially with regard to their southern (African) and southeastern (Asian) borders; the fencing off and militarization of the land crossings and narrow sea passages along the Spanish–Moroccan and Greek–Turkish borders have forced migrants to take the long and dangerous central Mediterranean route, resulting in many thousands of people drowning. The year 2016 was the deadliest year in migrant fatalities in the Mediterranean, while border crossings were down by roughly two thirds, compared to 2015.[1]

The archaeology of undocumented migration thus involves understanding the experiential encounter of moving bodies through diverse landscapes, and the accumulation of bodily knowledge through that movement. It also entails an analysis of the atmospheric and material components implicated in the process: space, natural and anthropogenic features; the weather; the appropriate clothing and gear for the journey; vehicles and boats; routes and paths, landmarks, and orientation signs; even the shrines and apotropaic traces left on the way (Soto 2016). It is also an archaeology which attempts to understand how these new engagements with spaces and landscapes relate to the long-term human interaction with these features, how perennial paths and routes are shared, and how and whether new knowledges rely on the existing reservoir of human movement through space. Understanding the materiality and sensoriality of mobility is thus central in what some authors have called the "viapolitical" conception of migration (Walters 2015), or what I would like to call, the sensorial economy of global flows.

During this movement, and in the migrants' border-crossing attempts, it is the lack of specific pieces of paper – of the appropriate passports and visas – in association with the materialized, enforced, and securitized border that results in an alien status: migrants are the *undocumented*, the *sans papiers* or the *sin papeles,* defined thus negatively by the lack of such documentation. It is a material object – a document, a piece of paper – which stands between the migrant and the country of destination (Cabot 2012). But beyond any single material object, it is the heterogeneous assemblage of material and immaterial entities which coheres to enact legality and illegality, and the performance and spectacle of border crossing (Deleuze 2004; Hamilakis and Jones 2017): border crossers are produced by the institutionalization, materialization, and enforcement of the border, which co-functions with the presence or absence of documents, human social actors such as guards, and a legal and an institutional apparatus. This is the sensorial assemblage of border crossing and migration (Hamilakis 2017).

Bodily and sensorial traits are also paramount in the construction of hierarchies of acceptability: primarily skin colour and complexion, but also foreign-sounding speech or alien attire. Odour and olfactory experience have long been a sensorial trope of distancing, othering, and racializing (Hamilakis 2013), and migrants are no exception. Taste and the multi-sensorial experience of eating work both negatively as separation and alienation as well as positively as

---

1. Deaths are tracked by the International Organization for Migration's Missing Migrants Project (http://missingmigrants.iom.int/).

affirmative biopolitics (Esposito 2008), as the production of positive home memories (Sutton 2001) and the creation of sensorial and affective, familiar worlds and atmospheres on the part of the migrants (Dudley 2011; Hamilakis 2013; see also below). In the Lesvos camps I visited, migrants would often reject the ready-made food provided by catering companies and find ways to cook their own food, using whatever fuel they could find in and around the camp.

The materiality of undocumented migration can also be encountered in the remnants that are left behind in the border-crossing attempts: material artefacts such as boats and dinghies, life vests, and discarded rucksacks, which are today scattered all over in regions such as the Mediterranean or the Arizona desert. In some cases, these artefacts become the subject of art projects or commemorative and museum exhibitions, and in others the raw materials for inventive initiatives, as they are transformed into functional biographical objects, carrying with them the affective memory of the migration experience (Figure I.2). Various makeshift camps *en route* leave often inconspicuous but highly significant traces, enabling a typology of transitory migration sites (De León 2015), and a detailed and almost forensic recording of their texture and materiality. Some of these camps, as we saw especially in Europe recently, can become substantial and highly organized structures despite their makeshift character, as has been happening in the so-called "Jungle", in Calais, or Idomeni, in northern Greece. Finally, there are the morbid material remnants of interrupted lives, be they shoes and clothing of those who did not make the crossing, unidentified bodies in the desert, or the anonymous and austere graves on a border island. These are burials that are often conducted without due process, be it in terms of funerary rites and religious customs, or in terms of documentation that can enable future identification of interred individuals, in the case of anonymous graves (Kovras and Robins 2016).

Even from the point of view of states and other apparatuses, however, it is the materialization of legality/illegality and of prevention that has become most prominent. Borders have recently acquired a more visible and tactile presence than ever before (cf. McGuire 2013): walls and fences are being erected along borderlines, and patrols are in operation on land and at sea, perhaps a futile material response to the sense of losing national sovereignty (Brown 2010). At the same time, the border effect has become more invisible and diffuse and can be encountered everywhere, and not just in borderlands themselves. These walls and borders are not there to protect against external enemies and military invasions, but seemingly to keep undocumented migrants out, to make the crossing more dangerous, and to perform the spectacle of securitization. Biometric controls have been introduced, detention centres – such as the one in Moria, Lesvos, discussed above – have been constructed, especially along borderlines, whereas recently many other "reception" facilities have sprung up in various countries, particularly those that are designated unofficially as buffer zones, such Greece and Turkey for the European Union. Islands seem to be particularly important in this process, leading some authors to speak of an "enforcement archipelago" (Mountz 2011), and alluding perhaps to their long history in the public imagination as places of detention, exile, but also sanitization. A closer look at the micro-scale, however, will show that such facilities are highly diverse, from the standard, UN-patterned ones to the impromptu temporary shelters constructed by migrants: in Lesvos, for example, in addition to the highly militarized detention centre at Moria, there is the relatively

Figure I.2. Life vests discarded by border crossers (top) and subsequently transformed into bags (bottom) by migrants at the PIKPA solidarity camp, Lesvos, Greece (photograph by author, April 2016).

open centre of Kara Tepe which is run by the municipality and is destined primarily for families, and the PIKPA solidarity structure which is run collectively by migrants and members of a small solidarity group and receives vulnerable people. Other camps include, for example, the various squats organized by "No Border Kitchen", an anarchist solidarity initiative, constantly under attack by the authorities, and the completely informal and temporary migrant shelters amongst ancient and medieval ruins. How does the materiality and spatial grid of all these structures shape migrant experience?

The archaeology of undocumented migration is not only about border crossing, though. The homes and material worlds that are left behind; the empty rooms and houses that are often kept as shrines, memorials to the departed, or even cenotaphs (cf. De León 2015, 276; Pistrick and Bachmeier, this volume); the houses and things that are left behind but are now occupied and used by others (Navaro-Yasin 2009); the material worlds and landscapes produced through the remittances migrants have sent back (e.g. Dalakoglou 2010; Lopez 2015; Byrne 2016): all can form worthwhile topics for further reflection and study. Also, how does migrant materiality transform the countries traversed, and the cities and countries of permanent or transitory relocation? How do undocumented migrants maintain a sensorial and affective connection with a homeland, and how do their own things and objects, the ones they have brought with them and the ones they have produced in their new home, shape their mnemonic world? Finally, do archaeology and material heritage discourses and practices in these transit and destination countries relate in any way to the migrant experience, and if so, in what way? How do museums react to the contemporary undocumented migration? Can the colonialist and nationalist heritage of modernist archaeology be countered by foregrounding migrant experience and mobility, past and present?

In studying the sensorial assemblage of migration, the voices of the migrants themselves – oral ethnographic encounters, histories, and narratives – are crucial, but undocumented migration cannot always be expressed in words. It can, however, be evoked in things, in sensorial and affective experiences and gestures, in non-linguistic utterances. This may be due to linguistic barriers, or to the intensity or the traumatic nature of the experience, which may not lend itself to the production of stories, narratives, or oral testimonies. In other cases, migrants may be reluctant to narrate their experiences because they are wary of their misuse and because they would rather stay under the radar, to be able to continue their transformative journey. Or they may resist what they see as the instrumentalization and the symbolic or literal commodification of their narrated lives by various social actors, including academics. Finally, they may be wary and tired of the constant demand to go over past events and circumstances for the benefit of various audiences, when they would rather express themselves in non-verbal ways, through art for example, or talk about their future plans and aspirations. In all these cases, it is things – material traces and artefacts, materiality and sensoriality – that are the primary means of understanding the phenomenon.

Migration thus is not just a matter of moving bodies but of a complex and heterogeneous, sensorial/material, multi-temporal assemblage. In understanding such an assemblage, an archaeological sensibility is paramount. And yet, there are still very few attempts by archaeologists and material culture specialists (e.g. Basu and Coleman 2008; Dalakoglou 2010) to engage with the phenomenon in a politically and ethically sensitive matter. The few exceptions include the pioneering and highly important Undocumented Migration Project on the Mexico–USA border (De León 2015), a couple of other studies in the same context (McGuire 2013; Soto 2016), the work of Dudley (2011) in refugee camps along the Tai-Burma border, or, for an earlier, historical example, the Archaeology Network of the Chinese Railroad Workers in North America Project (Voss 2015). The chapters that follow this introduction thus hope to explore the diverse intellectual, methodological, ethical, and political frameworks for an archaeology of forced and undocumented migration in the present, through both reflective ideas pieces and case studies. We invited short contributions from archaeologists, anthropologists, other specialists, artists, and activists, including items by migrants themselves, in different media, posing the following questions:

- How can we record, explore, and understand the materiality of the experience of forced and undocumented migration today, in its diverse forms?
- How can we communicate such work to scholars and to various publics?
- What kind of theoretical and methodological stances can we deploy, avoiding the instrumentalization of the phenomenon for purely academic purposes, and the aestheticization of an often painful and tragic experience?

The contributions cover a very wide geographical range, from Mexico and the USA to Finland, the Middle East, India–Pakistan, and Australia. Several deal with the contemporary situation as it is unfolding, especially in Europe's southern borders and on the Mexico–USA border, while others ask us to reflect on the historical dimensions of migration, and the lessons we can learn from major displacement episodes, such as that following the partition of the Indian subcontinent in 1947 or the war in Palestine in 1948. Finally, several contributions reflect on the museum and heritage presentation of the contemporary migrant experience, and critique the reluctance of heritage bodies and museums to engage with the political dimensions of the phenomenon and to connect it with earlier, celebrated and commemorated migration episodes.

Who Needs Such an Archaeology, What is its Nature, and How Can It be Conducted?

Archaeology of undocumented migration for whom? Who needs such an archaeology? One of the crucial roles of the archaeology of contemporary migration is to valorize the material remnants of mobility and border-crossing experience, especially when such remnants are seen as "trash" – another seemingly "environmentally sensitive" way to express xenophobic attitudes. In doing so, we complicate the notion of "trash", a highly situated, border concept itself: we decentre and undermine the divide between human and thing (Squire 2014), and we valorize migrants and border crossers as producers of valued materiality, worthy of attention, collection, and study. But it is worth reflecting for a moment on the fact that while archaeology valorizes such material traces, out of which it produces an "archaeological record" and an archive, such valorization is not necessarily shared by the migrants themselves. Indeed, as some contributions that follow show (see in particular Tyrikos-Ergas), migrants may want to forget the remnants of the border-crossing experience in particular; they would rather prefer not to recall and certainly not to memorialize traces such as life vests, or fragments of inflatable boats. More pertinently, our desire for documentation – a desire, it must be said, which we share with border authorities and states – seems to be at odds with the desires, aspirations, and practices of some migrants, such as those from West and North Africa attempting to cross into the EU through Spain and Italy. Many of them would rather burn any travelling documents to avoid identification with a specific country, thus lessening the risk of deportation to that country. The name "*haragas*" referred initially to those who burn their documents, but it is now an appellation which has come to denote metaphorically all those who would wish to "burn" their past lives and reinvent themselves in and through their journey (Andersson 2014; Alexander 2016). Some migrants, according to several media reports (e.g. *BBC News* 2004; Allen 2009), have even burnt their fingertips to evade biometric identification. To give another example, migrants on the Mexico–USA border take every effort to cover their tracks in order to avoid detection and arrest (for example, by wearing shoes with carpeted soles – De León 2015, 160–161), the tracks on the ground that a conventional archaeology would value in recording paths and itineraries. An archaeology that prioritizes preservation and documentation in the abstract is not an archaeology that would seem to work for the benefit of migrants, in these cases at least. In fact, it could potentially work against them: where do the surveillance of states and border agencies meet the surveying and documentation principles and practices of modernist archaeology?

It becomes evident that an archaeology of undocumented migration which begins from a position of active (but still critical) solidarity towards the border crossers and migrants cannot adopt the objectifying principles and the panopticism of modernist archaeology. It cannot import wholesale its documentation and recording apparatus. In other words, what is needed is a transformed, politically aware archaeology, and one which avoids the risk of becoming the heritage branch of the border control agencies and of the security apparatus.

The archaeologies of undocumented migration are currently in the making, and their constitution will be a collective endeavour. It is my suggestion, however, that they can operate at multiple levels:

(1) *Sensorial-material*: Studying up and studying down, directing sensorial attention to the securitization of human mobility and the militarization of border controls and thus turning the cameras towards the surveillance apparatus, and directing sensorial attention to the material remnants of the border crossing and migrant experience, including the vastly proliferating digital traces. We can thus foreground aspects of such experience that normally go unnoticed by scholars, by media, and by the border spectacle with its reliance primarily on vision: the textures, the smells, and the sounds, especially of the rarely exposed backstage situations (cf. Andersson 2014, 153–154).

(2) *Epistemic*: Understanding contemporary migrant experience through the study of natural and anthropogenic materiality, and helping us rethink archaeological categories and concepts through this experience. This is an *archaeology of care* which valorizes and activates small and seemingly insignificant material things, as well as the more imposing material edifices. It is *archaeology as witnessing*, which objectifies neither the migrants nor the migrant material traces but foregrounds both as subjects and agents in the world.

(3) *Affective*: Foregrounding the material traces and things that will enable us to be touched, to be affectively moved and empowered by the desire of migrants to become authors of their own destiny and by some of the associated tragic side-effects of such a drive for liberation.

(4) *Archival*: Producing a counter-archive, a partial and situated record of contemporary undocumented migration, and preserving and curating some of its remnants as material and affective agents of an important social process; and exploring the entanglement of materiality with temporality as well as the entanglement of the temporality of contemporary migration with other temporalities, such as that of long-term human mobility, of the never-ending era of colonialism, and of other episodes of forced migration in the recent past. Some of the key questions here should be: How do the material memories of previous forced migration episodes shape contemporary reactions? What is the temporality of the border crossing, of the migrant and refugee camp? How is migrant time, primarily a time of waiting, enacted and performed? How does it differ from other conceptions of time?

Shipwrecked boats, shoes, and rucksacks left in the desert or in beaches, small personal items, can attract public attention and generate concern and support. But they can also often invite a twenty-first-century ruin lust, and can become the subjects of a photographic "refugee porn" phenomenon. A reflexive archaeology of undocumented migration should resist such urges, and at the same time reflect on and debate the public fascination with such images. Nevertheless, such archaeology encounters a transitory and unstable materiality, one that is being transformed rapidly, inviting thus some sort of recording, of counter-counting. While the encounter with the border-crossing experience gives the impression of material abundance, these material traces disappear very fast, either because they are cleared off beaches, deserts, and other landscapes, since they are seen as "environmental pollution", or because they are transformed and recycled into other objects, including art installation projects. At the same time, the migratory landscapes are replete with traces of *accelerated ruination*: makeshift structures such as temporary camps are built, used, and abandoned over the space of a few months or even weeks (Figure I.3).

The archaeology of contemporary undocumented migration is also faced with the phenomenon of what can be called *compressed materiality*. The most characteristic example of this is the mobile phone, perhaps more valuable to the migrant than any other object. This is a hyper-object (Morton 2013) that compresses time and space, and merges communication, sociability, entertainment, storage, and archival functions (including the storage of digital photos of loved ones and of favourite places and home locales), emotion, and affect. This is a key tool in the migrants' urge to establish connection, a multi-temporal object that harbours so many promises for the future. In recent years, one of the most pertinent and telling sights of the border-crossing experience has been the image of temporary posts established in detention and solidary centres and equipped with multi-plug devices, used to charge dozens of migrant phones simultaneously.

An archaeology of contemporary undocumented migration should be a reflexive, multi-sited and multi-temporal archaeological ethnography (cf. Hamilakis 2011) which produces a shared space of encounters, a multi-temporal contact zone. It centres around materiality and temporality and fetishizes neither the thing and the object, nor the oral account and

Figure I.3. Accelerated ruination: tent platforms at the "Better Days for Moria" solidarity camp, outside the detention centre of Moria, Lesvos (photograph by author, April 2016).

the personal narrative. Both are deemed important, as are the other sites and arenas. Ideally, it should be a collaborative effort not only among scholars from different disciplines and social and cultural backgrounds but also between researchers and migrants of diverse backgrounds. This is an improvised research and activist endeavour that is constantly under suspension, ready to abandon any research practices that may harm the migrants, and give up archaeological work when a more pressing activist and solidarity task is required. It is archaeology-cum-activism for both the migrants themselves – who will have their own take on the materiality of migration – and for the people of the transit and destination countries, themselves potentially migrants or affected directly by the migration experience.

Finally, archaeologists and critical heritage specialists should encourage museums to accession remnants of contemporary migration, something that most of them seem to be reluctant to do. But there is an inherent danger of museifying the border-crossing and migrant experience, and an archaeology of contemporary migration is particularly susceptible to it. This is a danger of arresting and fixing the social life of a material relic of that experience. But such objects, like the migrants themselves, were meant to circulate and move, and as we saw, they get recycled and transformed into various biographical artefacts. There is also a danger of divorcing these material traces from the migrants themselves and from the other material and immaterial components of the migration assemblage; of entrapping them into the confines of an institutional framework and logic, such as a conventional museum; and of fixing them into a specific temporal moment. This temporal fixation is inevitably a futile attempt, as material, involuntary, biographical, and social memories of other migrations will be sensorially triggered and evoked (cf. Byrne, this volume). Attempts to counter such museification are, of course, already under way, and one recent proposal which addresses specifically Mediterranean migration speaks of a *liquid museum* (or *museaum*): a museum-ship which will be sailing from port to port in the Mediterranean, collecting as well as dispersing objects, stories, and narratives (Baravalle and Biscottini 2014), and incorporating the material memories of the sea. The world of museums needs to engage with contemporary undocumented migration, and to use this opportunity to imagine alternative museum horizons, including open, temporary anti-museums, or mobile, transitory or, as just mentioned, liquid museums.

Endnote

The archaeologies of forced and undocumented migration are long overdue. In the current climate of increasing xenophobia in the West, they are also politically and ethically essential. They are not just about migrants: they concern everyone, as the migration phenomenon reshapes the contemporary world overall. They merge research and activism and can become an essential component of the transdisciplinary and transcultural study of the phenomenon. At the same time, both archaeology and the museum world should welcome the challenge (to their foundational logic, their epistemologies, their politics) that an archaeology of contemporary undocumented migration can foment, the rethinking of key concepts and ideas it can engender, and the political work that it can facilitate.

References

Agamben, G. 1995. "We Refugees." *Symposium* 49 (2): 114–119. https://doi.org/10.1080/00397709.1995.10733798

Agamben, G. 1998. *Homo Sacer: Sovereign Power and Bare Life*. Stanford, CA: Stanford University Press.

Agier, M. 2002. "Between War and City: Towards an Urban Anthropology of Refugee Camps." *Ethnography* 3 (3): 317–341. https://doi.org/10.1177/146613802401092779

Alexander, I. 2016. "The Crossing." *Global Post Investigations*. Available online: https://gpinvestigations.pri.org/the-crossing-eb527318eb76#.b8l3agk96

Allen, P. 2009. "Calais Migrants Mutilate Fingertips to Hide True Identity." *Mail Online*, 22 July. Available online: http://www.dailymail.co.uk/news/article-1201126/Calais-migrants-mutilate-fingertips-hide-true-identity.html

Anderson, B. 1991. *Imagined Communities*. London: Verso.

_____. 1994. "Exodus." *Critical Inquiry* 20 (2): 314–327. https://doi.org/10.1086/448713

Andersson, R. 2014. *Illegality, Inc.: Clandestine Migration and the Business of Bordering Europe*. Berkeley: University of California Press.

Arendt, H. 1994 [1943]. "We Refugees." In *Altogether Elsewhere: Writers on Exile*, edited by M. Robinson, 110–119. London: Faber and Faber.

Azoulay, A. 2008. *The Civil Contract of Photography*. London: Verso.

Baravalle, C. and G. Biscottini. 2014. "The Liquid Museaum: Culture Hybridisation on Mediterranean

Shores." In *The Ruined Archive*, edited by I . Chambers, G. Grenchi, and M. Nash, 307–330. Milan: Mela Books.

Basu, K. and S. Coleman. 2008. "Introduction: Migrant Worlds, Material Cultures." *Mobilities* 3 (3): 313–330. https://doi.org/10.1080/17450100802376753

BBC News. 2004. "Sweden Refugees Mutilate Fingers." 2 April. Available online: http://news.bbc.co.uk/1/hi/world/europe/3593895.stm

Brown, W. 2010. *Walled States, Waning Sovereignty*. New York: Zone Books.

Byrne, D. 2016. "The Need for a Transnational Approach to the Material Heritage of Migration: The China-Australia Corridor." *Journal of Social Archaeology* 16 (3): 261–285. https://doi.org/10.1177/1469605316673005

Cabot, H. 2012. "The Governance of Things: Documenting Limbo in the Greek Asylum Procedures." *Political and Legal Anthropology Review* 35 (1): 11–29. https://doi.org/10.1111/j.1555-2934.2012.01177.x

Christopoulos, D. 2016. "Europe's Solidarity Crisis: A Perspective from Greece. Interview with G. Souvlis" *Roar*, 8 June. Available online: https://roarmag.org/essays/europe-refugee-solidarity-crisis-greece/

Dalakoglou, D. 2010. "Migrating-Remitting-'Building'-Dwelling: House-Making as 'Proxy' Presence in Postsocialist Albania." *Journal of the Royal Anthropological Institute* 16 (4): 761–777. https://doi.org/10.1111/j.1467-9655.2010.01652.x

De León, J. 2015. *The Land of Open Graves: Living and Dying on the Migrant Trail*. Berkeley: University of California Press.

Deleuze, G. 2004. *A Thousand Plateaus: Capitalism and Schizophrenia*. Translated by B. Massumi. London: Continuum.

Dudley, S. 2011. "Feeling at Home: Producing and Consuming Things in Karenni Refugee Camps on the Thai-Burma Border." *Population, Space and Place* 17: 742–755. https://doi.org/10.1002/psp.639

Esposito, R. 2008. *Bios: Biopolitics and Philosophy*. Minneapolis: University of Minnesota Press.

Fassin, D. 2012. *Humanitarian Reason: A Moral History of the Present*. Translated by R. Gomme. Berkeley: University of California Press.

Hamilakis, Y. 2007. *The Nation and its Ruins: Antiquity, Archaeology, and National Imagination in Greece*. Oxford: Oxford University Press.

_____. 2011. "Archaeological Ethnography: A Multitemporal Meeting Ground for Archaeology and Anthropology." *Annual Review of Anthropology* 40: 399–414. https://doi.org/10.1146/annurev-anthro-081309-145732

_____. 2013. *Archaeology and the Senses: Human Experience, Memory, and Affect*. Cambridge: Cambridge University Press.

_____. 2016. "The EU's Future Ruins: Moria Refugee Camp in Lesbos." *The Nation*, 15 April. Available online: https://www.thenation.com/article/the-eus-future-ruins-moria-refugee-camp-in-lesbos/

_____. 2017 "Sensorial Assemblages: Affect, Memory, and Temporality in Assemblage Thinking." *Cambridge Archaeological Journal* 27 (1): 169–182. https://doi.org/10.1017/S0959774316000676

_____. and A. M. Jones. 2017. "Archaeology and Assemblage." *Cambridge Archaeological Journal* 27 (1): 77–84. https://doi.org/10.1017/S0959774316000688

Harvey, D. 1989. *The Condition of Postmodernity*. Oxford: Blackwell.

Hirschon, R. 2007. "Geography, Culture and the Refugee Experience: The Paradox of Lesvos." In *Mytilene and Ayvalik: A Bilateral Historical Relationship in the North-Eastern Aegean*, edited by

P. M. Kitromilides and P. D. Michailaris, 171–184. Athens: Institute of Neohellenic Research, National Research Foundation.

Infomile. 2016. "My Shoes Burned in Moria. Before My Shoes Burned I Used to Run." 15 October. Available online: http://infomobile.w2eu.net/2016/10/15/my-shoes-burned-in-moria-before-my-shoes-burned-i-used-to-run/#more-3907

Khosravi, S. 2010. *'Illegal' Traveller: An Auto-ethnography of Borders*. Basingstoke, UK: Palgrave Macmillan. https://doi.org/10.1057/9780230281325

Kirtsoglou, E. and G. Tsimouris 2016. "'Il était un petit navire': The Refugee Crisis, Neo-Orientalism, and the Production of Radical Alterity." *Journal of Modern Greek Studies*. Occasional Paper 9.

Klein, N. 2007. *The Shock Doctrine: The Rise of Disaster Capitalism*. London: Penguin.

Kovras, I. and S. Robins. 2016. "Managing Missing Migrants and Unidentified Bodies at the EU's Mediterranean Border." *Political Geography* 55: 40–49. https://doi.org/10.1016/j.polgeo.2016.05.003

Lopez, S. L. 2015. *The Remittance Landscape: Spaces of Migration in Rural Mexico and Urban USA*. Chicago: University of Chicago Press.

McGuire, R. 2013. "Steel Walls and Picket Fences: Re-Materialising the US-Mexican Border in Ambos Nogales." *American Anthropologist* 115 (3): 446–480. https://doi.org/10.1111/aman.12029

Morton, T. 2013. *Philosophy and Ecology after the End of the World*. Minneapolis: University of Minnesota Press.

Mountz, A. 2011. "The Enforcement Archipelago: Detention, Haunting, and Asylum on Islands." *Political Geography* 30 (3): 118–128. https://doi.org/10.1016/j.polgeo.2011.01.005

Navaro-Yasin, Y. 2009. "Affective Spaces, Melancholic Objects: Ruination and the Production of Anthropological Knowledge." *Journal of the Royal Anthropological Institute* 15 (1): 1–18. https://doi.org/10.1111/j.1467-9655.2008.01527.x

Neocleous, M. and M. Kastrinou. 2016. "The EU Hotspot: Police War Against the Migrant." *Radical Philosophy* 200: 3–9.

Papadopoulos, D. and V. S. Tsianos. 2013. "After Citizenship: Autonomy of Migration, Organisational Ontology and Mobile Commons." *Citizenship Studies* 17 (2): 178–196. https://doi.org/10.1080/13621025.2013.780736

_____., M. Stephenson and V. Tsianos. 2008. *Escape Routes: Control and Subversion in the Twenty First Century*. London: Verso.

Papastergiadis, N. 2006. "The Invasion Complex: The Abject Other and Spaces of Violence." *Geografiska Annaler, Series B: Human Geography* 88 (4): 429–442. https://doi.org/10.1111/j.0435-3684.2006.00231.x

Papataxiarchis, E. 2016a. "Being 'There': On the Frontline of the 'European Refugee Crisis', Part 1." *Anthropology Today* 32 (2): 5–9. https://doi.org/10.1111/1467-8322.12237

_____. 2016b. "Being 'There': On the Frontline of the 'European Refugee Crisis', Part 2." *Anthropology Today* 32 (3): 3–7. https://doi.org/10.1111/1467-8322.12252

Rozakou, K. 2012. "The Biopolitics of Hospitality in Greece: Humanitarianism and the Management of Refugees." *American Ethnologist* 39 (3): 562–577. https://doi.org/10.1111/j.1548-1425.2012.01381.x

Said, E. 1996. *Representations of the Intellectual*. London: Viking.

Scalettaris, G. 2007. "Refugee Studies and the International Refugee Regime: A Reflection on a Desirable Separation." *Refugee Survey Quarterly* 26 (3): 36–50. https://doi.org/10.1093/rsq/hdi0241

Soto, G. 2016. "Migrant *Memento Mori* and the Geography of Risk." *Journal of Social Archaeology* 16 (3): 335–358. https://doi.org/10.1177/1469605316673171

Squire, N. 2014. "Desert 'Trash': Posthumanism, Border Struggles, and Humanitarian Politics." *Political Geography* 39: 11–21. https://doi.org/10.1016/j.polgeo.2013.12.003

Sutton, D. 2001. *Remembrance of Repasts: An Anthropology of Food and Memory*. Oxford: Berg.

United Nations. 2016. *International Migration Report 2015*. New York: United Nations.

Vaughan-Williams, N. 2015. "'We are not Animals!' Humanitarian Border Security and Zoopolitical Spaces in Europe." *Political Geography* 45: 1–10. https://doi.org/10.1016/j.polgeo.2014.09.009

Voss, B., ed. 2015 *The Archaeology of Chinese Railroad Workers in North America*. Thematic issue of *Historical Archaeology* 49 (1).

Walters, W. 2015. "Migration, Vehicles, and Politics: Three Theses on Migration." *European Journal of Social Theory* 18 (4): 469–488. https://doi.org/10.1177/1368431014554859

Acknowledgments

I am grateful to the journal editor, to two referees, and to Valia Kravva for their comments and suggestions on an earlier draft. Thanks are also due to the contributors to this volume for their bold and insightful contributions. To the people of Lesvos, locals and migrants, solidarians and border crossers, thank you for your affection and courage.

Yannis Hamilakis is Joukowsky Family Professor of Archaeology and Professor of Modern Greek Studies at Brown University. Address for correspondence: Joukowsky Institute for Archaeology & the Ancient World, Brown University, Box 1837, 60 George Street, Providence, RI 02912, USA. Email: yannis_hamilakis@brown.edu

Chapter 1

The 1947 Partition of India and Pakistan: Migration, Material Landscapes, and the Making of Nations

Erin P. Riggs and Zahida Rehman Jat

> The world of political possibilities in India seems to be simplifying into the frightening choice before most of the modern world's political communities: to try to craft imperfect democratic rules by which increasingly mixed groups of people can carry on together an unheroic everyday existence, or the illusion of a permanent and homogeneous, unmixed, single nation, a single collective self without any trace of a defiling otherness.
>
> —Sudipta Kaviraj (1994, 129)

The 1947 Partition: Mass Displacement and Emergent Nationhood

Archaeologists of forced migration need to take account of along with their considerations of the hardships of migration the ideas that drive displacement, statelessness, and migrant exclusion. The nation-state concept, through which a sense of cultural boundedness and timelessness legitimizes territorial sovereignty (Anderson 1983; McGuire 1992; Meskell 1998; Hamilakis 2007), is one such idea, and it is important to consider how it is sustained within different contexts and how it works to affix essentialist understandings of national belonging to different places. Hamilakis sees antiquities as playing a major role within this process, in the making of "national imagination" into "experiential truths" (Hamilakis 2007, 292–293). The 1947 Partition of India and Pakistan offers an interesting case study through which to consider, not only the role of antiquities, but also that of peoples' movement through historic landscapes in establishing such "experiential truths". Partition refugees materialized essentialist conceptions of nation by relocating their bodies, but, through their movement, they were simultaneously confronted with material landscapes shaped by the hybridity of both ancient and recent pasts.

Partition was the largest mass displacement in human history (Aiyar 1995; Brass 2003, 75), involving between 10 and 17.9 million people (Bharadwaj *et al.* 2008). The regions that became India and Pakistan were by no means culturally homogenous, but the mass migrations of Partition worked to make them more so – reshaping distributions of people to better suit understandings of whom the nation included and whom it did not.

The border area between India and Pakistan has been ethnically and religiously diverse for centuries, and Islamic and Hindu communities have cohabited for over 1000 years (Singh 2015, Chapter 5). Buddhism and Jainism also had long histories in the region (Von Glasenapp 1999, 49–55; Deol 2000; Grewal 2004, 6–10) as did Sikhism, which originated in the 1400s in what is now Pakistan (Deol 2000; Grewal 2004). Partition worked to separate these communities. As Muslim populations migrated towards Pakistan, a new Islamic homeland, Hindu and Sikh populations migrated in the other direction towards India.

The uncertainty, fear, and violence involved in this population exchange resulted in the deaths of millions. An estimated 3.4 million migrants went "missing" – nearly 19% of the estimated total migrant population (Bharadwaj *et al.* 2008, 40). With these displacements, complex and nuanced understandings of community and identity were abstracted. No longer was identity distributed across many social spheres (language, location, kinship, religious sect, occupation, and caste), arranged, as Kaviraj has described, "in the way colours are arranged in a spectrum, one shading off into another, without revealing closed systems with clear, demarcatable boundaries" (Kaviraj 1994, 117). National territories created clear boundaries between people, largely along religious lines. Arguably, Partition meant that even the ~540,000 non-Muslims who remained in what is now Pakistan (excluding modern Bangladesh) and the 35.4 million Muslims who remained in India (Malik 1969, 151; D'Costa 2011, 100 – both drawing from 1951 censuses) were, in a sense, displaced without moving. Perceptions of these non-migrants' historical and political legitimacy within the places they had inhabited for generations became precarious.

Built landscapes played a complex role within both responding to the refugee crisis and materializing the nations created through Partition. They served simultaneously as shelter for in-migrants and as persistent material reminders of out-migrants and their long histories within the regions they had left behind. In both India and Pakistan, many such buildings remain under the control of the state, have contested ownership, and/or are the subject of yet-evolving policies. In the following, we discuss the role of built landscapes and historical interpretation within refugee resettlement experiences. This discussion illustrates how out-migrant-associated spaces were (and are) a part of negotiations of who and what constituted both nations.

Why Preserve the Material Past of "Others"?

During times of conflict and displacement such as Partition, history becomes hyper-important in the negotiation of belonging. Bryant has suggested that at such moments of heightened anxiety, there is a "homomorphism between home and history [...] grounded in temporal alterity, a potential uncanniness of both objects and historical narrative" (Bryant 2014, 6). This was certainly the case during Partition. Many of the structures associated with Partition out-migrants are recognized as having artistic, architectural, and/or historic value. Famous example sites in Pakistan include the holy Sikh shrines at Hassan Abdal, Nankana Sahib, and Lahore, and the sacred Hindu sites of Hinglaj in Baluchistan and the Katas Raj temple complex in the Punjab. In India, they include the Hazratbal Shrine in Kashmir, the tomb of Sheikh Salim Chishti near Agra, the Char Minar in Hyderabad, and the many Islamic-period monuments scattered throughout Delhi. Such spaces are closely tied to the trauma

Figure 1.1. Devi Talab Mandir, a protected site in Gujranwala, Pakistan (photograph by Zahida Rehman Jat).

of displacement caused by detachment from sacred and historic places central to identity. The aesthetic gravitas of such places demands reverence and prescribes preservation. Yet, the governments have found ways to gesture towards preservation while balancing the needs of modern communities without strong cultural ties to these locations. This is the case in terms of managing both monumental spaces as well as smaller-scale buildings of historical importance, such as palatial homes, places of worship, and community buildings.

In Pakistan, one of us (Zahida Rehman) has spoken with many families who live in evacuee properties protected by heritage law. One Muslim family living in an Auqaf Department-protected Hindu temple in Gujranwala (Figure 1.1) stated that they had permission to change the exterior of the building according to their needs, but had been ordered to leave the *sanctum sanctorum* (i.e. the *garba griha*, where the presiding deity was kept) unaltered. Such protections decrease the monetary value of structures, rendering them less usable to occupants, which, ironically, often removes the incentive for residents to care for their home's preservation. For example, one interviewee who lived in a palatial building in Hyderabad, Pakistan built by Sobhraj Bherumal in 1932 (Figure 1.2) discussed the fate of such evacuee properties:

> As soon as new inhabitants come to know that this building [...] is a protected building, they know that its price would plummet and that brings them to desperation [...] So, they either sell it as soon as possible or raze it to the ground and make a plaza or small market [...] As far as I know, none of such acts have been challenged by anyone so far.

He went on to explain that one of his cousins owned Moti Mahal near Resham Bazaar Lane, a beautiful pre-Partition building in Hyderabad. When the cousin came to know that Moti Mahal was to become a protected property, he demolished it. It is inconclusive as to why these ineffective policies persist. Perhaps they serve to maintain the decorum and appearance of secularism and religious equity. In practice, however, gradual change is permitted.

In the larger-scale case of Delhi's world-famous Islamic architecture, preservation law has strictly forbidden alteration. However, preservation serves not only to protect historic spaces, but also to contain them, keeping them separate and distinct from the present. The Hindu Right, while still positioning itself as secular, wants to safeguard rights owed to the majority, and when this approach is applied to readings of India's architectural and archaeological landscapes, India (in total) is presented as the product of Hindu culture (Rajagopalan 2011). This is a difficult argument to make through an interpretation of Delhi, where pre-Islamic sites are few.

Figure 1.2. Sobhraj Bherumal building as seen from the street in Hyderabad (photograph by Zahida Rehman Jat).

This problem of historical incongruity has been addressed in numerous ways. One way has been to emphasize and add to Delhi's built past relics representative of the Hindu past. For example, Rajagopalan has discussed the recent construction of the monument statue of Chauhan, "the last Hindu King", and a 2011 event in which Hindu protestors held a *yajna* (ritual Hindu purification ceremony) at the thirteenth-century mosque complex that includes the celebrated Qutb Minar. She interprets such actions as attempts to "reposition" Delhi's built heritage as Hindutva. The fact that archaeological research sponsored by the State has sought to focus on what little evidence there is related to "proto-historic", "pre-Islamic" sites, like the supposed site of mythical Indraprastha (Sharma 1964; Frykenberg 1986; Mani 1998; Rajagopalan 2011), is also a part of this attempt.

Another way the dearth of pre-Islamic sites in Delhi has been addressed is through presenting the Islamic past as a cautionary tale about a bygone era during which India was subjugated. As a previous Delhi minister of culture explained, his hope for sites like the Red Fort and Humayan's Tomb was that they would communicate "lessons from the past" about previous losses of and fights for independence (Jagmohan 2015). Strict preservation law helps in presenting sites in this way. Taneja has described it as an attempt to make Muslim monuments into "necrophilic" spaces – unused and unconnected to Delhi's modern populations (Taneja 2013, 24). The Archaeological Survey of India also distinguishes between "living" and "dead" monuments, denying people the right to worship at protected sites and designating no-construction zones around their peripheries. Ruin aesthetics and patina are privileged over upkeep and the bright colours preferred by contemporary worshippers, so that Delhi's Islamic relics do not appear too alive (Taneja 2013) (Figure 1.3).

Materiality of Partition Out-Migrant Evacuee Properties

National belonging can be negotiated through reinterpretations of historic landscapes as well as through reinterpretations of our own everyday surroundings. Partition refugees resettled into locations incongruous with their own pasts. In the wake of mass out-migrations, multiple cities-worth of built environment were left vacant. These evacuee properties became important resources for in-migrating groups and state-led rehabilitation. Occupation of evacuee properties happened both through authorized government allocation and unauthorized squatting. Many incoming refugees with raw memories of violence and few alternative options sought shelter and/or retribution by breaking open locks and seizing claim to buildings left by their out-migrating counterparts. For example, buildings in predominantly Hindu areas of Lahore (such as Krishan Nagar and Sant Nagar) rapidly became populated with incoming Muslim refugees. Similarly, in Delhi, many incoming Hindus and Sikhs found shelter in areas from which many Muslims had evacuated (such as the Nabi Karim, Jama Masjid, and Sadar Bazaar areas) (Zamindar 2007; Talbot and Singh 2009).

Both governments created numerous institutions to fill the overlapping roles of rehabilitating refugees and managing evacuee properties. In Pakistan such government institutions included the Auqaf Department and Evacuee Property Trust Board (ETPB). In India, they included the Ministry of Relief and Rehabilitation and the "Custodian" office. Having the power to reshuffle and grant access to evacuee properties legitimized the sovereignty of the

Figure 1.3. The Afsarwala Mosque (in Humayun's Tomb Complex) frozen and preserved in a state of ruination (photograph by Erin Riggs).

new national governments. It was a demonstration of the governments' ability to control resources, organize distribution, and provide for citizens. All of these institutions still exist (in altered forms) and are yet involved in controlling the use and ownership of evacuee properties. For example, today the Evacuee Trust Property Board (ETPB) in Pakistan manages ~109,404 acres of agricultural land and ~46,499 built-up urban sub-units.[1] In India, the Custodian of Enemy Property (CEP) still controls 16,000 "enemy properties" (*Times* News Network 2016).

The management of refugee property is steeped in a politically charged, ever-evolving subtext that encompasses far more than Partition histories. For example, the ETPB is a part of Pakistan's "Ministry of Religious Affairs and Inter-Faith Harmony", a government body established in 1947 in the hopes of protecting the safety of Muslim pilgrims abroad and non-Muslims domestically. This governmental organization demonstrates the recognized associations between the management of evacuee properties at home and the treatment of Islamic spaces abroad. The relabelling of a subset of "evacuee properties" as "enemy properties" in 1968, following the 1965 Indo-Pakistani War, is an opposing example from India. The legislation that resulted in this change reopened contentions over ownership of certain properties (some of which are

---

1. For further details, see see the Ministry and ETPB websites (http://www.mora.gov.pk/ and http://www. etpb.gov.pk/).

ongoing). It also affirmed EP management as an instrument of international aggression (Press Trust of India 2016; Raghavan 2016).

Evacuee property management has also been tied to government investment in modernization and development. For example, many evacuee properties in Pakistan are "trust" properties, attached to charitable, religious, or educational trusts or institutions. In Delhi, the ownership of ~3,500 of the ~190,000 original evacuee properties in the city was transferred to the municipal corporation for slum clearance, in the name of city development in the 1960s and 1970s (Datta 1986; *The Hindu* 2015). These examples demonstrate the diverse ways in which evacuee properties have functioned as assets of state – acting as leverage in international relations and as symbols of investment at home.

Conclusion: An Archaeology of Displacement Experiences in the *Longue Durée*

In the wake of heightening global refugee crises, archaeologists of the contemporary world have begun to focus on materials that elucidate the realities of hardship-filled border crossings and momentary homelessness (De León 2013; Hamilakis 2016; Kourelis 2017). However, we must recognize that refugee experiences encompass both migration and resettlement: the horrors of the journey, and the precariousness and anxiety of post-journey existence. One can consider this precariousness by focusing on the movements of displaced peoples through built landscapes associated with ancient and modern pasts that are not their own. To this end, contemporary archaeologists can draw from the critiques of nationalist readings of the ancient past, and continue such critical analyses into readings of the recent past. In this chapter, we offer such an analysis in our discussion of places associated with Partition out-migrants. Our discussion began with the politics of heritage preservation in India and Pakistan, and followed with a consideration of out-migrant homes (evacuee properties). We argue that the management of these more unexceptional buildings is just as seeded with political symbolism, as is the management of historic monument spaces. In so doing, we highlight how archaeology can help build a more complete understanding of displacement experiences – one that includes the development of exclusionary ideas that write some people out of a nation's past, present, and future.

References

Aiyar, S. 1995. "'August Anarchy': The Partition Massacres in Punjab, 1947." *Journal of South Asian Studies* 18 (1): 13–36. https://doi.org/10.1080/00856409508723242

Anderson, B. 1983. *Imagined Communities: Reflections on the Origin and Spread of Nationalism*. London: Verso Books.

Bharadwaj, P., A. I. Khwaja, and A. R. Mian. 2008. "The Partition of India: Demographic Consequences." Available online: https://papers.ssrn.com/sol3/papers.cfm?abstract_id=1294846

Brass, P. R. 2003. "The Partition of India and Retributive Genocide in the Punjab, 1946-47: Means, Methods and Purposes." *Journal of Genocide Research* 5 (1): 71–101. https://doi.org/10.1080/14623520305657

Bryant, R. 2014. "History's Remainders: On Time and Objects after Conflict in Cyprus." *American Ethnologist* 41 (4): 681–697. https://doi.org/10.1111/amet.12105

Datta, V. N. 1986. "Punjab Refugees and the Urban Development of Greater Delhi." In *Delhi Through the Ages: Selected Essays in Urban History, Culture and Society*, edited by R. E. Frykenberg, 287–306. Delhi: Oxford University Press.

D'Costa, B. 2011. *Nationbuilding, Gender and War Crimes in South Asia*. London and New York: Routledge.

De León, J. 2013. "Undocumented Migration, Use Wear, and the Materiality of Habitual Suffering in the Sonoran Desert." *Journal of Material Culture* 18 (4): 321–345. https://doi.org/10.1177/1359183513496489

Deol, H. 2000. *Religion and Nationalism in India: The Case of the Punjab*. London and New York: Routledge. https://doi.org/10.4324/9780203402269

Frykenberg, R. E., ed. 1986. *Delhi Through the Ages: Selected Essays in Urban History, Culture and Society*. Delhi: Oxford University Press.

Grewal, J. S. 2004. "Historical Geography of the Punjab." *Journal of Punjab Studies* 11 (1): 1–18.

Hamilakis, Y. 2007. *The Nation and its Ruins: Antiquity, Archaeology, and National Imagination in Greece*. Oxford: Oxford University Press.

____. 2016. "Decolonial Archaeologies: From Ethnoarchaeology to Archaeological Ethnography." *World Archaeology* 48 (5): 678–682. https://doi.org/10.1080/00438243.2016.1209783

The Hindu. 2015. "683 Evacuee Properties Subject of Legal Strife." 11 March. Available online: http://www.thehindu.com/news/cities/Delhi/683-evacuee-properties-subject-of-legal-strife/article6980320.ece

Jagmohan. 2015. *Triumphs and Tragedies of Ninth Delhi*. New Delhi: Allied Publishers.

Kaviraj, S. 1994. "Crisis of the Nation-state in India." *Political Studies* 42 (1): 115–129. https://doi.org/10.1111/j.1467-9248.1994.tb00008.x

Kourelis, K. 2017. "The Archaeology of Refugee Crises in Greece: Diachronic Cultural Landscapes." Paper Presented at the Society of Historical Archaeology Conference, Fort Worth, Texas, January.

Malik, H. 1969. "The Muslims of India and Pakistan." *Current History* 56 (331): 151.

Mani, B. R. 1998. *Delhi: Threshold of the Orient*. New Delhi: Aryan Books International.

McGuire, R. H. 1992. "Archeology and the First Americans." *American Anthropologist* 94 (4): 816–836. https://doi.org/10.1525/aa.1992.94.4.02a00030

Meskell, L., ed. 1998. *Archaeology Under Fire: Nationalism, Politics and Heritage in the Eastern Mediterranean and Middle East*. London and New York: Routledge.

Press Trust of India. 2016. "Govt's Move to Amend Enemy Property Act Faces Opposition from Four Parties." *Indian Express*, 8 May. Available online: http://indianexpress.com/article/india/india-news-india/govts-move-to-amend-enemy-property-act-faces-opposition-from-four-parties/

Rajagopalan, M. 2011. "Postsecular Urbanisms: Situating Delhi within the Rhetorical Landscape of Hindutva." In *The Fundamentalist City? Religiosity and the Remaking of Urban Space*, edited by N. AlSayyad and M. Massoumi, 257–282. London and New York: Routledge.

Raghavan, P. 2016. "Enemy Property: Why India Is Still Struggling with a Political Legacy of Partition." *Scroll.in.*, 16 January. Available online: http://scroll.in/article/801926/enemy-property-why-india-is-still-struggling-with-a-political-legacy-of-partition

Singh, Y. P. 2015. *Islam in India and Pakistan: A Religious History*. New Delhi: Vij Books.

Sharma, Y. D. 1964. *Delhi and Its Neighbourhood: XXVI International Congress of Orientalists*. New Delhi: Archaeological Survey of India.

Talbot, I. and G. Singh. 2009. *The Partition of India*. Cambridge: Cambridge University Press.

Taneja, A. V. 2013. *Nature, History, and the Sacred in the Medieval Ruins of Delhi*. PhD diss., Columbia University.

Times News Network. 2016. "16,000 'Enemy Properties' Worth Crores in India, Several in City." *The Times of India*, 14 January. Available online: http://timesofindia.indiatimes.com/city/mumbai/16000-enemy-properties-worth-crores-in-India-several-in-city/articleshow/50582909.cms

Von Glasenapp, H. 1999. *Jainism: An Indian Religion of Salvation*. Delhi: Motilal Banarsidass.

Zamindar, V. F.-Y. 2007. *The Long Partition and the Making of Modern South Asia: Refugees, Boundaries, Histories*. New York: Columbia University Press.

Erin Riggs is a PhD candidate and Teaching Assistant at Binghamton University. Address for correspondence: Department of Archaeology, Binghampton University, State University of New York, 4400 Vestal Parkway, East Binghamton, NY 13902, USA. Email: eriggs1@binghamton.edu

Zahida Rehman Jat is Lecturer of Anthropology at the University of Sindh. Address for correspondence: Department of Anthropology and Archeology, University of Sindh, Allama I.I. Kazi Campus, Jamshoro-76080, Sindh, Pakistan. Email: zahida.jat@usindh.edu.pk

Chapter 2

"We Palestinian Refugees" – Heritage Rites and/as the Clothing of Bare Life: Reconfiguring Paradox, Obligation, and Imperative in Palestinian Refugee Camps in Jordan

Beverley Butler and Fatima al-Nammari

Introduction: "Configuring the Refugee"

> As I write this essay, 425 Palestinians expelled by the state of Israel find themselves in a sort of no-man's-land. These men [sic] according to Hannah Arendt's suggestion certainly constitute "the vanguard of their people". (Agamben 1995, 118–119)

The "figure of the refugee", synonymous with the iconic "We refugees" theses of Arendt (1994 [1943]) and Agamben (1995), is marked by a series of "grim paradoxes" (Siddiq 1995) that in the specific "figure of the Palestinian refugee" have deep-seated implications, primarily for refugee communities, and, we argue, for critical heritage discourse and contemporary archaeology. Arendt's (1994 [1943]) prescient essay articulates a crucial turning point in which the "figure of the refugee" is confined within the paradox of increasing if not absolute dependency on "Refugee Committees" and yet simultaneously charged with being the "vanguard of their people". Written half a century later, Agamben's essay offers a revised commentary on the "figure of the refugee" in new circumstances of mass displacement, migration, and extremis while taking forward this central paradox and explicitly referencing the on-going Palestinian refugee experience.

The legacy of Arendt's "Refugee Committee" is now the domain of new sovereign "actors" in the form of the UN/UNHCR (and in the Palestinian case, UNRWA), who orchestrate powerful "biopolitical" "rites of passage". This grim drama, synonymous with the unmaking and remaking of "displaced persons" into "refugees", has its fullest expression in the "cornerstone of humanitarian and host state responses to an influx of the displaced" – "the refugee camp" (Peteet 2005, 28). The camps themselves, and more particularly Palestinian refugee camps, are characterized as "non-spaces", "spaces of exemption", "laboratories" of "control and surveillance" in which the "refugee" is actively reduced to "passive victim", "homo sacer", and "bare life" (Peteet 2005; Hanafi 2009).[1] The legacy of Arendt's "figure of the refugee" as vanguard connects to alternative yet coexistent characterizations of refugee camps as "little Palestines" and as "spaces of resistance" and "refusal" (Peteet 2005; Hanafi 2009). As multi-layered spaces of "attachment and belonging" they function as "symbol and archive" and as everyday spaces for "living", "work", "shelter", and "services" (Misselwitz 2012; al-Nammari 2014).

We must add a further grim and exclusively "Palestinian paradox": the Palestinian "Right of Return", claims to which are bound up in obligations and imperatives to sustain both the "temporary" nature of the camp and a Palestinian identity centred upon *al-Nakba*, the Catastrophe of 1948 (Peteet 2005, 3–4). Thus the "unresolved" nature of the Palestinian refugees' humanitarian *rite de passage* creates a situation of "permanent impermanence" in which lives "interrupted" take on further extremis.

Ethnographic Journeys, Popular Heritage Rites

We draw on on-going ethnographic work to explore the diverse responses of refugee communities to these complexities, paradoxes, obligations, and imperatives, while highlighting other emergent themes and issues. The point of departure for our fieldwork is Talbiyeh Camp on the outskirts of Amman. Our research subsequently expanded to include a further four Palestinian camps in Jordan: Baqa'a, Husun, Jerash, and Wihdat/New camps. Conceived of as "heritage ethnographies", our broad framework elicits reflections and perspectives on how "heritage" is understood, perceived, articulated, experienced, deployed, performed, and transformed in these refugee contexts. Participants were drawn from women's, men's, and youth groups, in order to elicit specific gender and generational viewpoints. Our qualitative methods comprise of participant-observation, workshops, focus groups, and formal/informal discussion. Participants were encouraged to bring in "heritage objects" to prompt discussion and to reflect on diverse heritage forms (such as place, memory, performance, skill etc.) and on significance and value in terms of affective and emotional connectivities, embodiment, and aspects of wellbeing and illbeing (Butler 2011).

Heritage (*Turath*)

Initial workshop sessions began with participants exploring the specific vocabulary and connotations of Arabic words synonymous with "heritage", primarily "*turath*". It was clear that this word was typically identified with *one* particular item: the Palestinian embroidered cross-stitch dress, or *thobe*. It was particularly apt that the first of our pilot workshops at Talbiyeh Camp began with a woman whose chosen "heritage object" was an intricately worked front panel of one such *thobe*. Many women in this and other sessions spoke of having historical examples of such embroidery handed down within the family, and of more modern examples made in the camps (Figure 2.1).

The multilayered meaning was of undoubted importance: participants described how particular designs and patterns were immediately identifiable with specific Palestinian cities,

---

1. Obviously, the "Palestinian refugee experience" is not homogenous and requires research responsive to specificity. See the UNRWA website, "Where We Work" section for Jordan (http://www.unrwa.org/where-we-work/jordan). Details are provided for each camp.

villages, and locales, while collectively the dresses were iconic embodiments and identifiers of a broader unified and unifying Palestinian identity. Thus the *thobe* expressed a duality capable of rooting heritage, identity, and tradition within regionality/locality and also within the broader homeland of Palestine. This was the starting point of an on-going dynamic in which participants positioned *Palestine* as *the* centred "meta-object" of discussions and debates.

Figure 2.1. Front panel of a thobe (photograph by authors).

Unique Fingerprints

A pattern emerged of "heritage-equals-*turath*-equals-Palestine-equals-*thobe*". In gender terms many women expressed pride that women and women's heritage played a key custodial role in transmission. The men's groups similarly reiterated the importance of the *thobe*. Participants delved into the various designs and symbols used – some to identify "if person is married or a widowed", etc., and some used "as protection" and imbued with amuletic powers. As activated material forms, *thobes* offer on-going efficacies. The embroidered front panel is invested with transformational powers: it can be recycled, reused, transported, and transformed when cut off an old dress and placed on a new one. The panels continue to be used by younger women to learn embroidery skills and thereby engage in rituals of cultural transmission. Writ large, the *thobe* as "mobile" heritage and as "fused" or "bridging" object thus connected participants in Jordanian camps with their Palestinian origins. When worn for special events the dresses had the power to bring "Palestine to the camp". Fusing persons-object and metaphorically asserting a sense of Palestinian "cultural patterning", one participant eloquently stated: "The thobe is the unique fingerprint of Palestinian heritage and identity." Heritage as a form of ritual protection against the disintegration of self / selfgroup / world featured here and elsewhere as powerful coping strategies, repertoires of care, comfort, and wellbeing.

"Kept", "Lost" Objects

Discussions also opened up into a more general interest in heritage as "kept objects", typically synonymous with "heirlooms" (*mirath*): when able families passed down jewellery and craft items, thus iterating intimacies between heritage and inheritance (*irth*). The crucial importance of photographs and documents featured in discussions, notably "title deeds" to land and homes in Palestine. Keys to former homes and properties emerged as iconic objects that were transfused with the desire and promise of return. "Palestine" itself was thus regarded as the ultimate "lost object" and as an entity elicited deeply felt connectivities with lost homes, lost land, and lost family members and with expressions of mourning, melancholy, and nostalgia. The need to nurture, care for, and memorialize such connections was expressed in the desire to repair, repossess, redeem, and reconstitute such heritage. It was in turn inextricably connected in many people's minds to the duty and responsibility to make good the "right of return" as a – if not *the* – definitive aspiration.

Figure 2.2. Artwork depicting Palestinian suffering, Baqa'a Camp (photograph by authors).

Life, Death

Underpinning and motivating all discussions of heritage – as specifically *Palestinian* heritage – is the obligation and imperative "to remember". Here the extremes of memory-work (Sa'di and Abu-Lughod 2007) are indicative of the contradictory double-edged nature of being Palestinian. As one male elder put it, "Palestine is a source of pride and inspiration in life but also a heavy burden." National identity as a burden is a common trope and not unique to Palestine and Palestinians; however, it does bring into view the specific "pharmakonic" nature of Palestinian heritage and dynamics of wellbeing and illbeing (Butler 2011). Participants thus reflected on heritage as synonymous with the transmission of historical trauma and dispossession – notably the violent catastrophes of *al-Nakba* of 1948 and *al-Naksa* of 1967 – but also experiences of the "on-going *Nakba*" that threaten further traumatic episodes, thus exacerbating the extremis of refugee life (Sa'di and Abu-Lughod 2007).

Displacement, Suffering

This obligation and imperative to articulate and transmit "catastrophic" heritage is in turn inextricably linked to the quest to possess and repossess the authenticity of Palestine and Palestinianness, and sees persons-as-heritage further emerge as a potent force. Those elders who suffered originary violent dispossession and experienced the formation of the various Jordanian camps are afforded value as living embodiments of foundational experiences of displacement. They occupy a salient role – perhaps sacralized status – in memory transmission. As witnesses their testimony is deeply valued, and as one participant put it, it "is kept alive and remembered by everyone". Here obligation/imperative similarly demands that youth "take on" the emotional heritage of elders that sees both "joy" and "trauma" transmitted as "post-memory" and "intergenerational memory" (Hirsch 2012). Oral history projects have emerged in many camps – including at the Heritage Program at Talbiyeh Women's Centre – to "keep safe their [elders'] memories of Palestine and their experiences of the camp".

Curating Palestine

The ever-present threat of erasure and forgetting was responded to in ritual practices that again "brought Palestine to the camps". Alternative networks of archival, museal, commemorative, and memorial formations dedicated to collecting and curating Palestine emerged in discussions. One male participant brought objects from his personal collection of pots, head-dresses, a traditional camel-hair carpet, and maps of Ber Sheva. His friend joked that "it is almost a museum that he has. It is his hobby." As another participant stated, "*because* there are no official archives and museums", the lack of formal heritage institutions creates a dispersed network in which "certain people kept or collected certain items" that could be borrowed "on trust" to create temporary displays and exhibitions about Palestine. As such, heritage crossed-over and blurred private–public / personal–collective boundaries (see Butler 2008). Again, the creation of the Heritage Program at Talbiyeh Women's Centre and initiatives elsewhere saw increasingly organized approaches towards locating, reviewing, listing, consolidating, and nurturing such resources.

Communion, Sensorium, Magical Thinking

Interestingly, several participants refocused discussions on what they would have "*wished*" to have brought with them. One male participant's chosen object was "a prayer in Jerusalem". These imaginative acts as exercises in magical thinking and wish-fulfilment were extremely powerful and deeply felt. Prayer, acts of ritual communion and desire, featured in other articulations of powerful attachments to Palestine that unlocked further potent heritage cosmologies. Not only was this will to possess and commune with Palestine expressed in the crucially important fusion of heritage with faith, religion, and spirituality, but also in rituals by which "Palestine" was imaginatively reconstructed as a powerful "sensorium". Participants articulated the desire, for example, to "see Jerusalem", to "kiss the earth", and to "smell" and "eat the food". A common claim was made that "traditional Palestinian" foodstuffs (olives, figs, zaatar, and dates etc.) were "better" than and "superior" to Jordanian equivalents, and they were often afforded idealized status. Participants lamented that this desire was frustrated further by having few opportunities "to grow their own food in the camp". The idea of taking in or ingesting Palestinian food – and even the "air and scenery" of Palestine – was obviously regarded as bound up with wellbeing and with the belief that this was good for both "the mind and body". Conversely, not being able to commune in this way with Palestine was again seen as a source of illbeing.

Fragmentation, Belonging

The many paradoxes of living in a camp – a supposed temporary "non-place" (Augé 1995) that was simultaneously "home" – became centred in discussion. Attempting to describe her life as a refugee and the experience of living in a camp, one woman spoke of "suffering" in terms of on-going melancholic "sadness" brought about by the underpinning event of having "lost a home" and "further stress" synonymous with the everyday "poverty", "cramped conditions", and "unemployment", and the "enclosed nature" of the camp. She saw this as a "threat to identity" and to "Palestinian identity and tradition". Other participants reiterated the "injustice" of the situation. The sense of "not being able to plan and control the future" led to feelings of the fragmentation of self and selfgroup that were felt by many. However, a certain sense of belonging and diversity was evident too. One female youth explained that "each camp feels it is different and each of the camps are unique due to their composition […] We have specific Palestinian local culture (including Bedouin) and heritage in each camp based on where people have come from." The presence of "others" in the camps was commented upon, such as Iraqi refugees, Egyptian migrant workers, and, on-going at the time of field research, Syrian refugees.

Excavating the Camp

For many young people, particularly in Talbiyeh, there emerged a certain interest in the "archaeology" of the camp: the years of habitation revealing histories, memories, and a heritage of its own. One female youth explained:

> When the first refugees came to the camps they stayed in tents and then other structures were built. This is part of our history. Even the zinc roofing has become symbolic for

Figure 2.3. Zinc roof, Talbiyeh Camp (photograph by authors).

us. In the past people refused to move from the houses with zinc roofs even if it meant going to a better home, because they were afraid this would mean they had to live here permanently in the camp and the "right of return" would be lost. Most of the zinc has been replaced but items like this need to be documented [Figure 2.3].

This curiosity of youth, the materiality of place, and need to commune with and understand the history of the camp were obviously important agendas.

Self-Representation

The topic of representation, and more particularly self-representation, emerged further. A female youth argued:

> There is the need to address the stereotype of Palestinian refugee as dirty, hungry, barefoot, and needing aid. I feel that as a people we are tired of others speaking for us, they beg on our behalf, there is a "begging business" going on in our name – especially in the West […] This doesn't represent us and how we think and feel.

She powerfully added, "Now the battle is in the media. We are trying to represent ourselves as creative people, and strong, too." Her contribution to the Talbiyeh Heritage Program – a short film called *Lost in a Picture* (al-Hubeidi 2011a) – used irony, subversion, and juxtaposition to do this. The film consists of two young women recreating highly stereotyped historical photographs of the camp in which refugees are positioned as passive recipients of charity standing in front of UNRWA aid parcels and smiling gratefully. She reiterated that the "reconstructed image" provoked the self-conscious "truth" that "human beings are more than stereotypes" (al-Hubeidi 2011b, 12).

Mind Palaces, Memoryscapes

Palestinian refugee camps have been dubbed as "Little Palestines", in recognition of the ways in which such spaces have been constructed as metonyms. Participants spoke of attempts to establish potent and explicit memoryscapes by which "the camp and its different areas and its streets would take on the names of the places of origin that the refugees come from." These projects, although carried out in some camps, were rarely given official approval and therefore were typically informal constructions. However, the Palestinian flag and representations of the Dome of the Rock feature as repeated "heritage icons" in both domestic and public spaces. Naji al-Ali's Handala cartoons as important visual signs of resistance and the poetry of Mahmoud Darwish similarly carried a ritual efficacy of affirmation and affiliation to such heritage.

We Palestinian Refugees

While some camps, such as Talbiyeh, self-identified as "traditional", Baqa'a residents characterized their camp as a "political barometer". This in turn afforded them a claim to a certain intimacy, connectivity, authenticity, and synchronicity with the "cosmic" centre-point of Palestine; thus, "when something happens in Palestine, people in Baqa'a hear it first and we tell the others!" Wihdat in the east of Amman is one of the most "open" camps, and saw itself differently in an overarching way as "symbolic of all Palestinian camps" and as such a place that again was bound up in the obligation and imperative of nurturing, celebrating, and transmitting Palestinian heritage.

Other perspectives on "refugee identity" were again double-edged. In Husun Camp, members of youth groups spoke of the stigma towards them, with "neighbouring villagers" dubbing them the "Valley of the Wolves". This was interpreted as indicative of the dehumanization and "discrimination" felt towards them. The term "refugee" was regarded by many as both "a source of shame but also a source of pride and resistance": a paradox repeated in the statement that "we love and hate our camp". Frustrations emerged when attempts to create nicer environments within the camp became the subject of controversy. For example, a scheme to get young people to repaint building facades was halted by authorities[2] who felt "it may seem that we no longer need donor money." This raises the question of what a refugee camp should look like and the ethics of the motivation to either instigate change or prevent it.

Reflection of Suffering

Close to the iconic world heritage site of Jerash is located Jerash Camp (commonly known as "Gaza" Camp), a space that is subject to further discrimination and dehumanization.

---

2. The Jordanian Government Department of Palestine Affairs.

Figure 2.4. Key in the colours of the Palestinian flag (photograph by authors).

Participants here highlighted their communities' complex history of multiple dispossession, resulting in them having fewer rights, less access to resources (including schooling, medicine), and, crucially too, to "identity cards".[3] One youth stated: "Even the maintenance of our camp is not like the other Palestinian camps in Jordan: it is a reflection of our suffering." He argued that "young people here have a heavy burden" which causes "psychological problems" in addition to material disadvantage. In a further paradox, he stated that "we have lots of time to analyse the 'situation' but this can bring about depression too when we find out we cannot change things."

Factness, Futures

A shared concern across all five camps was that heritage be activated as a key resource to define a liveable present and better futures. Here an increasing desire was evident to return to, revive, reflect upon, and rework certain cultural expressions and performances that iterate the Palestinian heritage canon while opening this up to new creativity and transformation (Figure 2.4). These popular ritual forms in turn endow a new "factness" and confidence to Palestinian

---

3. See "Jerash Camp" on the UNRWA website (http://www.unrwa.org/where-we-work/jordan/jerash-camp).

heritage. Authenticity and "creative licence" coexist in a creative and dynamic heritage spectrum that brings together such cultural phenomena as traditional Palestinian *dabka* dancing and rap. Similarly, traditional Palestinian embroidery has become the site of inspiration for an array of what one participant described as "new adaptions for new purposes".

Such new "heritage-fusions" create a genre of "made objects" that see the "famous Palestinian cross-stitch" infuse contemporary popular culture in the form of mobile phone covers, keyrings, glasses cases, bookmarks, etc. Perhaps the creative tradition of "mismemory"[4] can be seen to add interesting paradox and vitality here. It should also be highlighted that many social development initiatives – notably for women – promote heritage schemes that enhance local skills and "heritage pride" while generating income. Writ larger still, "heritage-work" is valued for its efficacy to secure greater life chances, greater wellbeing and thus to empower oneself in the present and to strive for "just" futures.

Promised Lands

These desires are also expressed in popular heritage rituals common across the camps: the quest to locate viewing places where it is possible to see the physical landscape of the homeland. For Palestinians in Jordan the heritage sites of Um Qais (north Jordan), the Western Heights of Salt, and Mount Nebo (both in central Jordan) offer particularly magical efficacies. Mount Nebo's potency is further enhanced through its association with Moses and his first sight of the Promised Land. While Palestinian refugees, like Moses, are similarly denied entry, these visions elicit, as one participant put it, "bitter-sweet feelings of happiness and of longing", and the comfort of intimacy and knowing that "when it is sunrise here it is sunrise in Palestine" (Figure 2.5).

Conclusion: Reconfiguring Heritage and/as the Clothing of Bare Life

In his closing thoughts in "We Refugees", Agamben casts his alternative vision of the "Promised Land" as he returns to Arendt's "figure of the refugee" as "the vanguard of their people". In his vision, it is the Palestinian refugee experience he turns to, arguing that this vanguard is one that may "not necessarily or not merely" hinge on being the "nucleus of a future national state", but one that symbolizes the very crisis of the nation-state itself. Agamben likens the refugee presence-in-exile to "a snow-covered hill" that implicitly "acts-back", rendering the nation state "perforated and topologically deformed" and thus, he argues, provoking "the citizen […] to recognize the refugee that he or she is – only in such a world is the political survival of humankind today thinkable" (Agamben 1995, 119).

As *we* write, over two decades later, the Palestinian experience of exile is without conclusion and many thousands more displaced persons – refugees and migrants – risk their lives undertaking journeys to other "promised lands" they may never see nor enter. It is perhaps similarly necessary to conclude on a note of paradox that reworks Agamben's "snow-covered hill" and "acting-back" metaphors. This we found in acts of hospitality made by Palestinian refugees despite anxieties that the arrival of Syrian refugees in Jordan would lead to compe-

---

4. See details of an exhibition, "At the Seams: A Political History of Palestinian Embroidery", curated by Rachel Dedman in Beirut in 2016 under the auspices of the Palestinian Museum (http://www.palmuseum. org/ehxibitions/exhibitions#ad-image-thumb-2041). The dynamic of "mismemory" features in the exhibit.

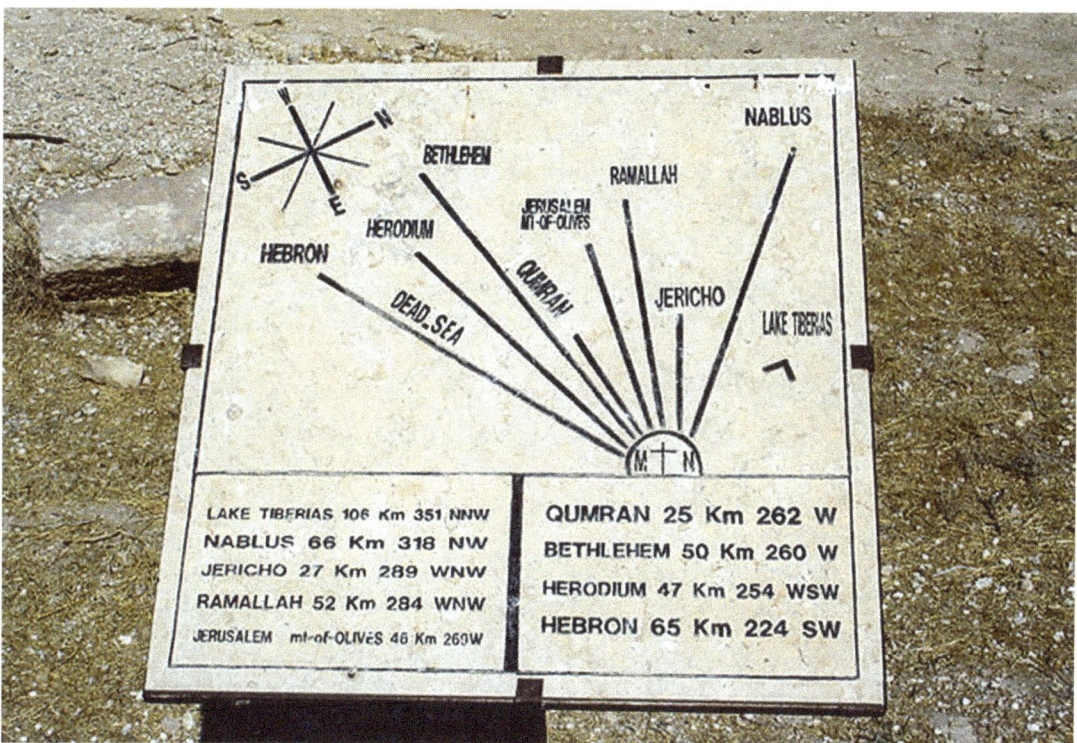

Figure 2.5. Mount Nebo – orientation signage (photograph by authors).

tition "for limited resources". Numbers of Palestinians actively empathized with the newly dispossessed. The core paradox to emerge also reworks Arendt's point that identities intensify in exile (Arendt 1994 [1943], 118). Thus, while being Palestinian intensifies in a refugee camp, the creative, multi-directional (Rothberg 2009) potential of "popular heritage rites" offers new acts of agency, empathy, and affiliation. This sense of solidarity was expressed in particular by a Palestinian youth: "The camp is not a place to live but a place to breath as a Palestinian in equity with other refugees […] It reminds you that you have a cause and that others are in the same position." We met young Palestinians from Husun Camp volunteering in Syrian camps such as Zataari[5] in order to "share knowledge of how to cope with the common experiences of suffering, distress, and other difficulty."

Perhaps this then is a small but important step in creating new "factness" and new "realities" that similarly challenge dominant impulses for heritage to remain harnessed to national identity, biopolitical discourse, top-down power-led rites of sovereignty and "objectivity"-based paradigms. Instead, the imperative and obligation is to recognize key shifts *vis-à-vis* the role of "popular heritage rites" as capable of creative and transformative engagements. As deeply felt and often magical acts, these new strategies of humanization are already being put

---

5. Details of Syrian refugees are tracked by the Syria Regional Refugee Response Inter-agency Information Sharing Portal, hosted by the UNHCR (http://data.unhcr.org/syrianrefugees/settlement.php?id=176&region=77&country=107).

in play *by refugees themselves*: including in relation to human and cultural rights discourses yet without reducing heritage to these agendas. Equally, the urgent need is to support and prioritize a reworked popular discourse of "heritage care" that heeds Arendt's warning: "The comity of the European peoples went to pieces when, and because, it allowed its weakest members to be excluded and persecuted" (Arendt 1994 [1943], 118).

Just as the Palestinian refugee voices cited in this chapter see the *thobe* as best expressing and encompassing their understanding of heritage, yet again without reducing Palestinian heritage solely to this, similarly "we/us", as heritage critics and contemporary archaeologists, should embrace a paradigm shift that resituates heritage within diverse theories, ontologies, and cosmologies of subjectivity and that recognizes the efficacy of popular heritage rites to "clothe" "bare life" in various, increasingly creative expressions and empowering persons not just in the future but in the present. Crucially, we should see this reconfigured heritage discourse as a fundamental part of wider quests for the "Good Life",[6] thereby taking on the complexities, paradoxes, and aspiration for fulfillment that being human means – especially in conditions of extremis.

Acknowledgments

We would like to thank all the people who took part in our heritage ethnographies. In particular we would like to extend our gratitude to the Department of Palestinian Affairs (DPA) and local committees, including the Women's Program Centres (WPC), Community Based Rehabilitation Centres (CBRC), and youth clubs, in all camps. Thanks also to Professor Yannis Hamilakis for his comments on our text.

Dedication

We would like to dedicate our paper to Waleed Al-Nammari, a proud Jerusalemite who will be remembered with love for embodying the very best of Palestinian heritage, hospitality, and kindness.

References

Agamben, G. 1995. "We Refugees." *Symposium* 49 (2): 114–119. https://doi.org/10.1080/00397709.1995.10733798

Augé, M. 1995. *Non-places: An Introduction to an Anthropology of Supermodernity*, translated by J. Howe. London: Verso.

Arendt, H. 1994 [1943]. "We Refugees." In *Altogether Elsewhere: Writers in Exile*, edited by M. Robinson, 111–119. London: Faber and Faber.

Butler, B. 2008. "'Othering' the Archive – From Exile, to Inclusion and Heritage Dignity: The Case of Palestinian Archival Memory." *Archival Science* 9 (1–2): 57–69.

_____. 2011. "Heritage as Pharmakon and the Muses as Deconstruction: Problematising Curative Museologies and Heritage Healing." In *The Thing about Museums: Objects and Experience, Representation and Contestation*, edited by S. Dudley, A. J. Barnes, J. Binnie, J. Petrov, and J. Walklate, 354–371. London and New York: Routledge.

Hanafi, S. 2009. "Palestinian Refugee Camps in the Palestinian Territory: Territory of Exception

---

6. Those existing as "bare life" are excluded from the "Good Life" (Agamben 1995).

and Locus of Resistance." In *The Power of Inclusive Exclusion: Anatomy of Israeli Rule in the Occupied Palestinian Territories*, edited by A. Ophir, M. Giovanni, and S. Hanafi, 495–517. New York: Zone Books.

Hirsch, M. 2012, *The Generation of Postmemory: Writing and Visual Culture After the Holocaust.* New York: Columbia University Press,

al-Hubeidi, M., dir. 2011a. *Lost in a Picture.* Amman: Talbiyeh Women's Programs Center Oral Heritage Program, funded by the Social Cultural Fund of GIZ.

al-Hubeidi, M. 2011b. *This is Our Story.* Publication accompanying Women's Program Centre, GIZ and UNRWA.

Misselwitz, P., ed. 2012. *Space, Time, Dignity, Rights*: *Improving Palestinian Refugee Camps,* Stuttgart: University of Stuttgart and UNRWA.

al-Nammari, F. 2014. "When the Global Impacts the Local: Revisiting Talbiyeh Camp Improvement Project." *Habitat International* 44: 158–167. https://doi.org/10.1016/j.habitatint.2014.05.007

Peteet, J. 2005. *Landscape of Hope and Despair: Palestinian Refugee Camps.* Philadelphia: University of Pennsylvania Press. https://doi.org/10.9783/9780812200317

Rothberg, M, 2009. *Multidirectional Memory: Remembering the Holocaust in the Age of Decolonization*, Stanford, CA: Stanford University Press.

Sa'di, A. H. and L. Abu-Lughod. 2007. *Nakba: Palestine, 1948, and the Claims of Memory.* New York: Columbia University Press.

Siddiq, M. 1995. "On Ropes of Memory: Narrating the Palestinian Refugees." In *Mistrusting Refugees*, edited by E. V. Daniel and J. C. Knudsen, 87–101. Berkeley: University of California Press.

Beverley Butler is Reader in Heritage Studies, UCL Institute of Archaeology. Address for correspondence: UCL Institute of Archaeology, 31–34 Gordon Square, London, WC1H 0PY, UK. Email: beverley.butler@ucl.ac.uk

Fatima Al-Nammari is an Assistant Professor in the Department of Architecture at the University of Petra and an Honorary Research Associate at UCL. Address for correspondence: University of Petra, P.O. Box: 961343, Amman, Jordan. Email: falnammari@uop.edu.jo

Chapter 3

Surveilling Surveillance: Counter-Mapping Undocumented Migration in the USA–Mexico Borderlands

Haeden Eli Stewart, Ian Ostericher, Cameron Gokee, and Jason De León

Introduction

Since 2001, the bodies of almost 2,500 migrants have been found in the Tucson Sector of the Mexico–USA border (Figure 3.1), the US federal border patrol zone that covers the majority of the Sonoran Desert in Arizona (Blust 2016). These bodies, the remains of undocumented migrants attempting to cross into the USA, are the direct result of a US Department of Homeland Security border strategy that actively funnels migrants into harsh, dangerous desert areas between Nogales and Sasabe. Though unwalled and ostensibly unguarded, this open desert is by design a key component of the US border security apparatus (Dunn 2009; De León 2015).

The Sonoran Desert is thus central to the US Department of Homeland Security's border policy, often referred to as Prevention Through Deterrence (PTD). By increasing security in and around urban ports-of-entry, migrants are funneled into more remote areas, where environmental conditions act as a natural barrier to movement and provide law enforcement with a "tactical advantage". This chapter both examines the ways in which mapping technology is central to how Border Patrol constructs and operates within this security apparatus and explores how the very same mapping technology can be used in opposition to the border security project, by analyzing the spatial patterning of migrant paths and deaths that are causally related to how US Border Patrol surveils the borderlands.

Drawing on the concept of counter-mapping, we use spatial data collected by the Undocumented Migration Project, a long-term anthropological project aimed at understanding various elements of the violent social process of clandestine migration between Latin America and the United States between 2009 and 2013, and mortality data from Humane Borders, a faith-based humanitarian organization dedicated to providing aid to migrants crossing the Sonoran Desert. Using these data, we critique the spatial ideology of PTD and the technological conditions of its production. In doing so, we also outline the tense contradictions that follow the seemingly paradoxical attempt to use spatial data and spatial analysis to critique and undermine spatial data and spatial analysis.

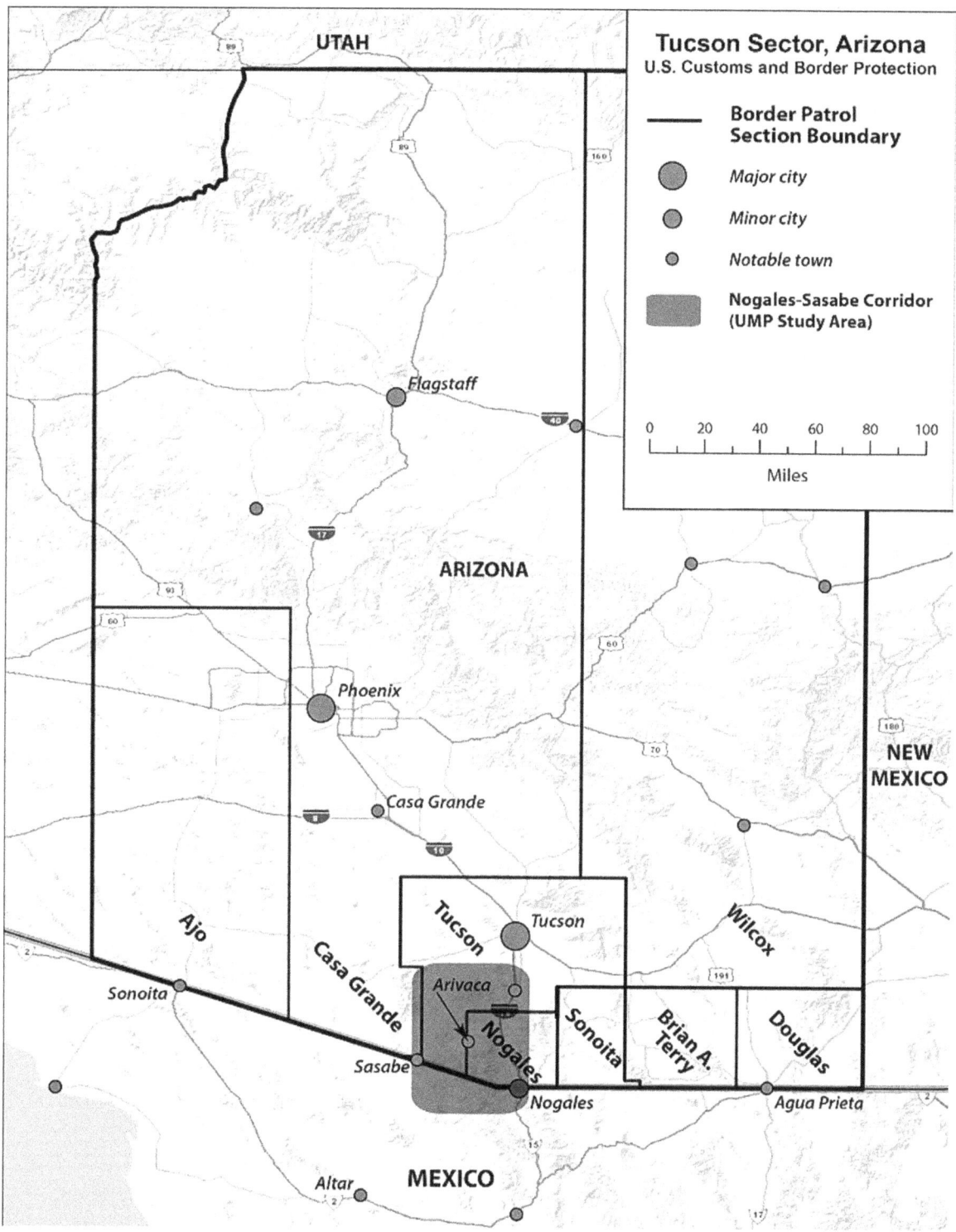

Figure 3.1. The Tucson Sector (US Border Patrol).

Denaturalizing the Desert

Prevention Through Deterrence (PTD), the dominant security paradigm that has organized US border security policy on the Mexico–USA border over the past two decades, was first officially developed in 1993 as a response to increasing numbers of people clandestinely crossing the border from the south through urban border towns like El Paso (for further discussion, see Nevins 2002; De León 2015). PTD's solution was a massive build-up of security infrastructure: specifically, military-grade walls and road checkpoints in cities and other easily crossable border zones, while leaving open areas of the border such as the section of desert between the towns of Nogales and Sasabe, where rugged terrain and severe environmental conditions (e.g. heat and venomous snakes) make crossings dangerous and deadly. In addition to funneling migrants through an already dangerous landscape, border security continually alters the desert, transforming it to make crossing more difficult and dangerous for migrants; for example, by dragging tires across large swathes of road and clearing foliage and underbrush, border agents create a landscape in which migrant footprints are easier to track, and migrants are easier to find.

The spatial ideology underpinning PTD naturalizes the border and differentiates human from non-human security. Border Patrol strategy appropriates, uses, and influences the Sonoran Desert as an element of border security, yet designates it as completely separate from explicitly human-built infrastructure. In the Border Patrol pamphlet in Figure 3.2, the desert is designated as a mortal threat beyond the control of border security. This separation veils the desert as a "natural" space, an area outside the control of human agents, rather than a constructed space actively supporting the intentional security apparatus.

In identifying the desert as a natural barrier, PTD also casts the international border itself as a natural dividing line, as opposed to something created through the security process. As such, the desert appears as a boundary that is simultaneously a form of protection for the nation and something whose "nature" requires defending. In this sense, as "nature", the desert becomes a useful ally to serve as a moral alibi (Doty 2011) for Border Patrol, removing the culpability of their security strategies for violence to migrants during desert crossings. At the same time, the desert is an at-risk sector of the border security body, requiring protection against "invading foreigners" and their polluting trash (Sundberg 2008).

GIS, Border Patrol, and Counter-Mapping

The spatial ideology of PTD, which naturalizes the desert as border and differentiates between human and non-human security infrastructure, is not merely presumed by US Border Patrol; it is actively produced. This ideology is constructed and disseminated through the production of maps for public consumption which portray the USA as a coherent entity with constantly at-risk borders (Figure 3.3). Other maps distinguish between "controlled" or walled sections, and "monitored" or unwalled sections of the border (Schroeder 2012). The gaps in the border wall are, according to this spatial logic, beyond the control of border security (Sundberg 2008; Andreas 2009). This representation of remote spaces as uncontrollable at once highlights their need for security – the need to be monitored – and reinforces their status as natural, existing outside human security technology.

La próxima vez que intentes cruzar
la frontera sin documentos puedes:

terminar víctima
del crimen organizado

terminar víctima del desierto

terminar tras las rejas y sin
beneficios de inmigración

Figure 3.2. US Border Patrol-distributed pamphlet warning would-be migrants about the dangers of border crossing (photograph by Mike Wells).

Maps produced and disseminated by US Border Patrol are a small subset of a much larger phenomenon that employs mapping and spatial analyses as core technologies of border security surveillance. In 2001, ESRI – the producer and vendor of ArcGIS, the industry-standard commercial Geographic Information Systems (GIS) software – published a news article highlighting the usefulness of their products to "maximize" Mexico–USA border security enforcement (Sweeney 2001). They detailed how spatial analyses were the most vital tool for Border Patrol's ability to "patrol and protect" the border. According to William Veal, then Sector Chief in San Diego, GIS provides the ultimate technical backdrop to all levels of border policing activity (Veal 2003, 41). Used in conjunction with the vast network of remote sensors, lookout towers, and agent-carried GPS units, GIS provides a streamlined database of spatial information that can be marshalled to provide immediate real-time information of suspected migrant activity. Specifically, Veal argues that GIS facilitates surveillance of migrant activity "in remote border areas" (Veal 2003, 41). GIS thus provides the underpinning framework to the surveillance of those areas, such as the Sonoran Desert, that have been left open according to the precepts of PTD. It is GIS that facilitates the interconnection of these open, "natural" areas with those areas of explicit security infrastructure. At the same time, GIS – by not constructing clearly

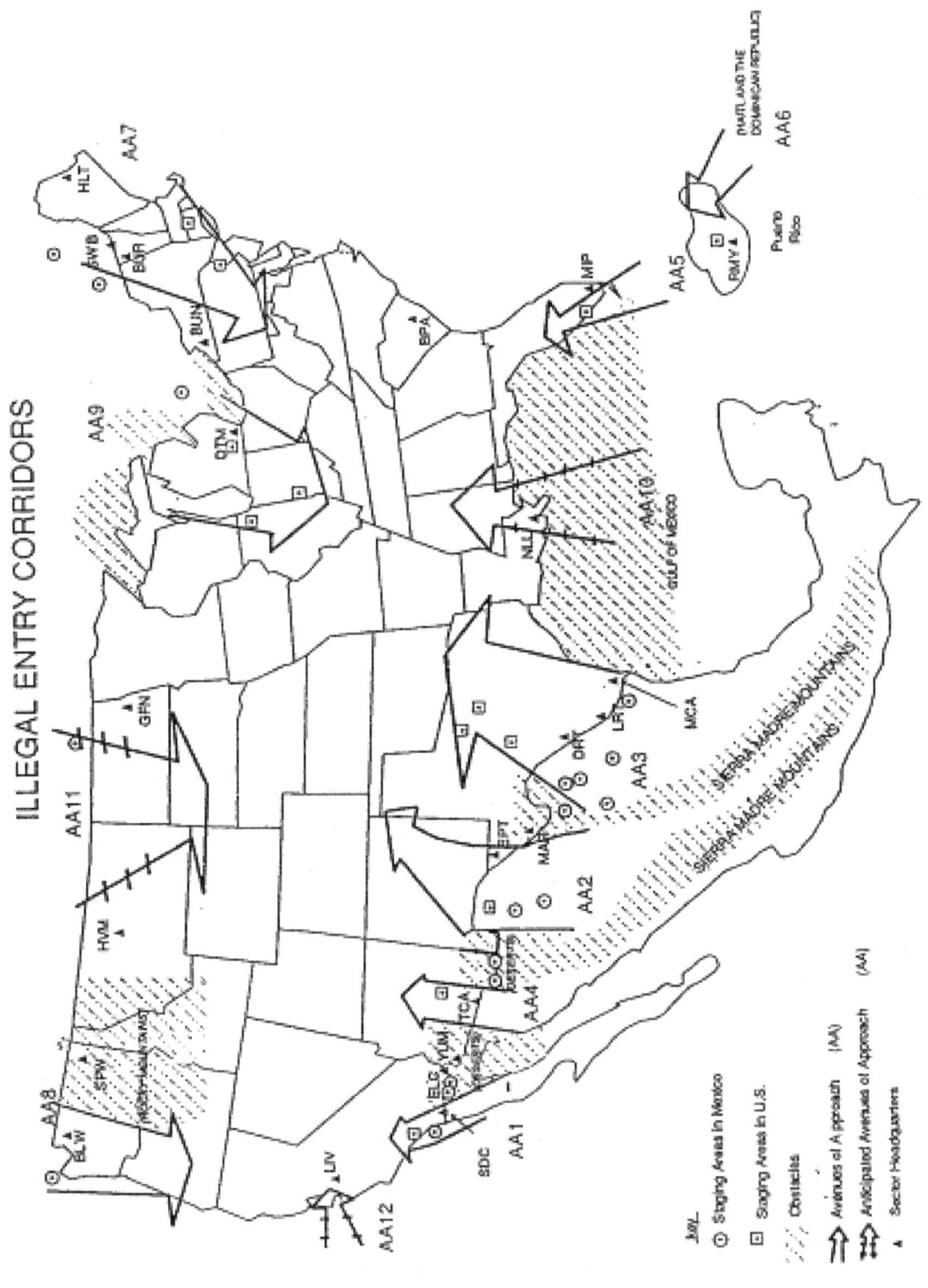

Figure 3.3. Map showing US borders as at risk of invasion (1994 Border Patrol Report Map, cited in Loyd 2014).

visible infrastructure such as walls and checkpoints – allows these areas to retain their "natural" appearance external to the border security apparatus.

This symbiosis between ESRI and Border Patrol is hardly surprising: following longstanding critiques of mapmaking as technology of power, GIS has been accused of being particularly suited to surveillance and control, and fetishizing a positivist and objectivist framework that cleanses the map of its own situatedness and conditions of possibility (Bondi and Domosh 1992; Smith 1992; Goss 1995; Kwan 2002; Elwood 2006). However, although GIS can serve as a tool of violence and control, it can also be used analytically to foreground spatial relationships that challenge and subvert structures of authority.

Since the mid-1990s, geographers have been exploring approaches to mapmaking, such as counter-mapping, that undermine dominant power structures enforced by institutional maps (e.g. Peluso 1995; Harris and Hazen 2006) by levying alternative forms of mapping (Wood 2010, 2015). Counter-mapping generally occurs where a disenfranchised group actively rejects imposed geographies and uses the authoritative voice of maps to stake claims on land rights, resource access, and historical narratives. Counter-mapping not only critiques how mapping technologies bolster imperial and state-level authority; it often actively combines mapping techniques with local knowledge to foster alternative forms of understanding, visualizing, and producing space.

Counter-mapping projects routinely resist the aesthetics and informatics of traditional mapping convention (Wood 2010; Kent 2012), using new ways of visualizing space and place to reterritorialize contested areas. More importantly for the topic of undocumented migration to the USA, counter-mapping reflexively engages with the politics of making the invisible visible, and attempts to map violence and marginalization without undercutting strategies of resistance (Tazzioli 2015). As Tazzioli writes, the "notion of 'counter' in counter-mapping has ultimately two meanings" (Tazzioli 2015, 4). First, it refers to making visible the effects of authority; in the case of migrants, these are the effects of immigration policy, borders, and border security. Second, it "challenges the very possibility of mapping" these effects (Tazzioli 2015, 4).

In the context of the Mexico–USA borderlands, the above tenets underpin our counter-mapping project. This chapter employs counter-mapping as a method of mapping the effects of the border security project, and of challenging the spatial ideology upon which border security is premised. This counter-mapping draws upon six years of field research in the Sonoran Desert mapping security infrastructure and migrant trails. By exploring how migrants are either forced or choose to move through surveilled landscapes and the resultant dangers they face, we aim to use counter-mapping both to surveil surveillance (i.e. reappropriate mapping authority to hold border policy accountable) and, in the process, reveal the mechanisms of silencing that such surveillance methods engender.

Unlike other counter-mapping projects (Hermann 2010; Wood 2010), we use conventional forms of data collection and visualization, while at the same time acknowledging that our maps are themselves artifacts of situated, incomplete, and politically motivated techniques of production. In our project, the priority is to make visible border security processes of erasure and not merely to unveil, but to unveil in a manner that is easy to understand and disseminate. However, our primary concern is that in using traditional modes of mapping, our data could be used to abet border security. Accordingly, we have waited over two years for publication and present our survey-based analyses in tabular format rather than as conventional maps.

Selective Surveillance: Risk, Death, and Invisibility

Our data is derived from surveying the desert between Nogales and Altar, from the border in the south to Three Points in the north, mapping 341 locations with concentrations of border-crossing material culture (Figure 3.4). These sites were typologized based on size, artifact concentration, and activity (humanitarian, migrant, or Border Patrol, smuggler, etc.). Sites were dated roughly with expiry dates on food packages, the presence of artifact types, and the state of object decay, which allowed a basic understanding of site chronologies. Furthermore, complete inventories of all objects found were performed for 80 of the largest sites.

Analyzing objects left in the desert became an entry point to better understand what border security is and does. Material traces track how people move through space over time, index the costs of existing in the landscape, and provide an optic onto how the desert has been constructed to control movement and enact violence on migrants over the past 15 years. Combining material and spatial data with ethnographic interviews of migrants who had recently crossed the border, we examined how the combination with desert and security defined migrant mobility. Using objects we had found in the desert as interview prompts, these ethnographic interviews outlined not only migrant strategies of preparation and movement, but experiences of the desert landscape itself.

Movement

Our initial mapping project, never published, examined the landscape position of different migrant site types to determine migrant movement strategy in relation to security infrastructure. The results, while interesting, were also deeply troubling and problematic, as they only made sense within border security enforcement strategy. Our data mimicked, rather than critiqued, surveillance data. Furthermore, this analysis maintained the naturalized fetish of the border as the organizing point of analysis. We redirected our analyses to focus less on migrants as a stable category with a single strategy, and more on the changing effects of the border security apparatus on migrant mobility over time.

The spatial patterning of migrant sites was combined with each site's Earliest Date (ED), the earliest identifiable date at the site. Instead of relating sites to distance from the border, each site was defined according to remoteness (distance from major roads). Three major trends of movement change are identifiable over the past 15 years. First, a decrease in trails in the flat areas of Altar and Green Valley (Figure 3.4), and increasing activity through the Tumacocori Mountains; and second, an increasing number of campsites closer to the border. Campsites, defined by high numbers of cans and packaging from protein-rich foods (e.g. tuna, sardines, beans), are frequently connected to either *ad hoc* built shelters, or sheltered, hidden areas within the landscape, and represent areas where migrants spend significant amounts of time resting or hiding (Gokee and De León 2014). Our survey indicates that in 2010–2013, campsites were situated on average over 3 km further south than was the case in 2000–2005. A southern shift in campsites suggests that crossing had slowed and was less direct.

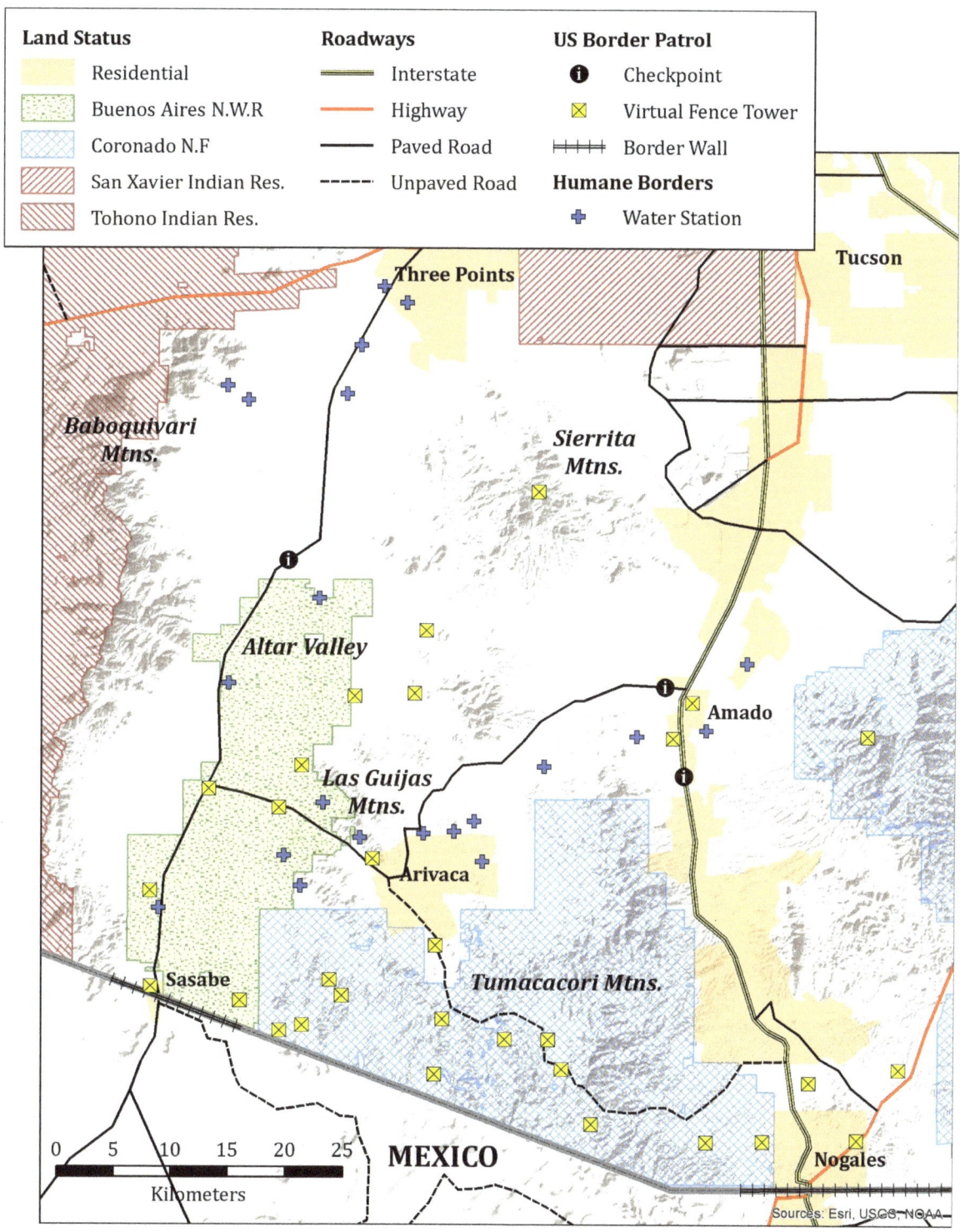

Figure 3.4. The Nogales–Sasabe corridor.

Figure 3.5. Photograph of two migrants in rugged terrain (photograph by "Memo" – see De León 2015 for detailed discussion of migrant photos shot *en route*).

The reduced speed of desert crossing is corroborated by a trend in site locations in increasingly remote areas, away from established trails and roads (Figure 3.5). In early sites (with an ED of 2005 or earlier) over half of the sites were located on major desert trails. Between 2010 and 2013, only a quarter of the sites were directly on trails (Table 3.1). Together, these patterns suggest that migrants have been moving away from established trails, taking more time to move through the desert, and moving through increasingly difficult areas to traverse as a means of avoiding detection. This at once increases the resource demand of the crossing (more food and water necessary) and the risk of injury or death.

Table 3.1. Migrant site locations.

	2000–2005	2006–2009	2010–2013
On trail (n-count)	26	20	14
Off trail (n-count)	18	33	40
Total sites	44	53	54
Percentage of sites on trail	59%	38%	26%

Complementary to our survey, mortality data from Humane Borders shows increasingly frequent migrant deaths in remote sectors of the desert. Migrant deaths in 2001–2004 were clearly grouped around the three arterial roads (Figure 3.6), with three-quarters of migrant bodies found in Altar and Green Valley. In 2005–2008 the total number of bodies found

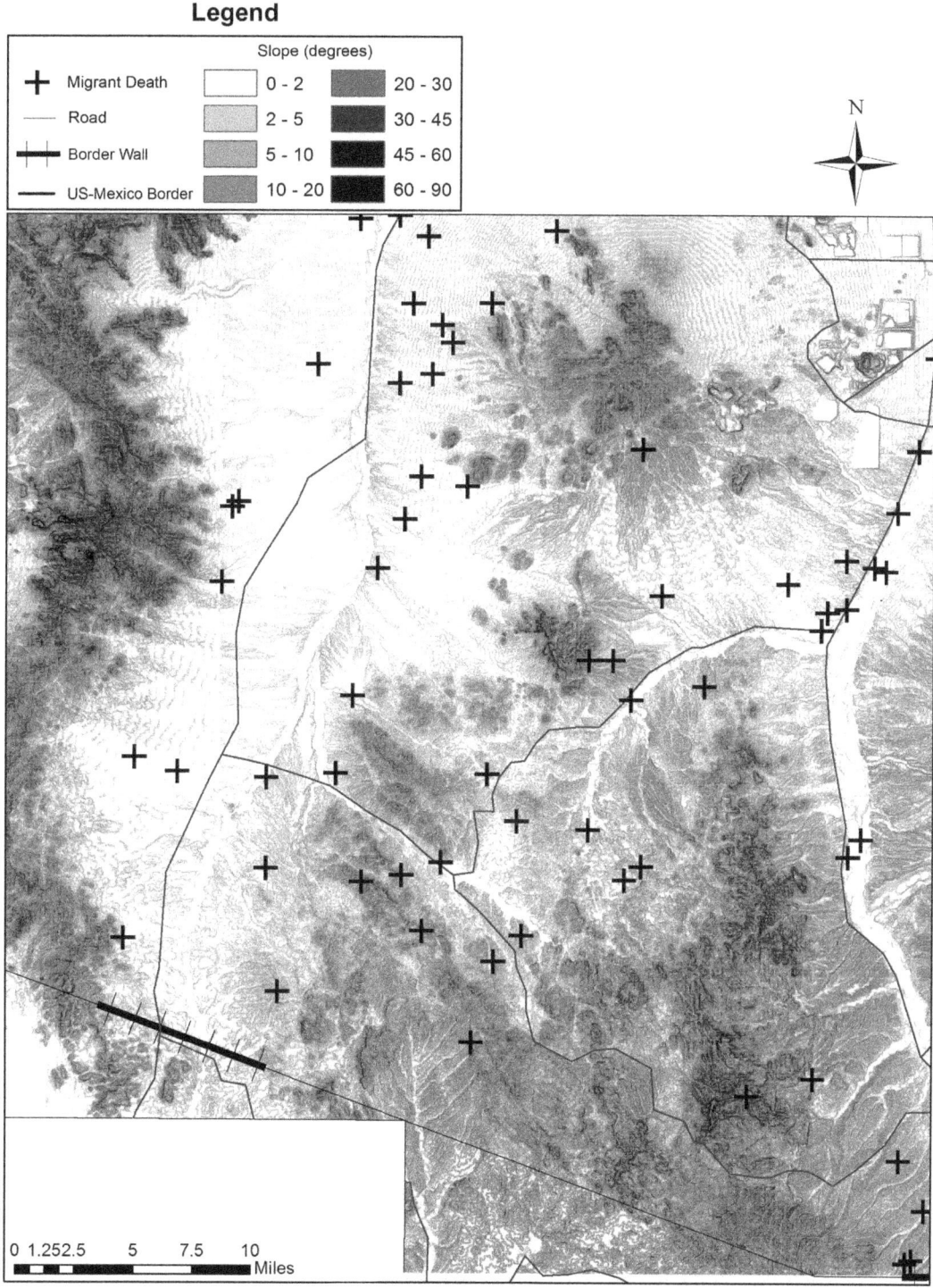

Figure 3.6. Migrant death locations in the Nogales–Sasabe corridor, 2001–2004 (data from Humane Borders).

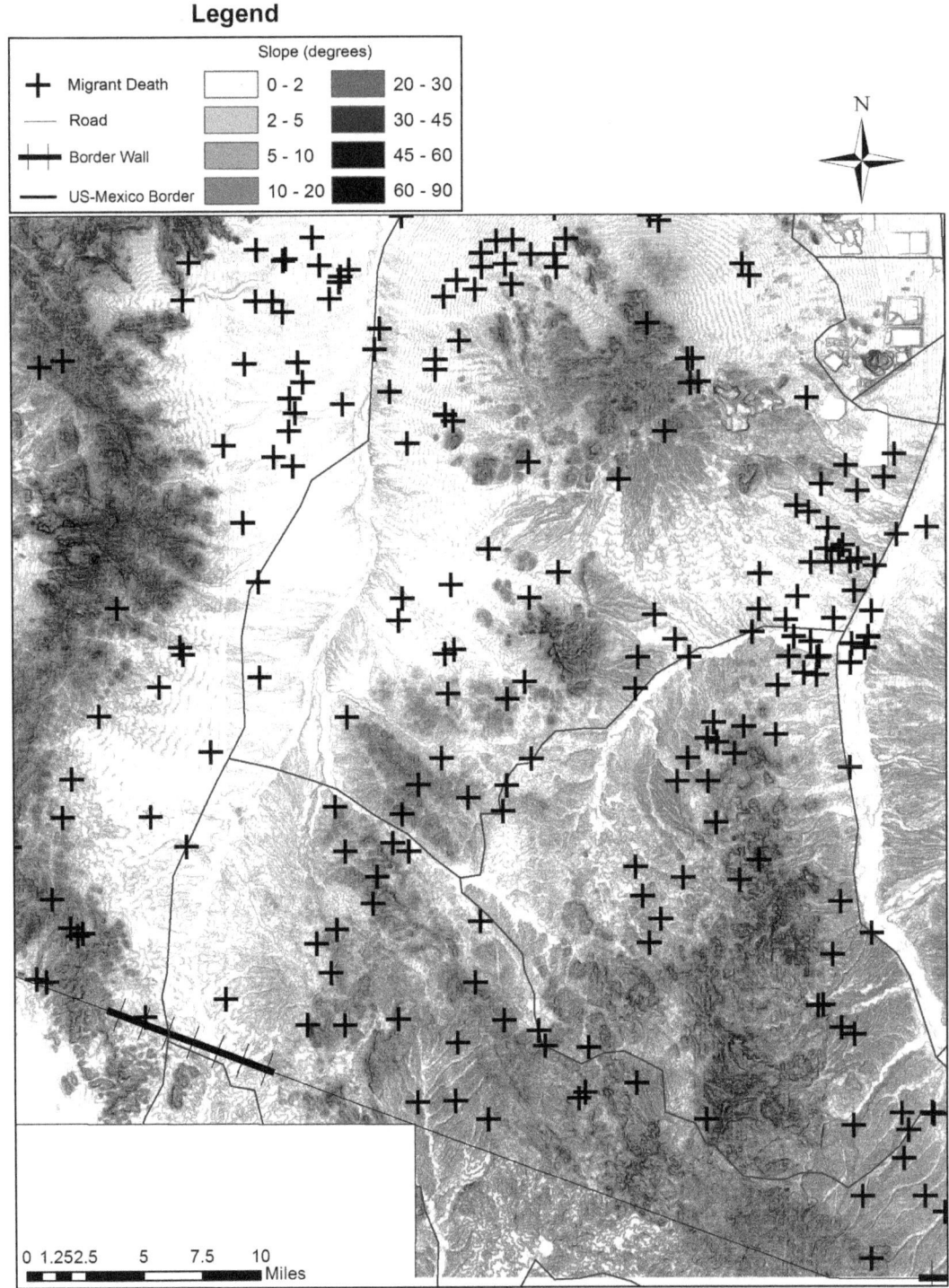

Figure 3.7. Migrant death locations in the Nogales–Sasabe corridor, 2005–2008 (data from Humane Borders).

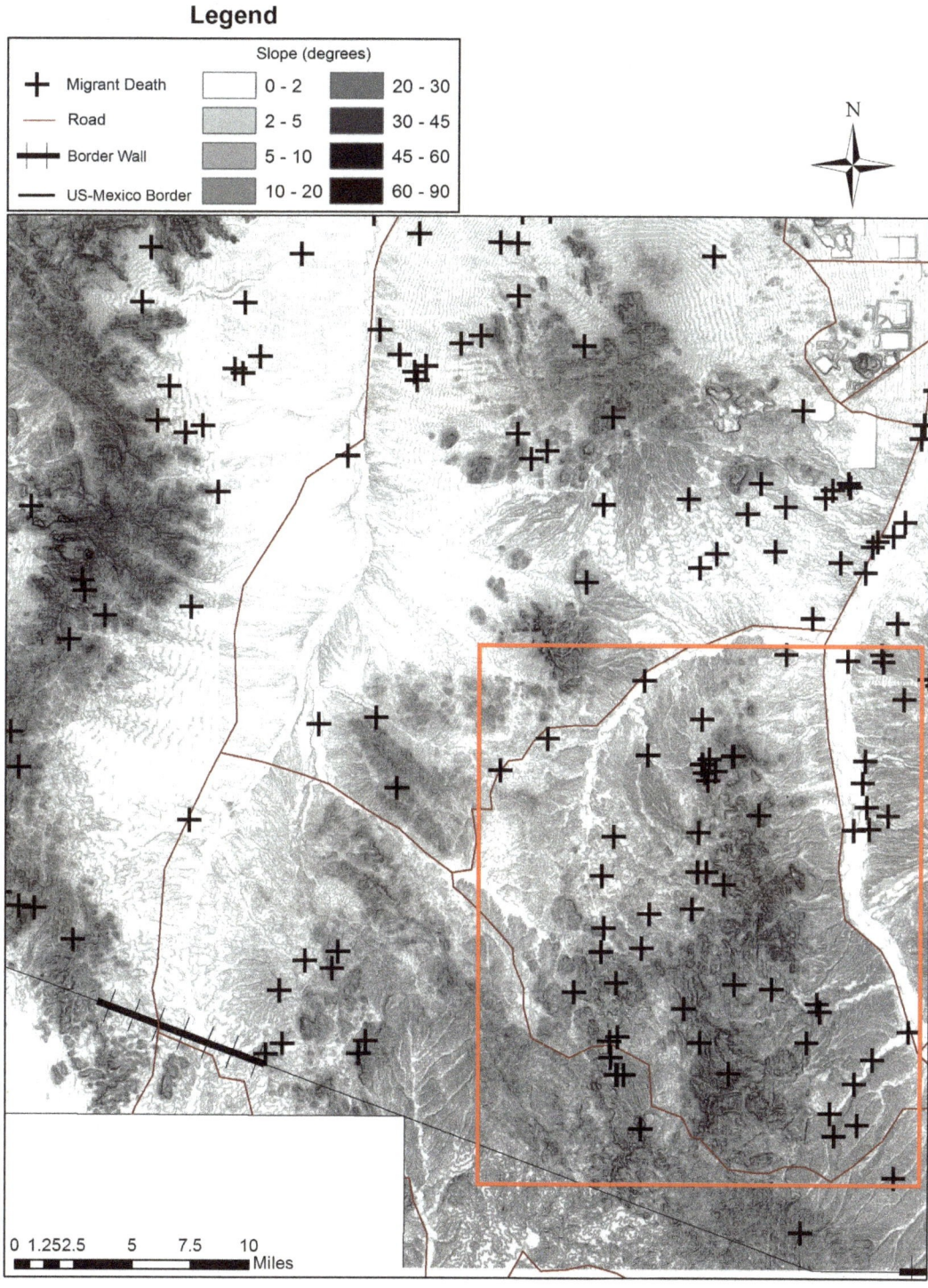

Figure 3.8. Migrant death locations in the Nogales–Sasabe corridor, 2009–2013. Box indicates southwestern portion of the Tumacocori Mountains (data from Humane Borders).

between Sasabe and Nogales had tripled, with half of the deaths occurring in the rougher terrain of the Tumacocori Mountains (Figure 3.7). In 2009–2013, nearly two thirds of all bodies were found in the mountains between Altar and Green Valley (Figure 3.8), and the latest statistics from Humane Borders show this trend continuing (Humane Borders 2016). Notably, one third of all bodies found during the same period were concentrated in the southwestern-most section of the Tumacocori Mountains, a much more rugged landscape closer to the border and where only 5% of bodies were found in 2000–2004.

The patterns of slower, off-path movement and higher occurrences of death in rugged and remote locations are direct results of migrants trying to avoid detection in the wake of PTD. However, a central paradox within Humane Borders's data, as well as the material culture data collected by the UMP, is that the general trends they identify suggest their own incompleteness. As migrants are forced into more remote areas where bodies are more difficult to find, the statistics and maps will account for fewer of the actual numbers of migrant deaths (see also Beck *et al.* 2014 for more on the effects of desert scavengers on corpse visibility). Therefore, the blank spaces in our maps may well indicate – by their inaccessibility – regions of higher potential for migrant deaths and extreme crossing conditions. In other words, not only does the security apparatus direct migrants to move through areas with a higher risk of death, it also forces them into areas where, if they do die, their bodies are unlikely to be found.

Conclusions

This mapping project intends to do two things. First, we aim to give presence to migrant traces and bear witness to those aspects of migration being erased jointly by the desert and the security apparatus. In pushing migrants into remote areas, border security intentionally directs migrants into the desert and outsources the resultant violence against migrants to landscapes concealed from public view. As migrants die in increasingly remote locations, the rapid decomposition of their bodies by the elements makes it less likely that their remains will be recovered (Beck *et al.* 2014). Accordingly, the number of migrant deaths will rise while the number of recorded deaths may stay the same or even decline.

Second, this project attempts to critique and undercut the naturalized violence and erasure that constitutes the border security apparatus. We argue that the desert, despite being touted as "nature", is not distinct from walls and checkpoints, and is utilized by security because it appears separate from and outside of human control. This critique, rooted in the very same technologies of spatial analysis used by security forces, reveals border security's reliance on a geographically based foundation of deniability and erasure. The purpose of counter-mapping the borderlands is not only to draw links between the violence of the security apparatus and the landscape, but to deconstruct the central conceptual pillars of the apparatus itself: i.e., that the border is a natural line, and that the desert is harsh and brutal but unconnected to human activities.

However, our mapping project – including the various maps both seen and unseen, published and those unpublishable – is not an objective representation of borderland interactions; they are products of specific conditions of possibility mediated by both border security and the desert. This project is itself situated, congealing the traces of our mapping process, identifying places we went and those we could not go to due to the limits of our own bodies and methods. Despite years of surveying this area, attempts to map and identify migrant sites were constantly constrained by the landscape itself. Large numbers of our sites were encountered at the very edge of our field of vision, at the edge of our own physical, financial, and personal limits of survey. Migrant sites are increasingly remote, hidden, and therefore beyond our limits as surveyors.

This is where the two points converge; our data represent the manners in which a changing border security apparatus remakes and remaps the desert as a violent tool for silencing and hiding the traumas of migration, and is itself an example of this silencing process. Both the content and gaps in our data point toward this erasure. At the same time, the ability of our maps and analyses to represent anything speaks to the unique discriminatory practices that the border security apparatus upholds, as our research was only possible due to our own positions within the regimes of citizenship, race, and class that border security recognizes. In other words, the data we collected indexed the ability of us, the researchers, to move through a contested landscape, unhindered and relatively unmolested, and juxtaposed our privileged position with those of the migrants. Despite walking the same desert paths, our outings were leisurely hikes dedicated to research, while those of the migrants were struggles for survival.

With clandestine migration occurring throughout the world, and public attention within Western nations flitting between sensationalized tragedies of Mediterranean crossings, bodycounts in the Sonora Desert, and the increasingly shrill rhetoric concerning the "threat" of immigrants to "civilization", the importance of politically engaged research on undocumented migration is incredibly high. To maintain its critical commitment to shedding light on the endemic violences of immigration policing and to doing no harm against the victims of this policing, this research on clandestine immigration can neither reject out of hand the use of rigorous data collection and dissemination techniques used by governing authorities, nor can it naively presume that these methods can be easily repurposed to speak truth to power. Counter-mapping, as we imagine it in this project, seeks to thread this needle through continual reflexivity over its methodology and constant concern over the potential value or harm of its data. Rather than attempting to reject spatial analysis as a technique *in toto*, or lionize it as the single tool to counter oppression, counter-mapping's approach to spatial analysis is much more modest. Relying on spatial analysis as a core part of long-term archaeological survey, counter-mapping provides a critical perspective on how a landscape has been designed and built. The survey is itself situated and historical, a fact which does not diminish the veracity of its data but helps to flesh out the contours of the landscape and the manner in which it has been produced. As a mode of critique which is reflexive, political, and committed to rigorous data-collecting fieldwork, counter-mapping provides an ethical and politically salient methodology for the archaeological study of clandestine migration.

References

Andreas, P. 2009. *Border Games: Policing the U.S.–Mexico Divide*. Ithaca, NY: Cornell University Press.

Beck, J., I. Ostericher, G. Sollish, and J. De León. 2014. "Animal Scavenging and Scattering and the Implications for Documenting the Deaths of Undocumented Border Crossers in the Sonoran

Desert." *Journal of Forensic Sciences* 60 (Supplement 1): S11–S20. https://doi.org/10.1111/1556-4029.12597

Blust, K. 2016. "Deaths per 10000 Border Crossers are up 5 Times from a Decade Ago." *Arizona Daily Star*, 21 May. Available online: http://tucson.com/news/local/border/deaths-per-border-crossers-are-up-times-from-a-decade/article_c1279aaf-4ad8-51c9-82d8-3143b836f52e.html

Bondi, L. and M. Domosh. 1992. "Other Figures in Other Places: On Feminism, Postmodernism and Geography." *Environment and Planning D: Society and Space* 10: 199–213. https://doi.org/10.1068/d100199

De León, J. 2015. *Land of Open Graves: Living and Dying on the Migrant Trail.* Berkeley: University of California Press.

Doty, R. L. 2011. "Bare Life: Border-Crossing Deaths and Spaces of Moral Alibi." *Environment and Planning D: Society and Space* 29 (4): 599–612. https://doi.org/10.1068/d3110

Dunn, T. J. 2009. *Blockading the Border and Human Rights: The El Paso Operation That Remade Immigration Enforcement.* Austin: University of Texas Press.

Elwood, S. 2006. "Critical Issues in Participatory GIS: Deconstructions, Reconstructions, and New Research Directions." *Transactions in GIS* 10 (5): 693–708. https://doi.org/10.1111/j.1467-9671.2006.01023.x

Gokee, C. and J. De León. 2014. "Sites of Contention: Archaeology and Political Discourse in the US-Mexico Borderlands." *Journal of Contemporary Archaeology* 1 (1):133–163. https://doi.org/10.1558/jca.v1i1.133

Goss, J. 1995. "Marketing the New Marketing: The Strategic Discourse of Geodemographic Information Systems." In *Ground Truth*, edited by J. Pickles, 130–170. New York: Guilford Press.

Harris, L. M. and H. D. Hazen. 2006. "Power of Maps: (Counter) Mapping for Conservation." *ACME: An International E-Journal for Critical Geographies* 4 (1): 99–130.

Hermann, M. 2010. "They Would Not Take Me There." *Cartographic Perspectives* 66: 31–40.

Humane Borders. 2016. Open-source GIS project. Available online: http://www.humaneborders.info/

Kent, A. 2012. "From a Dry Statement of Fact to a Thing of Beauty." *Cartographic Perspectives* 73: 37–60.

Kwan, M. P. 2002. "Feminist Visualization: Re-Envisioning GIS as a Method of Feminist Geographic Research." *Annals of the Association of American Geographers* 92 (4): 645–661. https://doi.org/10.1111/1467-8306.00309

Loyd, J. 2014. "One If by Land, Two If by Sea." *New Inquiry*, 16 May. Available online: thenewinquiry.com/essays/one-if-by-land-two-if-by-sea/

Nevins, J. 2002. *Operation Gatekeeper: The Rise of the "Illegal Alien" and the Making of the US-Mexico Boundary.* London and New York: Routledge.

Peluso, N. L. 1995. "Whose Woods are These? Counter-Mapping Forest Territories in Kalimantan, Indonesia." *Antipode* 27 (4): 383–406. https://doi.org/10.1111/j.1467-8330.1995.tb00286.x

Schroeder, R. 2012. *Holding the Line in the 21st Century.* US Customs and Border Protection. Available online: https://www.cbp.gov/sites/default/files/documents/Holding%20the%20Line_TRILOGY.pdf

Smith, N. 1992. "Real Wars, Theory Wars." *Progress in Human Geography* 16 (2): 257–271. https://doi.org/10.1177/030913259201600208

Sundberg, J. 2008. "'Trash-Talk' and the Production of Quotidian Geopolitical Boundaries in the USA–Mexico Borderlands." *Social and Cultural Geography* 9 (8): 871–890. https://doi.org/10.1080/14649360802441424

Sweeney, W. 2001. "US Border Patrol Maximizes Enforcement with GIS." *ArcNews Online*, Fall. Available online: www.esri.com/news/arcnews/fall01articles/usborderpatrol.html

Tazzioli, M. 2015. "Which Europe? Migrants' Uneven Geographies and Counter-Mapping at the limits of Representation." *Movements* 1 (2): 1–20.

Veal, W. 2003. "Protecting the Borders: GIS Technology and Command/Control Optimization." *Police Chief* 70 (6): 41–42.

Wood, D. 2010. *Rethinking the Power of Maps*. New York: Guilford Press.

_____. 2015. *Weaponizing Maps: Indigenous Peoples and Counter-Insurgency in the Americas*. New York: Guilford Press.

Haeden Stewart is a PhD candidate in Anthropology at the University of Chicago. Address for correspondence: Department of Anthropology, University of Chicago, 1126 East 59th Street, Chicago, IL 60637, USA. Email: haedenstewart@uchicago.edu

Ian Ostericher is a PhD candidate in Archaeology at the University of Cambridge. Address for correspondence: Division of Archaeology, Downing Street, Cambridge, CB2 3DZ, UK. Email: i.ostericher@gmail.com

Cameron Gokee is a Research Assistant Professor at Appalachian State University and manages spatial data for the Undocumented Migration Project. Address for correspondence: Department of Anthropology - ASU Box 32016 - Boone, NC 28608-2016, USA. Email: gokeecd@appstate.edu

Jason De León is an Associate Professor of Anthropology at the University of Michigan and Director of the Undocumented Migration Project. Address for correspondence: LSA Anthropology, University of Michigan, 101 West Hall 1085 S. University Avenue, Ann Arbor, MI 48109-1107, USA. Email: jpdeleon@umich.edu

Chapter 4

Place making in Non-Places: Migrant Graffiti in Rural Highway Box Culverts

Gabriella Soto

Rural Roads and Undocumented Migration In Southern Arizona: An Overview

This chapter describes a particular material phenomenon resulting from the mass movement of undocumented migrants across the border from Mexico into Arizona in the USA.
Focusing on the rural highways that weave through the borderlands, I examine how sites
of sanctioned interstate and international traffic overlap with irregular or undocumented
migration. Alongside and underneath these roadways, one finds traces of the clandestine foot
traffic of undocumented people. I argue that through these traces one can track the recent
history of migration in the region. Specifically, though one can currently (2016) find evidence
of undocumented migrants walking alongside the border region's remote highways, the dates
and context of this evidence point to a decrease in these sites' use for undocumented travel
in recent years. The evidence of use of rural highways by undocumented travelers, and the
evidence that such use has discontinued, are both fundamental to this story.

Undocumented migration at the Mexico–USA border is pre-planned and pragmatic, based
on long histories of undocumented travel in the region and established industries of human
smuggling (Durand and Massey 2004; Spener 2009; Hernández 2014; Sanchez 2015). "Clandestine" travel corridors have overlapped with existing trails and highway infrastructure as
much as possible, using and subverting sanctioned routes for migrants' own expedience of
movement (Durand and Massey 2004; Sheridan 2009; Sanchez 2015). Such acts leave traces
of history in the otherwise sterile spaces of mass transit – these rural branches of the US
highway system – and some of these traces are deliberately created as memory-markers.

At first blush, it is unsurprising that people would want to mark the places where they have
had a significant life experience, and a number of recent ethnographies with undocumented
migrants highlight how their cross-border journeys were indeed very significant life experiences
for them (Hagan 2008; Martinez 2001; Sheridan 2009; Martinez *et al.* 2013). The prevalence
of acts of "place-making" through history forms much of the archaeological record, and the
quest to understand such acts features prominently in social theory (Bourdieu 1985; Lefebvre
1991; Hirsch and O'Hanlon 1995; Tilley 2006; Bowser and Zedeño 2009). What makes these

particular acts of place-making unique is that they occurred in the shadows; undocumented migration is possible to the extent that those undertaking it can remain invisible to authorities. The hidden nature of migrants' journeys is exacerbated by border policy, which pushes migrant travelers into ever more remote spaces.

In locating sites that express tension, contradiction, and hidden processes, one can gain insight into the particular power dynamics of a place (Gonzalez-Ruibal 2008; Harrison and Schofield 2010; de Certeau 2011). In this case, the US government promotes a narrative of necessary border security to ensure the stability of the nation (United States Customs and Border Protection 2016), but the presence of place-making activities of those deemed direct threats to that security calls some of that ideal into question. At play here are not only actors in a dynamic social movement, but also the resonance of things after they are created and abandoned by their human counterparts. What are the implications of migrants' attempts to memorialize their presence in a landscape where their presence is forbidden?

I argue that the rural highways of southern Arizona represent classic examples of what Marc Augé (1995) calls "non-places" – a term that describes sites of industrialized mass transit, where people pass through, but never reside. Consequently, non-places are also sites where there seem to be no meaningful traces of history or belonging. The rural roads discussed here superficially fit that definition. They are nondescript in their typicality for the region, being lightly maintained with overgrowth on both sides. Innumerable cracks spread throughout and the road shoulders have begun to crumble. Here, one can find a sparse yet steady stream of vehicles. Perhaps these roads' most tangible point of distinction is that the patrol vehicles of the United States Border Patrol (USBP) constitute the bulk of the local traffic. The USBP cars on the road indirectly signal the presence of illicit border-crossing activity.

If one looks beyond the highway, material traces of undocumented migration are often scattered in the overgrowth on either side. Archaeological analysis of the practical yet ephemeral materials that migrants carry with them to survive an undocumented journey have been found to illuminate a dialectical struggle between those continuing to cross borders without official sanction and the social controls that aim to prevent them from doing so (Gokee and De León 2014; De León 2015; De León et al. 2015). Migrant materials commonly include backpacks, water bottles, food containers, clothing, and hygiene products. Ultimately, although these materials hold important information about the hidden social processes of migration, they are also transient. I visited the highway sites discussed below multiple times over a period of years, and the portable and ephemeral material belongings of migrants never stayed in place or the same: belongings were removed by those who consider such materials "trash" (Sundberg 2008; Banks 2009; Bureau of Land Management Arizona 2015), particularly highway clean-up crews; these materials were moved and buried by water flows after rains; and they decayed. Thus migrant belongings left along roadsides one day may be cleaned away the next, or experience active destruction by the elements, and ultimately decay beyond recognition.

On my last visit to these sites, I found only highly degraded materials associated with migration, and these remained only at some distances from the roadsides where clean-up crews may not have ventured. Absence, invisibility, and erasure of evidence characterize the decades-long interplay between the illicit social movement of undocumented migration in this space and the state-based efforts to interdict it through amassed paramilitary force. But then of course, traces of undocumented migrants walking along these remote rural highways *en masse* is almost wholly a result of US border policy, designed to deter undocumented migration by funneling migrants towards more dangerous geography (Rubio-Goldsmith *et al.* 2006; Magaña 2008; Doty 2011; and in this volume, Stewart *et al.*). Historically, undocumented migration into the USA through Mexico occurred at urban sites located at the borderline, where migrants could easily blend with local populations (Cornelius 2005; Nevins 2010).

Beneath rural highways, hidden beyond one's direct vision from a passing car, one may find graffiti markings by migrants carved into concrete underpasses. Unlike the traditional suite of migrant materials, graffiti markings are tethered to the space where created and thus create a sense of heritage in migrants' own terms. With a focus on migrant graffiti, I use this chapter to discuss how rural highway non-places are deliberately transformed in this particular migration context, and to narrate the stories generated from such sites.

Rural Roads as Non-Places

The designation of "non-place" may initially seem passive, but the context of undocumented migration may transform non-places into important points of controversy between what nations see as legitimate travel and the continued and rising rates of irregular or undocumented

Figure 4.1. A snapshot of the road near Site 1, looking south towards the border. In the grass on the other side is a pile of decaying clothing, likely left by migrants (photograph by author).

travelers (Bender 2001; Heyman 2014). When Marc Augé coined the term ("*non-lieux*"), its counterintuitive and contentious nature was deliberate. Non-places are refugee camps, airports, highways, and slums. Such sites are a specific outgrowth of neoliberalism with its mass international transit, growing globalized marketplace, and increasing privatization of resources (Augé 1995; Harvey 2005; Graeber 2009).

Augé also coined the term "supermodernity", to describe these polar facets present in this contemporary era of globalization, working on the premise that "the world of supermodernity does not exactly match the one in which we [those from the affluent Western world] believe we live, for we live in a world we have not yet learned to look at" (Augé 1995, 35). As globalization trains the (mainly) Western eye to see a small world slowly conforming to its seemingly democratic and capitalist ideals (see Fukuyama 1989), these processes simultaneously make it harder to see that not everyone may travel so easily; and those who cannot travel are relegated to non-places where they often lack rights or representation, are deprived of their means of production, and live precariously and in informal conditions (Augé 1995; Bender 2001; Davis 2007; Papadopoulos *et al.* 2008; Robinson 2011). Some must risk their lives to travel a few mere miles across international borders.

To document the contradictions implicit in supermodernity, Augé calls for a look behind the proverbial curtains of non-places, through locally-grounded (versus foreign and exotic) lines of anthropological inquiry that pinpoint "factors of singularity" (Augé 1995, 40). Through localized inquiries, one might also find points of non-conformity and subversion as well as displacement and suffering. As Gonzalez-Ruibal (2008, 2013) points out, an archaeological lens allows for a focus on the tangible contradictions within the prevailing tides of supermodern world order. Non-places are sites to which one can physically go, and the "factors of singularity" within them have tangible material signatures: "[As archaeologists] we have to look at the unstable zones of […] power, excavate (metaphorically and literally) under its façade and at its margins. We have to examine the crack in the walls of the […] monument[s] or the hidden shantytowns where the […] subaltern dwells" (Gonzalez-Ruibal 2013, 604).

Following both Augé (1995) and Gonzalez-Ruibal (2013), I look at the non-places that are rural roads in southern Arizona. Studies of social transformation tend to look for major public events and upheavals, but remind us that upheaval is always an end point within prolonged processes of dissent that are often not readily recognizable as they occur (Papadopoulos *et al.* 2008; de Certeau 2011; Scott 2012). By looking at margins, and even "cracks in the wall", one can find elements indicating incipient social change, or at least points that problematize official narratives of border security as necessary even to the extent that they cause mass suffering and the deaths of migrants (Augé 1995; Papadopoulos *et al.* 2008; Das and Randeria 2015).

As non-places, rural highways are for passing through, and points where the delineation between "belonging" citizens and undocumented migrants is policed (Heyman 2001, 2014; Kearney 2004; Nevins 2010). Initially, it would appear that the highways are stark contrasts to traditional "anthropological places" where one can reside, where belonging can be carved into the place, and history accumulated. When one starts to look at the rural highways more closely, a different image emerges. These non-places tell a distinct material story of temporary residence, and simultaneously that migrants' use of these spaces has declined in recent years.

In other words, they are indeed spaces of both residence and history. Further, they represent a subversion of the intended use of the infrastructure of the state, as seen in the use of culverts (discussed below): Augé, citing de Certeau, refers to this kind of thing as

> "tricks in the art of doing" that enable individuals subjected to global constraints of modern […] society to deflect them, to make use of them, to contrive through a sort of everyday tinkering to establish their own decor and trace their own personal itineraries. (Augé 1995: 38; see also de Certeau 2011)

Methods

This study stems from a cumulative six months of archaeological data collection for masters and pre-doctoral fieldwork between 2010 and 2013 in corridors of undocumented migration in southern Arizona. During this period, I documented 37 southern Arizona sites where undocumented migrants had attempted clandestine passage into the USA (Figure 4.2). These were sites where they left materials behind, a host of things including, as noted above, backpacks, water bottles, food containers, and a number of more personal items. Such materials have been comprehensively documented by Jason De León's Undocumented Migration Project (De León 2012, 2013, 2015; Gokee and De León 2014; see also Stewart *et al.*, this volume). However, where De León's publications focus mainly on cumulative interpretations of the migrant materials found in the borderlands wilderness in one time period, this chapter focuses on a specific class of sites: the multiple examples of graffitied markings by migrants, carved into the landscape through various vernacular means, and the specific history they represent. While numerous sites with individual carved or graffitied markings attributed to undocumented migrants were found within known migrant travel corridors, two of these sites (here referred to as Site 1 and Site 2) stand out, representing 34 to 51 individual graffiti markings. They were both found in rural highway box culverts.

Box culverts are structures underneath built-up roadways, designed to mitigate the flow of wildlife and natural water sources that would be otherwise interrupted by the barrier posed by roads (Figure 4.3). More specifically, culverts ease the impact of nature on roadways, where otherwise a major rain could perhaps wash away a state's significant investment in the infrastructure. Culverts' manufactured purpose – an imperative within a state's expected investment and maintenance of infrastructure for travel – does not account for the possibility of one or many persons residing within one. But, in the landscape of undocumented migration and its policing, these culverts present opportunities for migrants to navigate highways unseen.

Highway culverts present places for undocumented travelers to hide while following formalized state travel routes. That migrants used to follow roadways was both confirmed archaeologically – as I will discuss below – and corroborated through numerous informal conversations with Border Patrol agents met in the areas of Sites 1 and 2. When asked about the state of undocumented migration in the area, the agents explained that migrants "used to" (but no longer) hide under specific culverts while awaiting vehicle transport. The agents did not say anything about the graffiti I found underneath the culverts. Piles of migrants' abandoned materials and the graffiti left behind at both sites indicated that the culverts were places where migrants likely passed some time. The materials left included backpacks, clothing, empty water

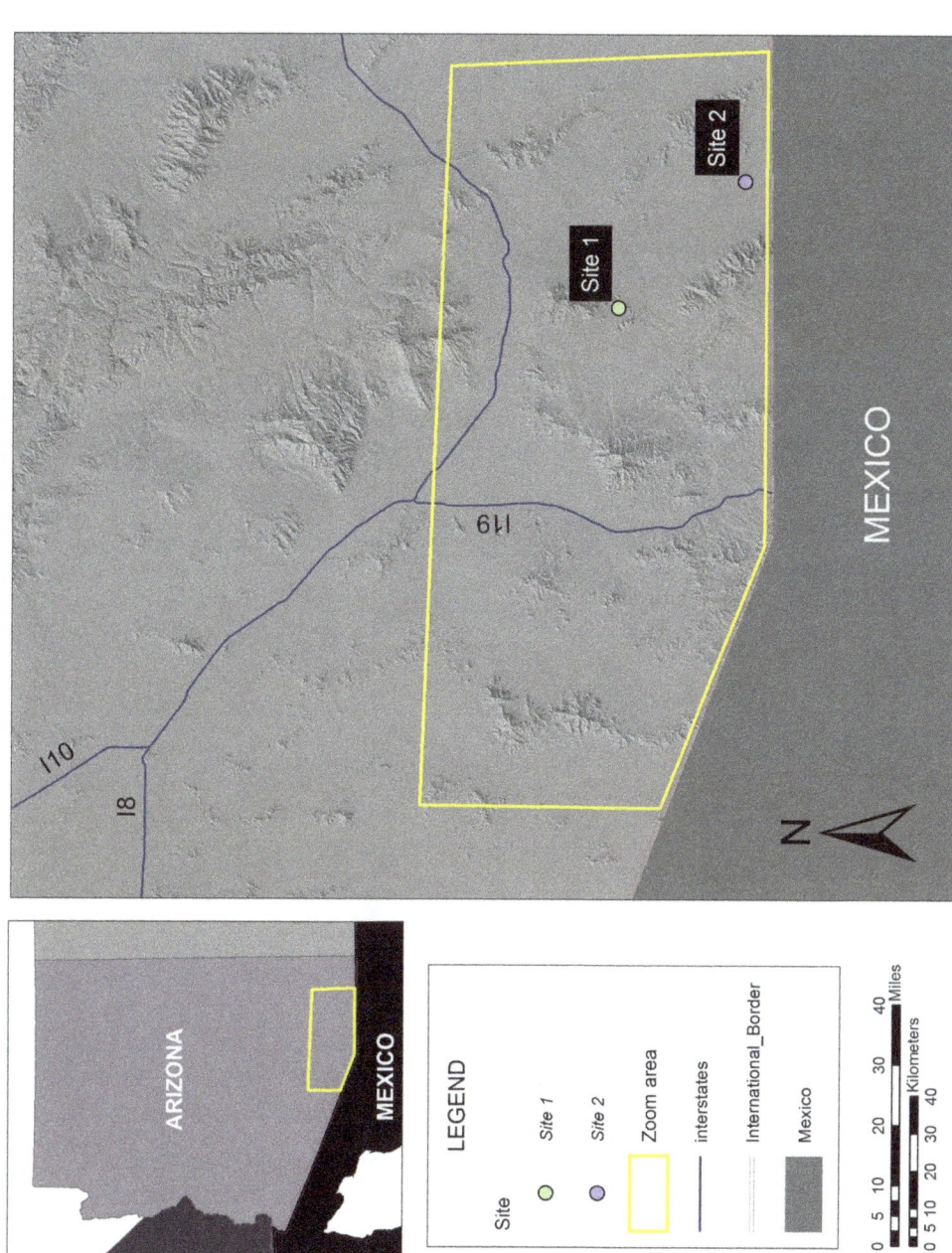

Figure 4.2. The location of the sites in relation to major highways (state routes are have not been included, to prevent others from locating these sites. Map by author).

Figure 4.3. The box culvert at Site 1 (photograph by author).

and juice bottles, toothbrushes, toothpaste, and small packs of powdered laundry detergent. The concrete surfaces of two culverts were covered by vernacular marks. These marks were not done with spray paint – graffiti done with spray paint evidences some forethought and planning on the part of its authors – but were opportunistic, written on the wall with a range of materials that could be found on the landscape: sharp rocks to etch, soft limestone used as chalk, and charcoal or lead pencil.

I initially visited Site 2 in 2010 and Site 1 in 2013, at which point I extensively photographed and documented their contents. Both sites were then revisited in 2016, when only one additional mark was found at Site 2 (Table 4.1). The revisit confirmed that the sites had remained (mostly) dormant since being initially encountered. The chalked and charcoaled marks were greatly faded, expressing in microcosm the widespread ephemerality of migrant materials on this landscape given their prolonged exposure to intense heat and aridity. Though faded, the graffiti did persist longer than the ephemeral and portable belongings encountered on my initial visits to the sites that were either removed, washed away, or decayed beyond recognition. In 2016, there were almost no new migrant materials at either site, which contrasted markedly with the preceding years of site visits.

At both sites, all but one instance of writing surveyed was in Spanish, providing another line of strong indication, in addition to the suite of typical migrant materials left behind (described

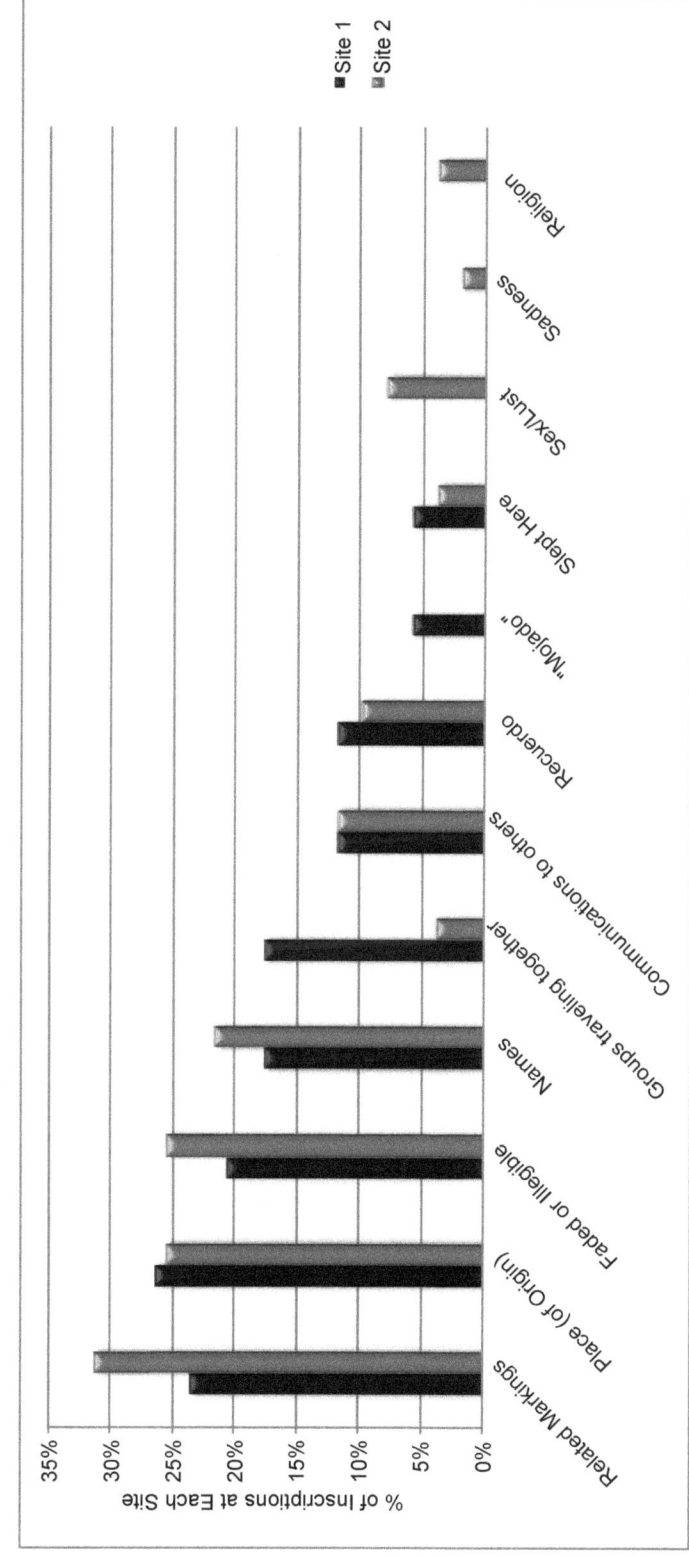

Table 4.1. Themes present in the inscriptions from Sites 1 and 2 are quantified by the frequency at which they occurred. Notably, at both sites over 20% of inscriptions were faded or illegible.

Figure 4.4. "Aqui Durmio Manuel Garcia from Guatemala" (Manuel Garcia from Guatemala slept here), at Site 2 (photograph by author).

in De León 2012; Gokee and De León 2014), that these marks belonged to undocumented migrants (Figure 4.4). Multiple persons were represented in the graffiti, evidenced by several names, handwriting styles, and multiple instances of overwritten graffiti, establishing some measure of chronology and repeated use of the sites over time. Many marks were in conversation, and many relayed messages to others in the same circumstance, voicing encouragement, humor, and frustration. They recorded migrants' places of origin and names, and repeatedly invoked the need for remembrance. Among the marks were: "*Recuerdos de su hamigo* [sic] *de Puebla, Abraham Perli Tobins*" (Remember your friend from Puebla), "*Hotél 5 Estrellas*" (Five Star Hotel), "*La Aventura de los putos emigrantes es algo inolvidable*" (The adventure of fucking migrants is unforgettable), and "*Feliz viaje a todos*" (Happy travels to all).

Place-Making In Non-Places: Aqui Durmio Manuel Garcia De Guatemala (Manuel Garcia From Guatemala Slept Here)

At the two sites, one finds a deliberately made and tangible record of the undocumented migration journey (Table 4.2). Represented among the 85 total inscriptions (34 at Site 1 and 51 at Site 2) were several themes: invocations to other migrants, records of individuals' places

Table 4.2. All inscriptions from (a) Site 1 and (b) Site 2, along with translations, noting the medium in which each inscription was recorded, whether it was related to any others' given content, and whether an inscription was overwritten. The last two elements help to establish relative chronology, and also establishes multiple recording events.

(a)   Site 1

Inscription	Translation	Notes	Medium	Over-written?	Related to Other Marks?
Bads Barrio	[*Barrio* = a neighbourhood]		Scratched	No	No
Recuerdos de 7 Jochitecos y un Copalieco que se binierón de mojados	Memories of 7 Jochitecos and one Copalieco who came up as wetbacks	A *Jochiteco* is a resident of the town of Juchitán, Oaxaca, Mexico; a *Copalieco* is a resident of town of Copales, Guanajuato, Mexico.	Pencil	No	No
Jose Edith Junior Pepe	[Names]	Likely from the same group as the "mojados de Molino" (see below).	Pencil	No	Yes
Recuerdos de 3 mojados Hermosillo y Obregon	Memories of 3 wetbacks from Hermosillo and Obregon	Hermosillo and Obregon are both major cities in Sonora, Mexico.	Pencil	No	No
Atoyac de Alvarez Gro		Atoyac de Alvarez is a city in Guerrero, Mexico. *Gro* = abbreviation for Guerrero.	Scratched	Yes	No
Puro Sonora	Pure Sonora	Sonora is a state in northern Mexico.	Scratched	Yes	No
La Hacha ocura (?)	[*Hacha* = axe; *ocurra* = happen]		Scratched	Yes	No
El Sitío	The Place		Scratched	Yes	No
aqui	here		Scratched	Yes	No
Mamon	Idiot/Sucker		Scratched	Yes	No
--rui Hol-y -Ato ---os	[Indecipherable]		Scratched	Yes	No
TCA	?		Scratched	Yes	No
Hotel 5 estrellas	5-star hotel		Scratched	Yes	Yes
Q aventura putos emigrantes es algo inolvidable	[The] adventure [of] fucking migrants is something unforgettable		Scratched	Yes	No
Feliz viaje a todos	Happy travels to all		Etched	Yes	No
[Drawing of a broken heart with an arrow through it]			Scratched	Yes	No
Hotel 5 estrellas [appears again]	5-star hotel		Scratched	Yes	Yes
Jalpan		Jalpan is a city in the state of Querétaro, Mexico.	Etched	Yes	Yes
Cal de --- [Boxed]	?		Etched	Yes	No
Los chicos del Barrio la colgada	The neighborhood kids hanging		Scratched	Yes	No
Feliz día de las madres un prospero nuvo año	Happy mothers' day, happy new year		Scratched	Yes	No
Queretaro		Querétaro is the name of a state and of a city in Mexico.	Scratched	Yes	Yes
Toña la diabla	Toña the she-devil		Scratched	No	No
Nike [drawn inside a Nike logo]			Scratched	No	No

Table 4.2 (continued)

Inscription	Translation	Notes	Medium	Over-written?	Related to Other Marks?
los mojados de aljapan y yerbabuena	the wetbacks from Aljapan and Yerbabuena	Aljapan is a city in the state of Puebla, Mexico; Yerbabuena is a city in the state of Jalisco, Mexico.	Scratched	No	No
Junior		Next to the entry below, probably from the Molino group.	Pencil	No	Yes
Recuerdos de 4 mojados de Molino Chih Junior Edith Jose Pepe	Memories of 4 wetbacks from Molino, Chihuahua [each signed their names with distinct signatures]		Pencil	Yes	Yes
recuer	remem…	Probably *recuerdo*, interrupted.	Etched	No	No
Jose y Betty	Jose and Betty		Pencil	No	No
Jalpan		Jalpan is a city in the state of Querétaro, Mexico.	Scratched	Yes	Yes
[Unintelligible first word] Valentino [unintelligible 3rd word] Bertran	4 names		Pencil	Yes	No
4 col-- 4 moreno [unintelligible final word]	?		Pencil		No
Guar--	?		Etched		No
[Unintelligible]	?		Etched		No

(b)   Site 2

Inscription	Translation	Notes	Medium	Over-written	Related to Other Marks?
Yambao Iztapalapa DF	[Name?]	Iztapalapa, DF is the most densely populated suburb outside of Mexico City.	Pencil	No	No
[Crude drawing of a man with spiky hair, glasses, and a goatee] Fox		"Fox" could be the English word or the Hispanic surname.	Pencil	No	No
Aqui Estubo Ron y Ronco	Ron and Ronco was here [sic]		Pencil	No	Yes
La Banda Leon	The Leon Band	León is a major city in the state of Guanajuato, Mexico.	Pencil	No	Yes
Estuvo Pancho As--- Maria Tontos 7	Pancho, [indecipherable name?], Maria was here [sic]; The Stupid 7		Scratched	Yes	No
Col. E Zapata	Colonia Emiliano Zapata	Colonía is a neighborhood or development. Neighborhoods named after the turn-of-the-century indigenous revolutionary figure, Emiliano Zapata, are very common throughout Mexico.	Scratched	No	No
Jerfo 34B	?		Scratched	No	No
S.S.D. Kukin	?		Pencil	No	No
Paco	[Name]		Scratched	No	No

continued/

Table 4.2 (continued)

Inscription	Translation	Notes	Medium	Over-written	Related to Other Marks?
RMS 7 BC		"RMS" undetermined; BC is the state abbreviation for Baja California, Mexico, perhaps indicating seven people traveling from the state?	Scratched	No	No
Sigan [an arrow pointing north]	Continue	The arrow pointing north instructs other migrants to keep going north.	Scratched	Yes	No
--tubo	[Maybe *Estubo*, meaning s/he was here]		Scratched	Yes	No
Aqui Durmio Manuel Garcia de Guatemala	Here slept Manuel Garcia from Guatemala		Pencil	No	No
Pirata	Pirate		Pencil	No	No
Omar Veracruz Mx	[Name]	Veracruz is the name of a city in the state of Veracruz, Mexico.	Scratched	No	No
East Side Viesa[?]	[*Viesa* = "crossbeam". Written in a more traditional graffiti style, so difficult to interpret]		Pencil	No	No
---cho	?		Scratched	Yes	No
BL----	?		Scratched	Yes	No
Recuerdo	Remember		Scratched	No	No
Veracruz		Veracruz is the name of is the name of a state and of a city in Mexico; MX is a common abbreviation for Mexico.	Scratched	No	No
Fr-r---	?		charcoal	No	No
Yajan Isack Sinaloa	Isack arrived from Sinaloa	"Yajan" (pron. yëgan) may be a misspelling of *llegan* = "they arrived"; Sinaloa is a state in Mexico.	charcoal	Yes	Yes
PB Sinaloa	[Name?]	Sinaloa is a state in Mexico.	Pencil	Yes	Yes
Recuedos	Memories [misspelled]		Pencil	Yes	No
Dormi Tono--- DF	I slept [Name?]	"DF" is the abbreviation for Mexico's capital city, Mexico City in Districto Federal (DF), analogous to "DC" for Washington, DC.	Pencil	No	No
Guero PB Locos	The light-skinned guy [name/nickname?] Crazy Ones	*Güero* is slang for someone with a light complexion or blonde hair.	Pencil	Yes	Yes
Recuerdos de El Ru-o y El Muecas de Mexico DF	Remember [*rudo* = "rough one" or *ruso* = "russian"] and the smiling one from Mexico City		Pencil	No	No
Recuerdos de Antonio	Remember Antonio		Pencil	Yes	No

continued/

Table 4.2 (continued)

Inscription	Translation	Notes	Medium	Over-written	Related to Other Marks?
Los emigrantes son mas am----	Immigrants are the most [unknown word, perhaps *amable* = friendly, kind, or good]		Pencil	Yes	No
Recuerdos de Nicolas Domingues -- cerca de Guadalajara	Remember Nicolas Domingues [indecipherable] from around Guadalajara	Guadalajara is a major city in the Mexican state of Jalisco.	Pencil		Yes
Calle Damian Carmona ----	Damian Carmona Street	Many streets in Mexico are named after historic figures. Damian Carmona was a famous soldier under former Mexican President/ army general Benito Juarez.	Pencil	Yes	Yes
San Juan Bosco	Saint John Bosco	The patron saint of youth, and especially young boys. Juan Bosco is also the name of migrant shelter in the Mexican border city of Nogales, to where many migrants are deported.	Pencil	Yes	Yes
[Drawing of a front-facing headless naked woman with legs spread open] Arriba	[*Arriba* = "get up", "come on" (as in, "come on, let's go")]		Pencil	No	Yes
siga la flecha	follow the arrow	Written near the arrow pointing north, but in different handwriting and using a different medium for inscription.	Pencil	No	Yes
sano de Guanajua--	healthy from Guanajuato	Faded, but Guanajuato is a state in Mexico and is the most likely meaning.	Pencil	No	No
[Indecipherable]	?		Pencil	No	No
Allahu Akbar	[Islamic phrase, meaning "God is great"]	The only trace of Islamic writing or religious practice I ever saw while working within the southern Arizona migration landscape.	Pencil	No	No
Recuerdos de su Hamigo de Puebla Abraham Perli Tobins [words below faded]	Remember your friend from Puebla Abraham Perli Tobins	Puebla is the name of a state and of a city in Mexico.	Pencil	Yes	No
Estubo Tala	He was cutting down	*Tala* = to cut or fell, as a lumberjack might cut or fell lumber.	Scratched	Yes	No
[Indecipherable]	?		Scratched	No	No
[Sticker of alien with the phrase:] Te reto a apagar las luces si no las usas	I challenge you to turn off the lights if you're not using them		Other	Yes	No
[Indecipherable]	?		Scratched	No	No
[Dollar sign with 2 vertical lines]	[Dollar sign]	The dollar signs are written in different mediums and seemingly different handwriting styles.	Pencil	Yes	Yes

continued/

Table 4.2 (continued)

Inscription	Translation	Notes	Medium	Over-written	Related to Other Marks?
$	[Dollar sign]	The dollar signs are written in different mediums and seemingly different handwriting styles.	Scratched	No	Yes
[Indecipherable]	?		Pencil	No	No
[Squiggly lines drawn inside pencilled dollar sign]	?	Someone filled in between the two vertical lines of the dollar sign, using a different drawing medium.	Scratched	Yes	Yes
M			Pencil	No	No
[Another drawing of a front-facing headless naked woman with legs spread open – less vaginal detail than the first]		This and the next two drawings are much smaller and are inscribed in a different medium than the first.	Scratched	No	Yes
[A drawing of a side-facing naked woman sitting with legs in front of her]			Scratched	No	Yes
[A cruder drawing of a side facing naked woman, legs only]		This looks like someone was practicing for the slightly better drawing that is done a similar style right next to it.	Scratched	No	Yes
La Migra Estubo Aqui	The Border Patrol was here	*Migra* is a common slang term for the Border Patrol. This mark was the only additional marking found at this site when revisited in 2016, six years after the initial visit.	Scratched	No	No

of origin, names, and the repetition of the word "*recuerdo*" (remember), which invokes both the need for memory and the creation of mementoes on behalf of memory. Twenty-four per cent of the inscriptions at Site 1 were in conversation with others, as were 31% at Site 2.

In some cases, it appeared that groups traveled underneath the culverts and wrote a unified inscription. One example of this was "*Recuerdos de 4 mojados de Molino, Chih.: Junior, Edith, Jose, Pepe*" (Memories of 4 wetbacks from Molino, Chihuahua: Junior, Edith, Jose, Pepe – Figure 4.5), which appeared alongside separate and individual records by two of the group members (Junior and Edith) of their names and sentiments. This inscription from the Molino group represents some of the other possible lessons from the graffiti panels. First, at the given point in time recorded by the graffiti series, most of the group markings indicated people traveling together from shared cities or villages. In other words, these travel groups were less likely formed by happenstance than pre-planned at individuals' locations of origin, whereas evidence indicates at present groups are more *ad hoc* (Martinez 2015; Slack and Campbell 2016). Equally, almost all of the inscriptions indicated travelers' origins in Mexico rather than locations further south. This also represents a bygone era, as now the majority of individuals are form areas further into the south of Mexico and Central America (Massey *et al.* 2010; Vogt 2012; Woody 2015).

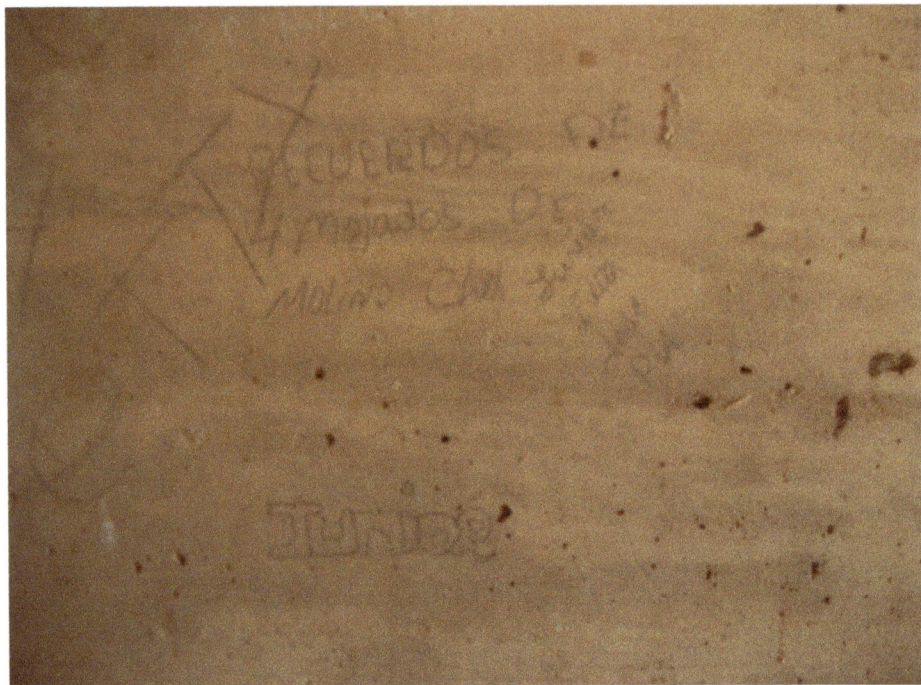

Figure 4.5. Recuerdos de 4 mojados de Molino, Chih' (Memories of 4 wetbacks from Molino, Chihuahua), at Site 1 (photograph by author).

Figure 4.6. The group from Molino and many others directly invoked the need to remember. In some cases the Spanish word for "remember" was written alone, as it was here at Site 2 (photograph by author).

Second, the word "*recuerdo*" appeared nine times between the two sites, spelling out the wider implicit purpose of many of the inscriptions: to create a tangible memento of migrants and their journeys in the landscape (Figure 4.6). With no other audience, all of the inscriptions at both sites, accompanied by the repeated directive "*recuerdos*", seem implicitly directed at fellow travelers. This implies that the journey will also not be soon forgotten by those who undertook it, including and especially those who invoked the need for memory on the walls of box culverts.

Third, the Molino group self-identified as *mojados*. The word is traditionally a derogatory racial epithet for undocumented Hispanic migrants, originally referring to those who surreptitiously crossed into the USA via the Rio Grande River border between Mexico and Texas. Those individuals literally entered the USA with wet backs. Those crossing the border in Arizona encounter a decidedly dry land border, yet the term perpetuates. There is a double-subversion at the site where (1) this negative racial term is appropriated by migrants to valorize their own identity and journey, and then (2) inscribed on the highway infrastructure of the USA in order to commemorate when they passed undetected to this point in the country. One other unrelated inscription at Site 1 also used the term as a self-descriptive.

Among other trends in the inscriptions were the 12% of writings at Sites 1 and 2 communicating messages to other migrants. Among them: "*Feliz viaje de todos*" (Happy travels to all); a drawing of an arrow pointed north, with the message "*Sigan*" underneath (Continue, or keep going); and nearby, in a different script, someone had written "*Sigan la fleche*" (Follow

Figure 4.7. "*La Migra Estubo Aqui*" (The Border Patrol was here) was the only new inscription recorded at Site 2 when the place was revisited after six years. The message is a stark warning (photograph by author).

the arrow), likely referring to the only arrow in the vicinity, that pointing north. The last two examples also mark an instance of two inscriptions in conversation. Perhaps the most poignant example of messages written to other migrants came with the only new inscription found at Site 2 when it was revisited after six years: "*La Migra Estubo Aqui*" (The Border Patrol was here – Figure 4.7). There was no evidence of new use at either site, but the message that USBP knew about the place warned all against stopping to rest here.

At both sites were several examples of inscriptions that may have been inspired by others. For example, no one from Site 2 described themselves as *mojados*, but the term was used twice at Site 1. In another case, someone at Site 2 had drawn a rough picture of a naked woman with her legs spread open. Several nearby inscriptions were rougher copycats of the same image, done with different recording mediums and in slightly different styles that would indicate multiple individuals. No such drawings existed at Site 1. As the majority of the names inscribed at both sites were male names, the naked series gives insight to the lust, longing, and loneliness felt by travelers.

Only two inscriptions invoked a spiritual higher power. One of them was the traditional Islamic greeting "*Allahu Akbar*" (God is great), written in Roman script. The inscription does provide evidence that individuals of Islamic faith cross the Mexico–USA border, though this does not mean they are of Arab ethnicity or even from somewhere other than Mexico. Estimates suggest that there is increasing Islamic conversion in Mexico, especially as a means of rebellion against Mexico's Spanish colonial heritage, harkening to a time when indigenous people were historically converted (often by force) to Catholicism (Marco 2002; Glüsing 2005; Debusmann 2013; Hootsen n.d.). The Spanish *Reconquista* – of which early colonization of the Americas formed a branch – opposed Jews and Islamic Moors, and promoted mass proselytization of the indigenous in the Americas, all as a means of unifying Spanish identity (Beezley *et al.* 1994; Joseph 1994). Islamic conversion is occurring especially among those affiliated with the Zapatistas, the forerunners of the anti-globalization movement (Marco 2002; Graeber 2009). Some argue that in some cases, undocumented migration extends from the same sort of rebellious anti-colonial spirit (Martinez 2001; Crostwaithe *et al.* 2003; Papadopoulos *et al.* 2008).

Not all of the writing was profound. In one case, the drawing was no more than a doodle comprised of squiggly lines. Another attempted to draw the logo for the athletic brand Nike. To avoid confusion, that individual also wrote "Nike" over the top. Still, the physical placement of so many inscriptions by undocumented travelers in such a rough and inauspicious location speaks volumes about the migration journey. If nothing else, the series of marks under both culverts provides clear evidence that the two structures temporarily housed undocumented travelers on the move. Indeed, as stated above, evidence points to the idea that the journeys of undocumented migrants have become more difficult in recent years as border security forces continue to funnel people towards increasingly treacherous passages (Magaña 2008; Doty 2011; Martinez *et al.* 2013).

Concluding Thoughts

The context of supermodernity presents an ideal frame for studies of global displacement, migration, and refugee crises. Specifically, in the study of non-places, points of subversion or resistance will stand out, as things "out of place" (Augé 1995; Bender 2001; Papadopoulos *et al.* 2008; de Certeau 2011). Globally, displacement is occurring at record levels for those affected by forces such as war, state violence, state failure, economic precarity, and environmental instability. The ability to stay in place and, correspondingly, to be defined by nationality and static spatial boundaries, are less and less viable. Emerging is a new paradigm of place making in transit (Parkin 1999; Bender 2001), exemplified here by the graffiti inscriptions by migrants in two rural highway box culverts. Notably, the examples described in this chapter are merely sites that stand out for the multitude of individuals who participated. There are many other sites where similar actions occur on a smaller scale, and likely even more prominent sites that I simply never encountered. The southern border is, after all, a vast place.

This leads to an important point in my conceptualization of undocumented migration in this space. A growing scholarly movement explores undocumented migration as an act of collective agency. Undocumented migration can be an important vehicle for informal politics by merit of the parallel collective efforts of thousands and their actions' continuity despite the widening net of draconian policing tactics at borders (Bender 2001; Papadopoulos *et al.* 2008; Mezzadra and Neilson 2013; Das and Randeria 2015). In fact, the conception of current migration as a "crisis" impedes a consideration of undocumented movement as a necessary result of economic and militaristic foreign policy incursions by Europe and the USA into less developed and poorer countries. In fact, "the very word 'crisis' is misleading for it implies a passing moment of danger that will eventually come to an end" (Blair 2016), but both migration as a means of substantively changing one's material circumstances and attrition-based paradigms of border security are increasingly becoming more economically and socially embedded (Bacon 2008; Menjivar and Kanstroom 2014; Mezzadra and Neilson 2013; Miller 2014).

This understanding necessitates that scholars rethink their prioritization of state-based and formalized political power, and attempt to view informal and illegal actions as alternative politics (Comaroff and Comaroff 2006; Papadopoulos *et al.* 2008; Das and Randeria 2015; Slack and Campbell 2016). We must ask how these forms of power relate, and explore these interactions locally. As Augé (1995) demonstrates, localized and intimate views inside non-places may help highlight these points of relation. This discussion essay ultimately poses an example of a way in which one might translate a theory of non-places into a research agenda.

Finally, the inscriptions at Sites 1 and 2 embed memorial commemoration of undocumented migration into the very landscape forbidden to their authors. These graffiti markings at once exemplify both the agency and profound precarity of those who created them. Migrants transformed the spaces from sterile routes of mass transit into places of memory. This transformation also demonstrated the risks of migration – the newest mark warning other migrants to flee because "The Border Patrol was here" – and the hardships of the journey, with many of the marks commemorating their authors' sleeping in hiding under a rural highway. One would not dwell in or mark place in such a location unless under duress. These marks are not the result of an uninhibited process of migration, but the result of border enforcement policy that deliberately pushes migrants into increasingly difficult territory. And as precarious as sub-highway dwelling may seem, undocumented travelers have been pushed to increasingly remote locations since these marks were created.

References

Augé, M., 1995. *Non-Places: An Introduction to an Anthropology of Supermodernity*, translated by J. Howe. London: Verso.

Bacon, D. 2008. *Illegal People: How Globalization Creates Migration and Criminalizes Immigrants.* Boston: Beacon Press.

Banks, L. 2009. "Trashing Arizona: Illegal Immigrants Dump Tons of Waste in the Wilderness Every Day – And It's Devastating the Environment." *Tucson Weekly*, 23 July. Available online: http://www.tucsonweekly.com/tucson/trashing-arizona/Content?oid=1168857

Beezley, W. H., C. E. Martin, and W. E. French, eds. 1994. *Rituals of Rule, Rituals of Resistance: Public Celebrations and Popular Culture in Mexico.* Lanham, MD: Rowman & Littlefield.

Bender, B. 2001. "Landscapes on-the-Move." *Journal of Social Archaeology* 1 (1): 75–89. https://doi.org/10.1177/146960530100100106

Blair, D. 2016. "The Migrant Crisis Will Never End: It Is Part of the Modern World." *The Telegraph*, 8 May. Available online: http://www.telegraph.co.uk/news/2016/05/07/the-migrant-crisis-will-never-end-it-is-part-of-the-modern-world/

Bourdieu, P. 1985. "The Social Space and the Genesis of Groups." *Theory and Society* 14 (6): 723–744. https://doi.org/10.1007/BF00174048

Bowser, B. J. and M. N. Zedeno. 2009. *The Archaeology of Meaningful Places.* Salt Lake City: University of Utah Press.

Bureau of Land Management Arizona. 2015. *Southern Arizona Project Report Fiscal Year 2015.* Phoenix: Bureau of Land Management. Available online: http://www.blm.gov/style/medialib/blm/az/pdfs/undoc_aliens.Par.34239.File.dat/Southern_Arizona_SAP_FY15_508.pdf

Comaroff, J. and J. L. Comaroff. 2006. "Law and Disorder in the Postcolony: An Introduction." In *Law and Disorder in the Postcolony*, edited by J. Comaroff and J. L. Comaroff, 273–298. Chicago: University of Chicago Press. https://doi.org/10.7208/chicago/9780226114101.001.0001

Cornelius, W. 2005. "Controlling 'Unwanted' Immigration: Lessons from the United States, 1993-2004." *Journal of Ethnic and Migration Studies* 31 (4): 775–794. https://doi.org/10.1080/13691830500110017

Crosthwaite, L. H., J. W. Byrd, and B. Byrd, eds. 2003. *Puro Border: Dispatches, Snapshots and Graffiti from La Frontera.* El Paso, TX: Cinco Puntos Press.

Das, V. and S. Randeria. 2015. "Politics of the Urban Poor: Aesthetics, Ethics, Volatility, Precarity." *Current Anthropology* 56 (Supplement 11): S3–S14. https://doi.org/10.1086/682353

Davis, M. 2007. *Planet of Slums.* New York: Verso.

de Certeau, M. 2011. *The Practice of Everyday Life.* Translated by S. F. Rendall. Berkeley: University of California Press.

De León, J. 2012. "'Better to Be Hot than Caught': Excavating the Conflicting Roles of Migrant Material Culture." *American Anthropologist* 114 (3): 477–495. https://doi.org/10.1111/j.1548-1433.2012.01447.x

_____. 2013. "Undocumented Migration, Use Wear, and the Materiality of Habitual Suffering in the Sonoran Desert." *Journal of Material Culture* 18 (4): 321–345. https://doi.org/10.1177/1359183513496489

_____. 2015. *The Land of Open Graves: Living and Dying on the Migrant Trail.* Oakland: University of California Press.

De León, J., C. Gokee, and A. Schubert. 2015. "'By the Time I Get to Arizona': Citizenship, Materiality, and Contested Identities Along the US-Mexico Border." *Anthropological Quarterly* 88 (2): 445–479. https://doi.org/10.1353/anq.2015.0022

Debusmann, B. Jr. 2013. "Muslim Converts in Mexico Make Up A Diverse, Fast-growing Community." *Fox News Latino*, 29 July. Available online: http://latino.foxnews.com/latino/lifestyle/2013/07/29/muslim-converts-in-mexico-make-up-diverse-fast-growing-community/

Doty, R. L. 2011. "Bare Life: Border-Crossing Deaths and Spaces of Moral Alibi." *Environment and Planning D: Society and Space* 29 (4): 599–612. https://doi.org/10.1068/d3110

Durand, J. and D. S. Massey. 2004. *Crossing the Border: Research from the Mexican Migration Project*. New York: Russell Sage Foundation Press.

Fukuyama, F. 1989. "The End of History?" *The National Interest* (Summer): 1–18.

Glüsing, J. 2005. "Praying to Allah in Mexico: Islam Is Gaining a Foothold in Chiapas." *Der Spiegel*, 28 May. Available online: http://www.spiegel.de/international/spiegel/praying-to-allah-in-mexico-islam-is-gaining-a-foothold-in-chiapas-a-358223.html

Gokee, C. and J. De León. 2014. "Sites of Contention: Archaeological Classification and Political Discourse in the US-Mexico Borderlands." *Journal of Contemporary Archaeology* 1 (1): 133–163. https://doi.org/10.1558/jca.v1i1.133

Gonzalez-Ruibal, A. 2008. "Time to Destroy: An Archaeology of Supermodernity." *Current Anthropology* 49 (2): 247–279. https://doi.org/10.1086/526099

____. 2013. "Modernism." In *The Oxford Handbook of the Archaeology of the Contemporary World*, edited by P. Graves-Brown, R. Harrison, and A. A. Piccini, 306–320. Oxford: Oxford University Press.

Graeber, D. 2009. *Direct Action: An Ethnography*. Oakland, CA: AK Press.

Hagan, J. M. 2008. *Migration Miracles: Faith, Hope and Meaning*. Cambridge, MA: Harvard University Press.

Harrison, R. and J. Schofield. 2010. *After Modernity: Archaeological Approaches to the Contemporary Past*. Oxford: Oxford University Press.

Harvey, D. 2005. *A Brief History of Neoliberalism*. New York: Oxford University Press.

Hernández, A. 2014. *Narcoland: The Mexican Drug Lords and Their Godfathers*. New York: Verso.

Heyman, J. M. 2001. "Class and Classification at the U.S.-Mexico Border." *Human Organization* 60 (2): 128–140. https://doi.org/10.17730/humo.60.2.de2cb46745pgfrwh

____. 2014. "'Illegality' and the U.S.-Mexico Border: How It Is Produced and Resisted." In *Constructing Illegality in America: Immigrant Experiences, Critiques, and Resistance*, edited by C. Menjívar and D. Kanstroom, 111–137. Cambridge: Cambridge University Press.

Hirsch, E. and M. O'Hanlon, eds. 1995. *The Anthropology of Landscape: Perspectives on Place and Space*. Oxford: Clarendon Press.

Hootsen, J. A. n.d. "Islam Is the New Religion in Rebellious Mexican State Chiapas." *RNW Media*. Available online: https://www.rnw.org/archive/islam-new-religion-rebellious-mexican-state-chiapas

Joseph, G. M., ed. 1994. *Everyday Forms of State Formation: Revolution and the Negotiation of Rule in Modern Mexico*. Durham, NC: Duke University Press.

Kearney, M. 2004. "The Classifying and Value-Filtering Missions of Borders." *Anthropological Theory* 4 (2): 131–156. https://doi.org/10.1177/1463499604042811

Lefebvre, H. 1991. *The Production of Space*. Malden, MA: Blackwell.

Magaña, R. 2008. *Bodies on the Line: Life, Death and Authority on the Arizona-Mexico Border*. PhD Diss., University of Chicago.

Marco, L. K. 2002. "¿El Islam En Chiapas?: El. EZLN Y El Movimiento Mundial Murabitun." *Revista Académica Para El Estudio de Las Religiones* 4: 79–91.

Martínez, D. 2015. "Coyote Use in an Era of Heightened Border Enforcement: New Evidence from the Arizona-Sonora Border." *Journal of Ethnic and Migration Studies* 42 (1): 1–17.

____., R. Reineke, R. Rubio-Goldsmith, B. E. Anderson, G. Hess, and B. Parks. 2013. *A Continued*

Humanitarian Crisis at the Border: Undocumented Border Crosser Deaths Recorded by the Pima County Office of the Medical Examiner, 1990-2012. Tucson: Binational Migration Institute, University of Arizona Department of Mexican American Studies.

Martinez, R. 2001. *Crossing Over: A Mexican Family on the Migrant Trail*. New York: Picador.

Massey, D. S., J. S. Rugh, and K. A. Pren. 2010. "The Geography of Undocumented Mexican Migration." *Mexican Studies* 26 (1): 129–152. https://doi.org/10.1525/msem.2010.26.1.129

Menjívar, C. and D. Kanstroom, eds. 2014. *Constructing Illegality in America: Immigrant Experiences, Critiques, and Resistance*. Cambridge: Cambridge University Press.

Mezzadra, S. and B. Neilson. 2013. *Border as Method, Or, The Multiplication of Labor*. Durham, NC: Duke University Press. https://doi.org/10.1215/9780822377542

Miller, T. 2014. *Border Patrol Nation: Dispatches from the Front Lines of Homeland Security*. San Francisco: City Lights.

Nevins, J. 2010. *Operation Gatekeeper and Beyond: The War on "Illegals" and the Remaking of the U.S.-Mexico Boundary*. London and New York: Routledge.

Nevins, J. and M. Aizeki, 2008. *Dying to Live: A Story of U.S. Immigration in an Age of Global Apartheid*. San Francisco, CA: City Lights.

Papadopoulos, D., N. Stephenson, and V. Tsianos. 2008. *Escape Routes: Control and Subversion in the Twenty-First Century*. London: Pluto Press.

Parkin, D. J. 1999. "Mementoes as Transitional Objects in Human Displacement." *Journal of Material Culture* 4 (3): 303–320.

Robinson, W. 2011. "Global Rebellion: The Coming Chaos?" *Al Jazeera*, 4 December. Available online: http://www.aljazeera.com/indepth/opinion/2011/11/20111130121556567265.html

Rubio-Goldsmith, R., M. McCormick, D. Martínez, and I. Duarte. 2006. *The "Funnel Effect" and Recovered Bodies of Unauthorized Migrants Processed by the Pima County Office of the Medical Examiner, 1990-2005*. Report for the Binational Migration Institute. Tucson: University of Arizona.

Sanchez, G.E. 2015. *Human Smuggling and Border Crossings*. London and New York: Routledge.

Scott, J.C. 2012. *Two Cheers for Anarchism: Six Easy Pieces on Autonomy, Dignity, and Meaningful Work and Play*. Princeton, NJ: Princeton University Press.

Sheridan, L. M. 2009. *"I Know It's Dangerous": Why Mexicans Risk Their Lives to Cross the Border*. Tucson: University of Arizona Press.

Slack, J. and H. Campbell. 2016. "On Narco-Coyotaje: Illicit Regimes and Their Impacts on the US-Mexico Border." *Antipode* 48 (5): 1–20. https://doi.org/10.1111/anti.12242

Spener, D. 2009. *Clandestine Crossings: Migrants and Coyotes on the Texas-Mexico Border*. Ithaca, NY: Cornell University Press.

Sundberg, J. 2008. "'Trash-Talk' and the Production of Quotidian Geopolitical Boundaries in the USA-Mexico Borderlands." *Social and Cultural Geography* 9 (8): 871–890. https://doi.org/10.1080/14649360802441424

Tilley, C. 2006. "Introduction: Identity, Place, Landscape and Heritage." *Journal of Material Culture* 11 (1): 7–32. https://doi.org/10.1177/1359183506062990

United States Customs and Border Protection. 2016. "About CBP." Washington, DC: Department of Homeland Security. https://www.cbp.gov/about

Vogt, W. A. 2012. *Ruptured Journeys, Ruptured Lives: Central American Migration, Transnational Violence, and Hope in Southern Mexico*. PhD diss., University of Arizona.

Woody, C. 2015. "Mexico Is Facing a Deadly Central American Migrants Crisis." *Business Insider*, 21 June. Available online: http://www.businessinsider.com/mexico-is-facing-a-cental-americans-migrant-crisis-2015-6

Gabriella Soto is a PhD candidate at the School of Anthropology at the University of Arizona. Address for correspondence: School of Anthropology, University of Arizona, P.O. Box 210030, Tucson, AZ 85721-0030, USA. Email: sotog@email.arizona.edu

Chapter 5

The Materiality of the State of Exception: Components of the Experience of Deportation from the United States

Agnieszka Radziwinowiczówna

According to the philosopher Giorgio Agamben (1998), sovereignty is created by exclusion from the political community – in other words, by the setting of a "threshold" between citizens and "aliens". The anthropologist Nicholas De Genova (2010) adds that deportation is a technology of citizenship (cf. Walters 2010, 71), and a manifestation of state power; a deportation regime[1] creates, or, more accurately, re-creates, sovereignty by the production of "aliens" and by their exclusion.

However, before an "alien" is deported, his or her body has to be detected, seized, controlled, and catalogued. The deportation literally translates into the reduction of a person to his or her bare life (Agamben 1998). Agamben (1998, 10) describes the process of incorporating this biological (bare) life into mechanisms and calculations of state power as the "state of exception". Dozens of artifacts are employed in the reduction of "unauthorized migrants" to bodies. By what means is the state of exception produced?

The analysis of the lived experience of deportation (cf. Radziwinowiczówna 2016) shows that the deportees have intensive and embodied experience of the material processes involved in their own removal. De León (2015) explains a corporeal relation between migrants and the objects they use on their way across the Mexico–USA border. Similarly, the objects employed in the course of deportation, such as guns, chains, handcuffs, uniforms, and syringes, are keenly experienced bodily by the deportees. These objects are non-human actors (Latour 1987) that embarrass, humiliate, and frighten deportees and thus produce the sovereign power of the deporting state. Similar to the material culture of border crossing (De León 2013), the artifacts of forced return migration need to be explored. This chapter discusses the role and impact of the material components of the deportation experience. More specifically, it seeks to examine the agency of the materiality of deportation and to explain functions that are important in the process of subordinating the deportees.

---

1. Peutz and De Genova (2010, 2) define a deportation regime as "a structure of power that produces compulsory removal of 'aliens' from physical, juridical and social space of the State".

Studying deportation is of particular importance in today's "age of deportation" (Boehm 2016; Walters 2010). The United States deports the biggest number of people annually, which makes that country a "laboratory" for the study of deportation. A record 434,015 individuals were removed from the USA in 2013, 71% of whom were Mexican citizens (US Department of Homeland Security 2016, 110–111). Due to the high volume of deported Mexicans, researchers regard Mexico as a "country of the deported".[2]

This chapter draws on the narratives of Mexicans deported from the USA. Between 2012 and 2018, I collected narratives of 29 former deportees in their hometown, a Mexican pueblo here given the pseudonym San Ángel (the names of interviewees have also been changed). San Ángel is in Oaxaca, in an impoverished and peripheral region of Lower Mixteca, which has been exporting workforce to the USA over the last six decades. However, due to the increasingly strict immigration and border controls introduced in the aftermath of the 9/11 attacks and the 2008 economic crisis, a number of migrants have since returned to their hometown as deportees. During my five-month ethnographic fieldwork in San Ángel I collected the life stories of 24 male and four female former deportees, and analyzed their removal narratives. All of the individuals quoted in the chapter were unauthorized immigrants in the USA and had crossed the US border without inspection.

The material components of the experience of deportation serve to *detect* the bodies of "unauthorized aliens". The 2005 border protection plan announced the Secure Border Initiative (SBI), which stressed the use of state-of-the-art techniques of border surveillance. US Border Patrol started to use "sensors, light towers, mobile night vision scopes, remote video surveillance systems and unmanned aerial vehicles" (Haddal and Gertler 2010, 1). However, this program was cancelled in 2011, having been found to be ineffective and costly. The US authorities decided instead to rely on the proven technologies of video and mobile surveillance and thermal imaging.

Many former deportees from San Ángel told me about the military methods of surveillance at the border: the helicopters and drones used against them during their border-crossing attempts. Even though many of them had crossed before the introduction of the SBI, they had been surprised by the use of modern technologies – a manifestation of US power. Here's what Daniel, who crossed the US border in 2001, told me:

> There was a moment, when they [i.e., coyotes] told us, "Get down on the ground! Lie down on the ground! We're going… Because…" They call it "a fly" [la mosca], that's how they call a helicopter, the security of the United States. And they had us lie down on the ground; they made us put ground on ourselves, basically bury ourselves into the ground so that they couldn't see us from above. And when this was over, they didn't capture us and we continued walking.

Soledad, who crossed in 1997, observed:

---

2. "En la dimensión de país de retorno, México se está convirtiendo en uno de deportados" (Alarcón and Becerra 2012, 126).

[Coyotes said,] "If you are wearing rings, if you are wearing anything, take it off, because a helicopter is flying." And sometimes because of a sparkle of an earring they realize that people are going.

Camilo, who migrated in 2000, recounted the following:

[Coyote] told us not to make any noise […] and to hide because, I think there was infrared [light] and they detected eyes or something like that at night.

Once they are detected and detained, material technologies employed by the US deportation regime put the bodies of the deportees under control. The control process of the detained immigrants is rationalized and bureaucratized (Bhartia 2010, 334): the means of "rationally organizing authority relations" (Weber 1978 [1922], 987) include the use of identifiers. For example, in a private immigration detention center in Tacoma in Washington State detainees have two identifiers: a card that they carry in a shirt pocket and a bracelet. Both contain the detainee's photograph, name, and nationality (Javier: "In order not to make a mistake and send him to another country"). Identifiers facilitate the surveillance of detainees' bodies and automatize discipline. The methods of control used also serve to follow the movement of people within the space of the immigration detention center. Here's how Acacio explained the panoptical function of the identifier:

The technology is very advanced there; this thing was like an ID card. It worked together with the alarm. If you went behind the bars with this thing, I guess it activated it, because if you went to the door when you weren't supposed to, it turned on the alarm […] They took a photo of me, I have a photo in my uniform, and it has a bar code. To go to the restroom, to go to the door, you had to (I guess they activated it) do it like that [he shows that he had to bring the card close to a reader] and the door opened. But if you wanted to go out, you notified them. They have a lot of power. The United States has a lot of power.

Knowledge-gathering generates power, as noted by Foucault, and the use of modern and expensive technologies evokes a feeling of the overwhelming supremacy of the US state in the deportees:

Power produces knowledge; […] power and knowledge directly imply one another; […] there is no power relation without the correlative constitution of a field of knowledge, nor any knowledge that does not presuppose and constitute at the same time power relations. (Foucault 1979, 27)

As already explained, material processes *rationalize* detention and confinement. Another means of rationalizing and intensifying control over detainees is the classification of inmates in an immigration detention center. People in such centers are divided into "categories" wearing uniforms in different colors. Here's how César described the way former offenders who had served a prison sentence in the USA were classified in GEO Group-operated Northwest Detention Center in Tacoma:

They give you a uniform; they are of three categories. I guess, they're blue, orange, and red. The blue ones are the people who have had a ticket, who have driven against a red light, small things like that. Those who wear orange ones are supposedly a little more dangerous, and those who wear red ones are people who have big problems.

The different uniforms not only facilitate the handling of detainees, but also *criminalize* them. Additionally, the orange and red uniforms stigmatize ex-prisoners. Another means of criminalizing the deportees is the use of handcuffs while they are convoyed between detention sites or during the transfer to the country of citizenship. Several former deportees from San Ángel interpreted convoy-like transfer to Mexico as criminalizing (Sergio: "I think that even offenders get a better treatment there. Who have we beaten or killed to be treated like that?"). Coutin (2010, 361) observed that "the shackles [… are] a particularly vivid marker of criminalized 'illegality' and aliengage". When on the bus and plane, detainees are constricted with handcuffs as well as ankle and waist chains, or reinforced mittens that immobilize and hurt hands. Two interviewees, Javier and Acacio, provided their accounts:

Javier: About 20 marshals boarded the plane.

Researcher: *Do they have weapons?*

J: Yes. For example, if you wanna go to the restroom, they take us [i.e., you], but tied. They only release one hand…

How do they tie you?

J: With handcuffs and with a chain. But there is another type in Arizona. They call it a "box" [*caja*]. It's like a box, they put it in the middle of the chain. And [we] got on the bus wearing those […] They drive badly, they seem to make the bus jerk on purpose and you want to stop it, but you can't stop and it keeps hurting.

What is the box made of?

J: Metal. And 'cause it's uncomfortable, you move it.

Acacio: As a matter of fact, they torture us psychologically by frightening us. When they threw me back to Mexico, they made me board the plane wearing a chain here [on the waist]. You can't raise your hands because they tie them. You get tired. That's how they treat the majority of people.

State-organized transfer to Mexico *frightens* deportees. The material signs of their criminalization are not only the shackles but also the Justice Prisoner and Alien Transportation System (JPATS) marshals, who supervise the transfer (the same ones who convoy criminal prisoners). Therefore, the vehicles used to transfer the deportees to Mexico are zones of phenomenological threat, where the "passengers" are surveilled and their bodies are disciplined. Thus, the vehicles are similar to immigration detention sites. Walters (2015, 98) has proposed the term "*brig*", by which he means a mobile space where prison materializes, and the bodies of detainees are controlled, disciplined, and repressed, under the hegemonic principle of security. We can take Walters's observation further and say it is not only prison that materializes on a plane or bus with deportees, but also the state of exception, for the voyage of the *brig* brings to an end the sovereignty-producing exclusion.

Another function fulfilled by the material components of the deportation experience is *dehumanization*. For instance, the uniforms I mentioned above deprive the detained individuals of their identity. A similar task is performed by controls and medical checkups. Upon detention in the US Immigration and Customs detention site, where they await a transfer to Mexico, detainees undergo compulsory controls and medical examinations. The site staff use lice-killing shampoo, syringes, vaccinations, pregnancy tests, or radiography. One of the former deportees from San Ángel, Jennifer, told me about personal controls and a series of medical tests she underwent in a detention center in Arizona:

> It's so bad to be there. When we arrived, they gave us a vaccine with a hepatitis test, I guess. They injected us and a bubble appeared on my arm. They gave us an injection, made pregnancy tests. They bathed us. They soaped us with lice-killing shampoo. Later, the policewomen arrived. They ordered us to undress; they checked our ears, our hair. They checked everything! And later they made us put on these ugly clothes […] I just kept asking, "Why?" Later, they made a lot of examinations on my chest. Yes, they made tests, made an X-ray examination. I don't know why. They never told me why. I was just asking, "Why are they doing that to me? What do I have?"

> *What kind of injection did they give you?*

> Supposedly it was against hepatitis, something like that. And a bubble appeared on my arm. Everyone [i.e., every detained woman] had a bubble.

In an immigration detention center, the experience of deportation becomes literally embodied, as the organisms of detainees are intervened into. Personal controls concern the most intimate spheres of migrants' lives – their bodies and health. At the same time, they humiliate and dehumanize detainees in pre-deportation confinement. Fischer (2015, 607) has observed that personal controls and medical checkups in an immigration detention center are degradation ceremonies (Goffman 1961), and they neutralize the detained people as bodies.

Humiliating medical checkups are also part of the practice of biopolitical othering. Fassin (2001, 2005) understands the biopolitics of otherness as politically driven decisions based on the attribution of certain characteristics to the individuals who share certain physical markers. The otherness should be construed here *à la* Simmel, as the feeling that "we" share little with "others". The other "is far from us, insofar [features of a national, social, occupational nature] extend beyond him or us, and connect us only because they connect a great many people" (Simmel 1950 [1908], 406). The otherness of unauthorized migrants is associated with body practices attributed to them (e.g., untidiness, or risky sexual behaviors that might cause hepatitis).

In this chapter, I have examined the artifacts employed by the US immigration enforcement and their subordination-producing functions. By shedding light on the material culture of deportation we might "excavate the more subtle forms of human suffering" (De León 2013, 22). The artifacts that constitute the US deportation regime are experienced in a deeply embodied way, by causing pain (e.g., *caja*), by making deportees stiffen (e.g., shackles used during transportation), by embarrassing them (e.g., lice-killing shampoo). The material components of detention, confinement, and transfer are the non-human actors that play an intermediary role in the power relation between the deportees and the deporting state. Their use results in the subordination of "aliens". The materiality of the deportation experience subordinates deportees by criminalizing and dehumanizing them, producing them as biopolitical others, as well as frightening and depriving them of their identity. In this way, the material components of deportation turn deportees into bare lives, create a state of exception, and contribute to the construction of the sovereignty of the US state.

References

Agamben, G. 1998. *Homo Sacer: Sovereign Power and Bare Life*. Stanford, CA: Stanford University Press.

Alarcón, R. and W. Becerra. 2012. "¿Criminales O Víctimas? La Deportación de Migrantes Mexicanos de Estados Unidos a Tijuana, Baja California." *Norteamérica* 7 (1): 125–148.

Bhartia, A. 2010. "Fictions of Law: The Trial of Sulaiman Oladokun, or Reading Kafka in an Immigration Court." In *The Deportation Regime: Sovereignty, Space, and the Freedom of Movement*, edited by N. De Genova and N. Peutz, 329–350. Durham, NC: Duke University Press. https://doi.org/10.1215/9780822391340-013

Boehm, D. A. 2016. *Returned: Going and Coming in an Age of Deportation*. Oakland: University of California Press.

Coutin, S. B. 2010. "Exiled by Law: Deportation and the Inviability of Life." In *The Deportation Regime: Sovereignty, Space, and the Freedom of Movement*, edited by N. De Genova and N. Peutz, 351–370. Durham, NC: Duke University Press. https://doi.org/10.1215/9780822391340-014

De Genova, N. 2010. "The Deportation Regime: Sovereignty, Space, and the Freedom of Movement." In *The Deportation Regime: Sovereignty, Space, and the Freedom of Movement*, edited by N. De Genova and N. Peutz, 33–65. Durham, NC: Duke University Press. https://doi.org/10.1215/9780822391340-002

De León, J. 2013. "Undocumented Migration, Use Wear, and the Materiality of Habitual Suffering in the Sonoran Desert." *Journal of Material Culture* 18 (4): 1–25. https://doi.org/10.1177/1359183513496489

_____. 2015. *The Land of Open Graves: Living and Dying on the Migrant Trail*. Oakland: University of California Press.

Fassin, D. 2001. "The Biopolitics of Otherness: Undocumented Foreigners and Racial Discrimination in French Public Debate." *Anthropology Today* 17 (1): 3–7. https://doi.org/10.1111/1467-8322.00039

_____. 2005. "Compassion and Repression: The Moral Economy of Immigration Policies in France." *Cultural Anthropology* 20 (3): 362–387. https://doi.org/10.1525/can.2005.20.3.362

Fischer, N. 2015. "The Management of Anxiety: An Ethnographical Outlook on Self-Mutilations in a French Immigration Detention Centre." *Journal of Ethnic and Migration Studies* 41 (4): 599–616. https://doi.org/10.1080/1369183X.2014.960820

Foucault, M. 1979. *Discipline and Punish: The Birth of the Prison*. New York: Vintage Books.

Goffman, E. 1961. *Asylums: Essays on the Social Situation of Mental Patients and Other Inmates*. Garden City, NY: Doubleday.

Haddal, C. C. and J. Gertler. 2010. *Homeland Security: Unmanned Aerial Vehicles and Border Surveillance*. CRS Report for Congress 7–5700. Washington, DC: Congressional Research Service. Available online: https://www.fas.org/sgp/crs/homesec/RS21698.pdf

Latour, B. 1987. *Science in Action: How to Follow Scientists and Engineers Through Society*. Cambridge, MA: Harvard University Press.

Peutz, N. and N. De Genova. 2010. "Introduction." In *The Deportation Regime: Sovereignty, Space, and the Freedom of Movement*, edited by N. De Genova and N. Peutz, 1–32. Durham, NC: Duke University Press. https://doi.org/10.1215/9780822391340-001

Radziwinowiczówna, A. 2016. *Living/Leaving the Deportation Regime? Power and Violence in the Experience of Deportation*. PhD diss., University of Warsaw.

Simmel, G. 1950 [1908]. "The Stranger." In *The Sociology of Georg Simmel*, by G. Simmel, edited and translated by K. H. Wolff, 402–408. New York: The Free Press.

US Department of Homeland Security. 2016. *2015 Yearbook of Immigration Statistics*. Washington, DC: US Department of Homeland Security. Available online: https://www.dhs.gov/immigration-statistics/yearbook/2015

US Department of Homeland Security: Office of Inspector General. 2010. *The Performance of 287(g) Agreements*. Washington, DC: US Department of Homeland Security. Available online: http://www.oig.dhs.gov/assets/Mgmt/OIG_10-63_Mar10.pdf

US Immigration and Customs Enforcement. 2014. *ICE Enforcement and Removal Operations Report Fiscal Year 2014*. Washington, DC: US Immigration and Customs Enforcement. Available online: https://www.ice.gov/doclib/about/offices/ero/pdf/2014-ice-immigration-removals.pdf

Walters, W. 2010. "Deportation, Expulsion, and the International Police of Aliens." In *The Deportation Regime: Sovereignty, Space, and the Freedom of Movement*, edited by N. De Genova and N. Peutz, 69–100. Durham, NC: Duke University Press. https://doi.org/10.1215/9780822391340-003

_____. 2015. "On the Road with Michel Foucault: Migration, Deportation and Viapolitics." In *Foucault and the History of Our Present*, edited by S. Fuggle, Y. Lanci, and M. Tazzioli, 94–110. New York: Palgrave Macmillan. https://doi.org/10.1057/9781137385925_7

Weber, M. 1978 [1922]. *Economy and Society: An Outline of Interpretive Sociology*. Berkeley: University of California Press.

Agnieszka Radziwinowiczówna is an Assistant Professor at the Centre of Migration Research, University of Warsaw and Marie Sklodowska-Curie fellow at the Univeristy of Wolverhampton (starting in November 2018). Address for correspondence: Centre of Migration Research, University of Warsaw, 7 Pasteur St, 02-093 Warsaw, Poland. Email: a.radziwinowicz@uw.edu.pl

Chapter 6

Lessons from the Bakken Oil Patch

William Caraher, Bret Weber, and Richard Rothaus

Introduction

The archaeology of temporary labor in the Bakken oil patch might appear to occupy a separate historical and even moral category from those undocumented migrants who have fled catastrophic military or political events. At the same time, the influx of temporary labor into the Bakken in the aftermath of the "Great Recession" of 2007–2009 reflects global trends that Saskia Sassen (2014) has summarized as expulsions. Displaced from their homes on account of the mortgage crisis, untethered from the historical fixity of middle-class life, and buffeted by the increased speed of an industrial boom-bust cycle, the migrant Bakken worker is another manifestation of the deterritorialized politics and economy of the twenty-first-century world. While the majority of the Bakken workforce are US citizens and retain the social and legal rights that transnational refugees have lost, the material culture of temporary labor in the Bakken nevertheless reflects the expulsions that shape a disrupted world and the tense emergence of new forms of settlement designed to accommodate and normalize the experience of the migrant, the refugee, and the modern worker. Our research speaks to several issues that resonate across the archaeology of the contemporary world: the accelerating pace of capital; the increasing fluidity of populations, labor, and places; the challenges of abundance and ephemerality in the contemporary world; and the potential for the practice of archaeology to amplify the experience of displaced groups.

The North Dakota Man Camp Project has used both interviews and archaeological techniques to document the wide range of short-term workforce housing in the Bakken oil patch in western North Dakota (Caraher 2016; Caraher *et al.* 2017; Caraher and Weber 2017) (Figure 6.1). Improvements in both drilling and fracking technology in the early twenty-first century and high oil prices reopened the Bakken and Three Forks formations to large-scale exploitation. The global economic crisis, which began in 2008, accelerated the arrival of workers from around the USA. Multinational corporations such as Halliburton and Schlumberger imported some of the workers to the region and housed them in temporary "crew camps" provided by global logistics companies like Target Logistics. In contrast, our work focuses more on those who moved to the region seeking employment and housing. The small and historically remote communities of western North Dakota were unprepared for the influx of both kinds of workers

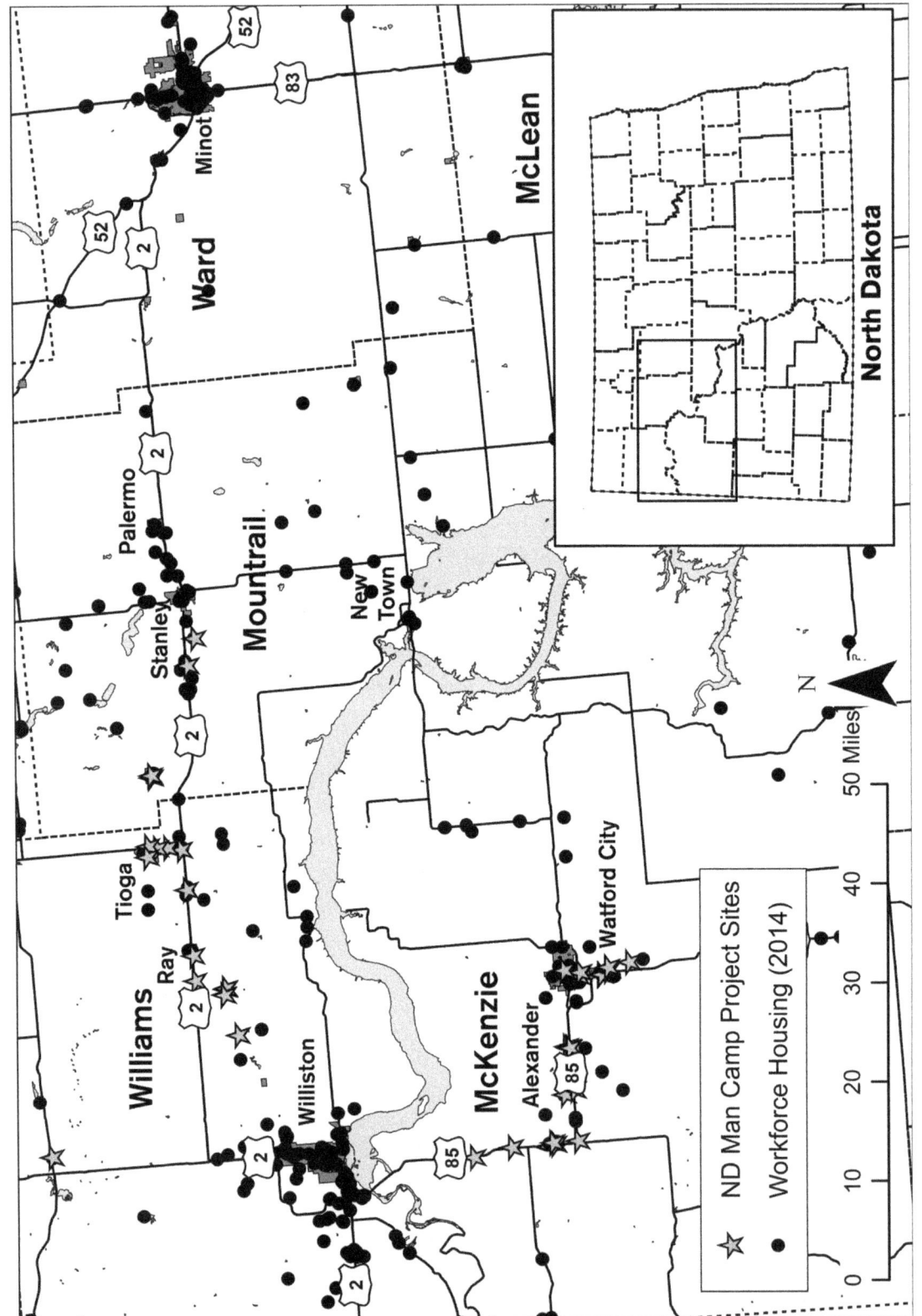

Figure 6.1. Map of the North Dakota Man Camp Project study area (W. Caraher).

and this led to many new arrivals squatting in public parks, living in recreational vehicles (RVs) in the Walmart parking lot, and paying exorbitant prices to park their RVs or campers, rent beds, or to stay in local hotels. The very fluidity of the Bakken workforce, the ambiguous state of its temporary lodging, and the inability of communities or the state to track the ebb and flow of housing and workers, framed our qualitative approach to the people and materiality of life in the Bakken as a lens through which to understand the experience of the twenty-first century.

Situations

If the relative dearth of projects for the politically and ethically productive engagement with forced and undocumented migrants has hindered new archaeologies of this phenomenon, it is worth exploring analogues like those provided by the experiences of temporary denizens of the Bakken. As Sassen's *Expulsions* (2014) argued, the development of "advanced capitalism" has transformed both economic and social relationships on a global scale; and as Arendt (1994 [1943]) and Agamben (1995) recognized, the displacement of people is more than just the movement of individuals from one situation to another, but the displacement of an individual's rights from the guarantees derived from status as citizens of a particular state to a new status dependent on a new set of political realities, definitions, and relationships. This situation does not deprive the refugee of all agency, of course, and Agamben has argued that the refugee has the potential to disrupt the political order of the nation-state by creating space for a kind of "pure human" to emerge in the gap between the individual as human and the individual as citizen.

If Agamben recognizes the transformative potential of the refugee as a "disquieting element" in the political order of the nation-state, the spaces of the western North Dakota Bakken oil patch represent a different expression of the deterritorialization of the individual. The movement of individuals into the Bakken followed the global flow of capital, ignoring national boundaries, demographics, or culture (Harvey 1989). Transnational companies contract with global logistics firms to fill prefabricated crew camps, which accommodate the largely male workforce involved in extractive industries. These "man camps" are set up to optimize access to work sites, to leverage local infrastructure, and to allow for the rapid deployment of personnel to remote locations. Their modular design enables them to be adapted to a range of conditions: generators, water treatment plants, cafeterias, laundries, security systems, and leisure spaces allow these camps to exist in self-contained and nearly self-sustaining ways (Rothaus 2013). The dehumanized space of the prefabricated crew camp seeks to standardize the experience of temporary residence and to maximize the labor extracted from each individual. The space of the crew camp is a "non-place" with no political or social community, and no distinguishing features to complicate or disrupt the seamless deployment of flexible, on-demand labor (Augé 1995; Caraher 2016).

The distinct character of the camps as an architectural form led Charles Hailey to describe them as the quintessential twenty-first-century space (Hailey 2009). The formal and industrial crew camps are the latest version of the mobile home deployed as a version of the mining camp, the work camp, and the company town. Our work focused particular attention on the RV parks, where a sizable portion of the Bakken workforce lived from 2008–2013, at the height of the Bakken oil boom. RVs are built to be mobile, to be lived in for little more than a week or two at a time, and are intended for recreation. In the Bakken, RV parks contort to man camps, with residents modifying their RVs to adapt to year-round occupation, to expand the useable space of individual units, and to define outdoor activity areas (Figure 6.2). These changes were both ubiquitous and as temporary and individualized as the residents who moved through these places.

Methods

The modern landscape changes at a remarkable rate, owing in part to the rapid movement of people both within and across boundaries. The emergence of generic non-places – like airports, hotels, mobile crew camps, and refugee camps – eradicates the differences between places that slow the movement of people. As a result, the archaeological record for late modernity and the physical manifestations of late capitalism can be exceedingly elusive. Traditional archaeological methods are relatively unsuitable for documenting the movement of individuals through spaces intentionally designed to obscure the accumulation of the material traces that would make these places distinct. In the Bakken settlements, housing for highly mobile populations tends to be short-lived, to occupy marginal spaces in the landscape, and to utilize ephemeral, portable, or ubiquitous materials.

The North Dakota Man Camp Project (2012–) has identified 50 workforce housing sites in the Bakken region of North Dakota for systematic investigation, and our methods fit within the broadly defined terms of archaeological ethnography as they bring together conventional archaeological approaches with methods grounded in a range of disciplines, from social work to history (Hamilakis and Anagnostopoulos 2009). Our research sites were visited regularly over a four-year period and documented through video, photography, text descriptions, and interviews. Systematic video and photography, in particular, offered an efficient way to document the changing situations within the RV parks that made up a significant share of workforce housing in the Bakken. To date, we have over 10,000 photographs and hours of georeferenced videos synced to time-stamped GPS coordinates.

In contrast to the ephemeral character of short-term settlement and the potential for archaeological invisibility, our documentation practice produced an abundance of largely digital objects that paralleled the abundance of objects in the modern world, and the speed and efficiency of video and photographic recording accommodated the speed of change in the Bakken. Our efforts to analyze our growing photographic archive, however, made clear that our method of documentation reproduced, to some extent, the chaotic dynamism of mobile populations and suggested the utter futility of grasping the scale both of human individuality and movement. Aerial photographs from satellites, airplanes, and kites allow for a sense of scale, while detailed photographs on the ground complemented with textual descriptions provide a sense of intimate immediacy, but, like our video archive, do little to dispel the feeling that parts of the Bakken continue to slip out of frame unnoticed. Our interviews reinforce the sense of elusiveness by demonstrating the disjunction between conversations and the objects present in these informal settlements.

With the collapse of oil prices in 2014, our work in the Bakken has come to focus increasingly on various forms of abandonment, as the number of temporary workers in the Bakken

Figure 6.2. Methods of defining personal space in an RV park in the Bakken Oil Patch (W. Caraher).

Figure 6.3. Frustration and abandonment in RVs in the Bakken Oil Patch (W. Caraher).

declined concurrently with the oil-rig count. Numerous coffee-makers in an abandoned RV revealed signs of methamphetamine use, trashed trailers smeared with human feces showed frustration and anger, and squatters' occupying empty rooms at defunct crew camps reflect a shifting reality (Figure 6.3). In contrast to the anonymity and hectic hospitality of the boom era, access to workforce housing sites has become more complex. Communities that had previously embraced temporary housing now litigate with cagey owners who position themselves politically for continued financial gain. Communities face the difficult reality of previously heralded development now transformed into hotel vacancies. Many of the RV parks and larger crew camps reflect million-dollar investments: some were highly profitable, others resulted in only disappointing returns. Rational calculations led workers to abandon their temporary homes rather than tow the long-stationary RVs to the next worksite. As a result, the fate of many of the abandoned crew camps remains unresolved even as the growing number of abandoned RVs fills the margins of RV parks and salvage yards. The foreman at a local salvage yard remarked that "people just leave 'em where they're at [... because] the landfill don't want 'em no more." The salvage yard had previously accepted RVs and then sold the parts, but now "we have to charge because we can't get rid of 'em", and the abandoned RVs are sometimes burnt on rainy days (interview with R. Wilson, 2015).

Our methods used to document the material culture created by the Bakken boom reveal various disjunctures. Any clarity regarding boom and busts exists only in hindsight. To illustrate: expressions of caution during the rise of the boom gave way to the desperate optimism that many clung to during the early stages of the bust. Accordingly, our photographic archive and interviews do not align precisely with the historical experience. The changing complexion of the Bakken and the shifting fortunes of migrant labor in the region destabilized our methods at the very moment when the material culture of the region was becoming archaeological through the process of abandonment. We see our work at the intersection of what Buell has described as "the marriage of catastrophe and exuberance". By focusing on material culture, we seek to escape the historicizing narratives that align experiences with an inevitable boom and bust cycle (Buell 2014). During the months leading to the height of the boom, interviews occasionally included warnings about the inescapable bust. These were soon to be juxtaposed with claims during the early stages of the bust that this was only a correction, and an ideal time to invest and move forward in preparation for the next phase of a boom destined to last for decades. During the summer of 2015 when the bust was, in retrospect, clearly underway, Jose Garcia admitted that prices were way down, and that "work is affected a lot." In fact, he had been laid off from his job as a welder. Nonetheless, his buoyant confidence comes through in his explanation that the large companies were creating this slowdown "to filter out all the workers who are not useful. That's what this whole thing is about. Everything is going to go back up" (interview with Jose Garcia, 2015). Indeed, during the interview he was installing a new deck on his trailer, for which he had just paid US$10,000, and Man Camp 77 was already exhibiting litter from abandoned trailers. Our dataset inevitably echoes, in a discordant way, those inconsistencies. Despite these limitations, our archive provides a foundation for interrogating the complex strategies that highly mobile populations adopt across a range of scales, from the regional to the personal.

Archaeology

From a strictly archaeological standpoint, the mechanical and financial efficiencies that have shaped these placeless crew camps threaten to obscure any persistent archaeological signature. The communities near where these camps were established generally sought requirements that the land be returned to its previous condition. At best, this impulse stems from a custodial attitude toward the land and environment. In most cases, however, local attitudes toward workforce housing are more complex. Prominent among them is a preference for "permanent housing", families, and the demographic and economic stability that allows for predictable growth, tax income, and government expenditures. There are also persistent class-based fears in relation to the presence of large numbers of temporarily unattached male laborers, pressures from developers eager to profit from high housing prices, and general apprehension from conservative communities, deeply averse to change. These factors combine to encourage temporary workforce housing to be particularly ephemeral, invisible, and low impact.

Many arrivals in the Bakken traveled at their own expense, towing RVs of various sizes and descriptions and setting up camp in hastily constructed RV parks. The RV parks projected a rigid ordering of space, with lots arranged in neat rows designed to provide efficient access to water, septic disposal, and electricity. Beneath this order, however, some parks lacked water, others had flawed infrastructure that let water-pipes freeze in the winter or overtaxed septic systems. For individual residents, the challenges associated with living in an RV year-around in the brutal climate of western North Dakota are not insignificant, but residents show a significant degree of ingenuity in adapting their moveable homes to new locales. Residents communicate through various social networks present in these temporary settlements the techniques necessary to make a narrow, light-weight streamlined box into a long-term home secure from the relentless elements. Some of the modifications are practical. For example, residents built wood frames around the base of the RVs to insulate the units from the cold winter and pounding winds of North Dakota (Figure 6.4). They also added "mud rooms" constructed from plywood and other scraps abundant in these RV parks. Other modifications adapted the space around the RVs to create elevated social areas, define boundaries, and create pathways. As a camp manager of a larger camp in the Bakken noted in 2012:

> [T]his is not an RV park. This is going to be a community. We're going to know our neighbors, we're going to be friends, we're going to help each other […] We had a thing where we put flower boxes and then there were folks that said, "those are cute, I can do that!" And pretty soon it spread. Now you get one person who does something like that over there and the little fence [around their unit] and then they come ask, "can I do that?" I say "sure". Once they see people starting, then they want to do it.
> (Interview with Beth Bartell, 2015)

The use of shipping pallets, scrap wood, cable spools, blue-tarp, and recycled material locate the Bakken RV park in a global tradition of informal architecture. The presence of discarded plywood, PVC pipe, extruded polystyrene, and other potentially useful material stacked at the edge of the camp reflects a global tradition of functional and opportunistic vernacular architecture that is only now being documented thoroughly.

Figure 6.4. Installing insulation in preparation for the North Dakota winter in the Bakken oil patch (W. Caraher).

Managed RV parks and modular workforce housing sites represent more formal settlements designed to accommodate the highly mobile workforce employed across the oil patch. The lack of sufficient, affordable housing, the extreme mobility of certain segments of the Bakken workforce, and the global economic downturn created a situation where people came to the area without resources or plans for accommodations. Groups set up small squatter camps first in city parks and the Walmart parking lot, and then in tree-lined wind breaks around farms and in secluded corners of the oil patch. The North Dakota Man Camp Project documented one such camp, where a group of construction workers from Idaho lived with a few unemployed economic migrants who had come to the Bakken looking for work. The camp consisted of a loose cluster of four RVs and a tent around an open space. The RVs lacked water and took electricity form a nearby construction site. The central area included a space where the group prepared food and a fire pit around which they socialized. This spatial arrangement contrasted with the neatly arranged rows of RVs and the rows of rooms projecting from long hallways in the large-scale crew camps imported to the region. The individuals living in this squatters' camp worked together, at least for a time, to share resources and a common space: "We're like brothers, like a family, brothers and sisters out here, like a family. We're close, tight-knit family [...] I own a construction company called Crystal Construction so we were working, we were all contracted in Idaho but a bunch of us just got together" (interview with Mrs Crystal, 2012). A return visit to the camp two months after our initial visit in the summer of 2013, found that the site was now abandoned, seemingly removed by authorities, leaving behind a thin scatter of trash.

Perspectives

As humans scramble to catch up with the speed of twenty-first-century capital, our traces in the landscape, and even our histories, become increasingly ephemeral. The speed and efficiency possible in documenting mobile populations has produced media – photographs, videos, descriptions – that are every bit as abundant and dynamic as objects and people in the modern world. This hyper-abundance of objects is characteristic of the modern world and complements the technologies that we can use to document them. At the same time, we will continue to struggle with this abundance of objects and media, which nevertheless represents a useful archive to an event that contemporary societies are only too eager to erase from the landscape. The desire to house undocumented migrants in temporary places in the Bakken reflects both longstanding moral attitudes toward the value of permanent housing as well as short-term concerns for property values, tax revenues, and infrastructure. In short, our urgency to document the experiences of undocumented migrants comes from social pressures to erase the lives of these workers from the landscape, the speed of capital and labor (which is always ready to depart for the next opportunity) in the twenty-first century, and our own disciplinary predilections to study abandonment rather than development.

Our efforts to document and to understand the social and material life in temporary workforce housing in the Bakken has produced several traditional articles, but our project has also explored several less conventional approaches. Bret Weber, who conducted many of the interviews for the project, has published on social policy, drawing upon his work with our project, and has integrated his findings with focus groups for social-service providers. His work brings together his interviews in the camps with concrete policy recommendations for communities in North Dakota. William Caraher has documented his experiences of the Bakken through the genre of the tourist guide. He argues that the modern experience of tourism marks the significance of fossil fuels for the creation of the modern world, and follows Dean MacCannell's work in seeing tourism as central to the formation of the middle or "leisure class" (MacCannell 1976). At the same time, the rise of tourism anticipated the kind of mobility and provided the critical RVs that have come to define both labor and capital in extraction zones of the twenty-first century. Finally, Richard Rothaus has seen fieldwork in the Bakken as part of an "archaeology of care" which regards the archaeological process as an expression of concern from the archaeological community. In our experience in the Bakken, the archaeological research in the daily life of oil patch workers found a receptive audience in the residents of workforce housing, who shared our view that something remarkable was occurring. The common ground between researcher and participant demonstrates that the practice of archaeology, despite its range of disciplinary baggage, can participate in a mutually significant dialogue with undocumented migrants.

Interviews

Beth Bartell, 2012
Jose Garcia, 2015

R. Wilson, 2015

Mrs Crystal, 2012

References

Agamben, G. 1995. "We Refugees." *Symposium* 49 (2): 114–119. https://doi.org/10.1080/00397709.1 995.10733798

Arendt, H. 1994 [1943]. "We Refugees." In *Altogether Elsewhere: Writers in Exile*, edited by M. Robinson, 111–119. London: Faber and Faber.

Augé, M. 1995. *Non-Places: Introduction to an Anthropology of Super Modernity*. Translated by J. Howe. London: Verso.

Buell, F. 2014. "A Short History of Oil Cultures; or, The Marriage of Catastrophe and Exuberance." In *Oil Culture*, edited by R. Barrett and D. Worden, 69–87. Minneapolis: University of Minnesota Press. https://doi.org/10.5749/minnesota/9780816689682.003.0004

Caraher, W. 2016. "The Archaeology of Man Camps: Contingency, Periphery, and Late Capitalism." In *The Bakken Goes Boom: Oil and the Changing Geographies of Western North Dakota*, edited by W. Caraher and K. Conway, 181–198. Grand Forks: The Digital Press at the University of North Dakota.

_____., K. Kourelis, R. Rothaus, and B. Weber. 2017. "North Dakota Man Camp Project: The Archaeology of Home in the Bakken Oil Fields." *Historical Archaeology* 51 (2): 267–287.

_____. and B. Weber. 2017. *The Bakken: An Archaeology of an Industrial Landscape*. Fargo: North Dakota State University Press.

Hailey, C. 2009. *Camps: A Guide to 21st-century Space*. Cambridge, MA: MIT Books.

Hamilakis, Y. and A. Anagnostopoulos. 2009. "What is Archaeological Ethnography?" *Public Archaeology* 8 (2–3): 65–87. https://doi.org/10.1179/175355309X457150

Harvey, D. 1989. *The Condition of Postmodernity*. Oxford: Blackwell.

MacCannell, D. 1976. *The Tourist: A New Theory of the Leisure Class*. New York: Schocken Books.

Rothaus, R. 2013 "Return on Sustainability: Workforce Housing for People, Planet and Profit." *Engineering & Mining Journal* 214 (12): 88–90.

Sassen, S., 2014. *Expulsions: Brutality and Complexity in Global Economy*. Cambridge, MA: Belknap Press at Harvard University Press. https://doi.org/10.4159/9780674369818

William Caraher is an Associate Professor in history at the University of North Dakota. Address for correspondence: Department of History, University of North Dakota, 221 Centennial Drive Stop 8096, Grand Forks, ND 58202, USA. Email: billcaraher@gmail.com

Bret Weber is an Associate Professor in history at the University of North Dakota. Address for correspondence: Department of History, University of North Dakota, 221 Centennial Drive Stop 8096, Grand Forks, ND 58202, USA. Email: bret.weber@email.und.edu

Richard Rothaus holds a PhD from the Ohio State University and currently runs Trefoil Cultural and Environmental, a privately owned cultural resource management firm. Address for correspondence: 2646 Lexington Drive, Bismarck, ND 58503, USA. Email: richard.rothaus@gmail.com

Chapter 7

Empty Migrant Rooms: An Anthropology of Absence through the Camera Lens

Eckehard Pistrick (text) and Florian Bachmeier (photos and text)

Local Talk, Vision, Perception: Empty Migrant Rooms as "Absence Signifiers"

On first sight, the periurban area of Krasta near the town of Elbasan looks like any other informal area at the outskirts of Albanian towns inhabited by people who have descended from the villages into urban areas in the postsocialist era in search of a better life: hastily erected reinforced concrete constructions, with a finished ground floor and an unfinished second floor, surrounded by gardens, olive groves, and plots of land with grazing cows or sheep. Some of these houses – built by villagers from Shpati, a mountain area 20 km from Elbasan – contain empty rooms, and some entire houses are vacant, with doors locked and called *shpi bosh emigranti* (empty migrant houses) by the local population. However, asking locals about these houses reveals a rich emic terminology which indicates that they are anything but empty: rather, they are charged with multiple layers of meaning which link the material construction to the migration histories (or biographies) of their owners, who had left for Greece and Italy. Several terms, according to Gerda Dalipaj (2016), point to the juridical-economic aspects of these buildings: they are built in times of economic instability and in a legal vacuum and are therefore called *shpit' e tranzicionit* (houses of transition) or *shpi pa letra* (houses without building permit). Other terms point to the social relevance of the house for the family as regards the continuation of the kinship lineage: *shpit' e çunave* (houses for the sons), *shpi për kallamajtë* (houses for the children), and *shpi për pleqni* (houses for the old age [of the parents]). Other terms again define the house in temporal terms: *shpi për të ardhme* (house for the future). Finally, a whole group of terms refers to the emotional aspects of such houses, built on the imaginary of a migration history of deprivation, suffering, and back-breaking work: *shpi me gjak e me djersë* (house with blood and with sweat), *shpi e dhimbshme* (painful house), and *shpi me kokë* (a house for which I could have been killed).

This local discourse developing around these houses excited our interest as a team consisting of a photographer (Florian Bachmeier, German), a foreign anthropologist (Eckehard Pistrick, a

German ethno[musico]logist), and an Albanian anthropologist (Gerda Dalipaj).[1] Access to such houses, kept usually by the elderly (grand)parents of the migrants, was granted to us through a local from the area of Shpati who himself had a building project in the area and who knew the people through kinship networks from his home village. Still, accessing these emotionally charged sites, these *lieux de mémoire*, these places with an almost ritual meaning for those caring for them, proved to be difficult. For the grandparents, parents, or siblings, entering any such room meant being confronted with emotions linked to experiences of displacement, rupture, and social separation. Opening it to an Outsider meant sharing this intimate emotional world. However, these places also revealed an emotional ambiguity when "those left behind" were talking about them: on the one hand they represented nostalgia for those absent, and on the other they represented a source of family pride, as these rooms or houses were primarily financed through remittances, pointing to the economic success stories of "those who left".

As such, they are indicative of the contradictory act of dwelling, comparable to a study relating to Albania by Dalakoglou (2010) but also to locations such as Australia (Lozanovska 2007), Mexico (Lopez 2015), and Turkey (Bürkle 2016). Lozanovska in particular has shown in her multi-sited ethnographic study of migrant houses of Macedonians in Australia's city of immigration (Melbourne) and in their home villages that such "remittance houses" confront us with trajectories, modes of travel, and forms of community which are essentially different from those in the diaspora setting. Her perspective, which emphasizes multiterritorial belongings and polytopic dwelling, leads us to question the currency of transnationalism, the binary structure of dwelling/travelling and the fabrication of community (Lozanovska 2007, 250). She points also to the fact that the construction and maintenance of such houses creates a "psychic landscape of migration" (Lozanovska 2007). Considering that houses are central to the migrants' struggle to locate a place of belonging, a place of human agency and dignity, the unfinished condition of such houses and rooms, their in-betweenness and polysemantic character, is indicative. What kinds of belonging are expressed through such empty spaces? What does their fragmentary interior equipment tell us about the agency of the migrant, his imaginaries? Does the unfinished state of the construction or the continuous rebuilding of one and the same place correlate with the migrant condition and his strategic choices? In which ways do the continuous reconfiguration and readaptation of the physical appearance of a home-place depend on the socio-economic adaption processes of the migrant, depending on his changing life circumstances in the diaspora? In which ways can such "homescapes" (Tschoepe 2016) and their design – the groundplan, architectural elements, patterns, rhythms, geometries, and intangible elements – be understood as a text "which encodes socio-cultural information about the identity of places and people, memories, local histories and cultures" (Tschoepe 2016, 418)? Does a visual-ethnographic analysis bring us closer to the "psychogram of the migrant", revealing his unsettled mental condition, his open-ended questions and imaginaries?

On first sight, many of the rooms in the half-finished houses in the Krasta area looked to us to be the same. The interior setting – particularly the bedrooms of migrant couples – seemed to follow a pre-existing logic: a neo-baroque bed made of plastic imitating dark wood, a wardrobe

---

1. The project was realized in April 2013.

of the same material, two night cabinets (on one of which a framed photo of the couple was standing), a cosmetics cabinet with a mirror decorated with souvenirs and photos. The room created immediately the idea of a "museum of nostalgia", of an uninhabited space, frozen in time, whose primarily function was to memorialize.

While looking more closely at the rooms – and particularly later, at the photos taken – we understood that they differed in details: in the colour of the wall, the violet curtains providing a surreal light to the interior, an iron left on an ironing board, mould spots on a moss-green wall. At times the rooms were left as if the migrant had just departed in a hurry: half-ironed laundry in a plastic basket, children's toys spread over the ground, a bridal veil left on the mirror, a ready-packed suitcase in the corner.

These details were often commented on by the parents of the migrants, providing the background for anecdotes or painful memories about "those who had left". The elderly parents also explained to us the time cycles within which the residents returned to this place (for Easter, New Year, once in four years, never), and that these rooms needed a kind of specific care to keep them ready for an unexpected return. This care included the weekly watering of the indoor plants, dusting, window cleaning, and the removal of spiders' webs on the ceiling. The refrigerator was sometimes "kept in use" for the (grand)parents needs, "to have it ready". The refrigerator hum was the only sonic testimony of a future human presence in these rooms. All this made us think of such places not only as *lieux de mémoire*, but also as material substitutes for the physical absence of the offspring. The obsessive ritual care given to these rooms was the care which was destined to the bodies of the absent; a care which made us understand that these places are material but at the same time material substitutes for physical bodies of flesh and blood, and "memory boxes" of the immaterial. Excessive hygiene and orderliness are their main feature – a striking counterweight to the physical disorder and inner confusion in which "those left behind" were left. It claims control over an uncontrollable situation and intends to reintegrate events of social rupture and detachment into a vision of continuity and hope.

Empty migrant rooms are real, hyper-real. They seem to be livable, but they are not. They seem to wait for being inhabited but at the same time resemble a museum, filled with requisites which do not serve everyday life and whose almost ritualistic order resists any change or adaption.

For the local people concerned, migrant rooms are stable constructions, a constant point of reference for "those who left", and an anchor for those who wait for their return. They represent the moral, social, and symbolic value of a continuing kinship connection as materialized in concrete. At the same time, they are anything but permanent. Their meaning is situational and ambiguous – they are half inhabited and half deserted, half empty and half full with meaning. At times these rooms/houses represent the "myth of return" (Bolognani 2007) and the idea of "migration as hope" (Pine 2014); at others they are reminders of life ruptures, uncompleted life cycles, impossibilities of return, and mental breakdowns.

A useful methodological tool to explain the conflicting meaning of such rooms is the recently established anthropology of absence (Bille *et al.* 2011), and the work of the Australian philosopher Patrick Fuery (1989), who argues that absence always exists in relation to the idea of presence. Absence (*boshllik*) and presence (*prani*) in Albanian popular culture are thought of as being directly related to the mental and physical state of a person. *Boshllik* is felt as an immense pain (*dhimbje*), as longing (*mall*), and as an incurable illness. Being absent from one's own place of origin is often associated in popular poetry with the idea of an inextinguishable thirst. In this light the meaning of such rooms – their inner logic, their emotional relevance – is constituted by the referent "presence". The room as such, as well as the sum of all home furnishings, therefore function as "absence signifiers", making the signified (the migrant) present and more apparent through pointing at his absence. Fuery insists that an absent signifier is always a potential: the encoding process through vision, or in our case through photographic representation, is therefore crucial, so that absence can unfold its meaning.

Photographing Absence

Photographing empty migrant rooms is a challenging task, as the material–immaterial is in a fragile balance here. Through photographing – visually representing – these spaces, one manipulates this balance, one works at the edge between the material and the immaterial and gives priority to the immaterial over the material, the real over the fictional, or *vice versa*. Photographing the rooms means producing traces of migrants' existence, making absences and emotional worlds visible as materialized in space. This poses problematic ethical questions, as this reveals and disseminates intimate family histories. As the parents' care for the keepsake of their migrated relatives transforms these rooms into "memory museums", the photographer conserves and "freezes" memory while capturing such places. But there is more to tell about these places beyond such a static, almost aestheticizing, perspective: of course the photographs should transmit the "emotional aura" of such places, but photography should also make these places "speak" to those who are not confronted with the existential aspects of migration on an everyday basis.

Here, we can find inspiration in the work of photographers and painters of the past. Perhaps the most influential figure in this respect is the Danish symbolist painter Vilhelm Hammershøj (1864–1916). In his paintings of interior settings, often inhabited by an anonymized female figure shown from behind, he reveals not only the constructedness of such spaces but also the fragile tension between closure and openness, often corresponding with respective psychological states. Some of the elements used to convey a certain atmosphere have been used in the photographic project: claustrophobic settings, the play with openings and closings (doors and windows), work with light, and monochromatic work, in order to "dematerialize" the fixed boundaries of the room. Also, the idea of constructing "still lives" inherent in Hammershøj's work, as well as the idea of an anti-temporal and anti-narrative stance, was relevant for the Albanian project (Monrad 2014).

If we turn to other photographic representations of absence, we must at once refer to Jean Mohr's dream-like images documenting the dehumanizing working conditions of migrants in the 1960s (Berger and Mohr 2010 [1975]). Mohr focuses on facial expression as revealing the "migrant condition", and only one image in his *A Seventh Man* explicitly contemplates space. This is a photograph of a Greek *gastarbeiter* in his room; the wall is clad with memorabilia – a rosary, family photographs, embroidery, an image of his hometown – on the edge of the bed, almost like in a Hammershøj setting, the worker reading a journal. This room seems to exemplify what Boym (2002) would call "retrospective nostalgia": the past absorbs the space, and all elements tend to transform the unknown space into one's home. The case of the Krasta migrant rooms represents the contrary vision of a "prospective nostalgia" (Boym 2002, 168): space is left in a suspended transitory state, ready to absorb new meanings.

As a photographer, I have been confronted with diverse forms of absence. In Pripyat, a town abandoned after the catastrophe of Chernobyl, the objects as remnants of extinguished life had a disquieting effect on me. In another project, on living conditions on the shores of the Strait of Gibraltar, I focused on the Mediterranean Sea as a symbolic space of absences, menacing and dissolving ideas of home, security, family bonds, and human trust. Such topics are of particular interest for photographers, as they allow going beyond journalistic coverage, taking objects such as an abandoned puppet, a clove of garlic wrapped in plastic foil against the evil eye, or a made-up bed as elicitors that reveal the narrativity of space and individual human destinies. At times, the interior arrangement in the empty migrant rooms in Krasta resembled a staging: an unused brand-new iron, most probably a wedding gift, left on a sideboard resembled an artistic object. I decided to photograph with a tripod and my Mamyia 7 on colour negative film with an 80 mm gauge, the standard focal length for this image format. With tripod and daylight I consequently had long exposure times, as I wanted to shoot with a small aperture in order to gain a relatively continuous sharpness. I tried to capture the hyperreality of the place frozen in time with technical equipment "mirroring" this static impression. Rooms are empty and immobile; the single movement was at times the curtain, moved through a breeze coming through an opened window – a ghostly presence of those who should have lived here. At times one feels observed, although the inhabitants do not even know that they are observed through a lens, and that someone has seen them and photographed. Roland Barthes wrote in *Camera Lucida* about such a paradox: "How can we look without seeing?" (Barthes 1981, 111). Barthes made this observation in a café about a boy who was looking at him, asking himself whether the boy was seeing him. One looks at these rooms and the faded photographs of its inhabitants and cannot resist the impression that one is looked at.

There were, however, physically present humans caring for these rooms: "Those left behind". I portrayed them with a digital camera – however, it would have made sense to photograph throughout the entire project with the same technical equipment and constant photographic parameters. Enlarging such a project, covering different regions of Albania in an attempt at "photographic mapping", would reveal regional variations and mentalities in dealing with the phenomenon of migrant absences.

Naming the project "Bridreams" (*Brautträume*) was a logical step. Such a term testifies to the uncompleted life cycles and fragmented character of migrant dreams. Many migrants left their families just days after their wedding, leaving behind objects such as veils, wedding presents, or wedding photographs. These relics, often exposed in an ostentatious way, reveal emotional ambiguity: they are reminders of a joyful celebration of a "rite of passage", but at the same time they recall the transience and the merciless passing of time. Photographing empty migrant rooms as a setting means to capture settings which have not changed over years, and are "frozen" in time – however, a feeling of ephemerality is omnipresent, the idea that the moment of the departure of the migrant could have been his final one. The Albanian self-definition of a migrant as a "living dead" materializes in such rooms.

Migrant Traces as an Issue of Permanence–Non-Permanence

Photos of such materialized absence are real and aesthetic at the same time. They document while they construct and contemplate a "prospective nostalgia", pointing to the many potentialities which have not been realized (Boym 2002, 168). They also ask questions about the tension between the material and the immaterial which concern the very nature and preservability of "migrant traces". Are these traces not all ephemeral and transitory, as migrants are constantly on the move? In which ways are these traces representative of the migrant's existential struggle? Are these traces "exposable" to a wider public?

Expositions like those in the Musée de l'Histoire de l'Immigration in Paris, the Museo delle Migrazioni on Lampedusa, or mostly recently that of Ai Wei Wei in the Museum of Cycladic Arts, Athens, make us think in a way that the only migrant traces worth being exposed are material ones. Material objects integrate well into our "museological mind", the idea of "heritage", and the network of inherited institutions, as they allow people to attach a fixed meaning even to people who are on the move. They allow us to believe that such objects are semantically stable, while in reality they circulate through contradictory social (and media) contexts of meaning. Exhibiting family photographs, teapots, copies of the Qur'an, or lifebelts converted into marble nourishes the fiction that the non-permanent can be turned into the permanent.

But what about the non-permanent, the floating meanings of migrant existence? What about the life jackets on the beaches of Lesvos – removed after migrants' arrivals – used by the media to make human tragedy visible without showing explicit images of death and suffering? What about the demolition of "the Jungle", the refugee camp in Calais (completed in October 2016)? What about the refugee camp of Idomeni, which in May 2016 was reduced to a dehumanized and denaturalized bulldozed surface, resembling the moon? Such acts did not aim to preserve and materialize non-permanent traces; rather, demolition teams supported by riot police covered over the improvised, non-permanent tracks of migrant existence: tents, and improvised places of worship, and housing conditions compared in media coverage to the *favelas* in Brazil.

If we look at the empty migrant rooms from this material–immaterial perspective we might think of such places as places of permanence; but if we take a second look we will realize that such a walled room is anything but stable. While the non-permanent tents of refugees in Idomeni are inhabited and filled with everyday life, these rooms that transmit an idea of permanence are only temporarily inhabited. They are not made for the present, everyday life; instead, they are a promise for a better future. Empty migrant rooms, in the words of Stewart, are places "caught in the ongoing density of sociality and desire", locations "to which 'we' might return – in mind, if not in body – in search for redemption and renewal" (Stewart 1996, 5).

Figure 7.1. Light study – bedroom, Krasta, Elbasan, Central Albania (photograph © Florian Bachmeier).

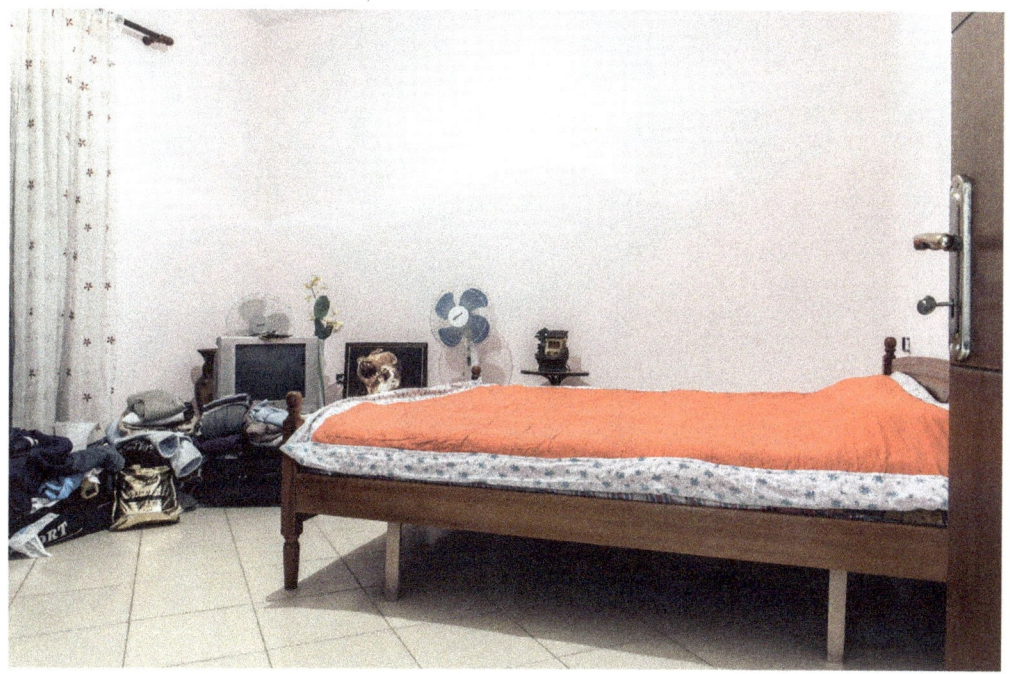

Figure 7.2. Bedroom, Krasta, Elbasan, Central Albania (photograph © Florian Bachmeier).

Figure 7.3. Marriage bed of a migrant couple, Krasta, Elbasan, Central Albania (photograph © Florian Bachmeier).

Figure 7.4. Marriage and children's beds, Krasta, Elbasan, Central Albania (photograph © Florian Bachmeier).

Figure 7.5. Marriage and children's beds, Krasta, Elbasan, Central Albania (photograph © Florian Bachmeier).

Figure 7.6. Single bed and socialist furniture of an old man "left behind", Tepelena, South Albania (photograph © Florian Bachmeier).

Figure 7.7. Children's room with bread oven (center), Krasta, Elbasan, Central Albania (photograph © Florian Bachmeier).

Figure 7.8. Elderly couple waiting for the return of their sons, Krasta, Elbasan, Central Albania (photograph © Florian Bachmeier).

References

Barthes, R. 1981. *Camera Lucida: Reflections on Photography*, translated by R. Howard. New York: Farrar, Straus and Giroux.

Berger, J. and J. Mohr. 2010 [1975]. *A Seventh Man*. London and New York: Verso.

Bille, M., F. Hastrup, and T. F. Sørensen, eds. 2011. *An Anthropology of Absence – Materializations of Transcendence and Loss*. New York: Springer.

Bolognani, M. 2007. "The Myth of Return: Dismissal, Revival or Survival?" *Journal of Ethnic and Migration Studies* 33 (1): 59–76. https://doi.org/10.1080/13691830601043497

Boym, S. 2002. *The Future of Nostalgia*. New York: Basic Books.

Bürkle, S., ed. 2016. *Migrating Spaces: Architecture and Identity in the Context of Turkish Remigration*. Berlin: Vice Versa.

Dalakoglou, D. 2010. "Migrating-Remitting-'Building'-Dwelling: House-Making as 'Proxy' Presence in Postsocialist Albania." *Journal of the Royal Anthropological Institute* 16 (4): 761–777. https://doi.org/10.1111/j.1467-9655.2010.01652.x

Dalipaj, G. 2016. "Migration, Residential Investment and the Experience of 'Transition': Tracing Transnational Practices of Albanian Migrants in Athens." *Focaal* 76: 85–98. https://doi.org/10.3167/fcl.2016.760106

Fuery, P. 1989. "Toward a Typology of the Absent Signifier." *Semiotica* 75 (1–2): 79–84. https://doi.org/10.1515/semi.1989.75.1-2.79

Lopez, S. L. 2015. *The Remittance Landscape: Spaces of Migration in Rural Mexico and Urban USA*. Chicago: University of Chicago Press.

Lozanovska, M. 2007. "Diaspora, Return and Migrant Architectures." *International Journal of Diversity in Organizations, Communities and Nations* 7 (2): 239–250. https://doi.org/10.18848/1447-9532/CGP/v07i02/39369

Monrad, K., ed. 2014. *Hammershøi and Europe*. London: Prestel.

Pine, F. 2014. "Migration as Hope: Space, Time, and Imagining the Future." *Current Anthropology* 55 (Supplement 9): S95–S104. https://doi.org/10.1086/676526

Stewart, K. 1996. *A Space on the Side of the Road: Cultural Poetics in an "Other" America*. Princeton, NJ: Princeton University Press.

Tschoepe, A. Y. 2016. "Diasporic Homescapes: Liminal to Permanent Spaces of Identity and Memory Practices." In *Migrating Spaces: Architecture and Identity in the Context of Turkish Remigration*, edited by S. Bürkle, 418–425. Berlin: Vice Versa.

Eckehard Pistrick is a Postdoctoral Researcher and Lecturer in Ethnomusicology at Martin-Luther-Universität Halle-Wittenberg. Address for correspondence: Institut für Musik, Medien- und Sprechwissenschaften (IMMS), Abteilung Musikwissenschaft, Kleine Marktstr. 7, 06108 Halle, Germany. Email: eckehard.pistrick@musikwiss.uni-halle.de

Florian Bachmeier is a socially engaged photographer with n-Ost Network for Reporting on Eastern Europe who has extensively reported on the conflict in eastern Ukraine and the "refugee crisis" in Greece. Address for correspondence: Frühlingstr. 13 a, 83727 Schliersee, Germany. Email: mail@florianbachmeier.com

Chapter 8

If Place Remotely Matters: Camped in Greece's Contingent Countryside

Kostis Kourelis

Introduction

This chapter lays out an agenda for an archaeology of cultural landscapes that situates new migrant camps in Greece within a longer history of settlement and occupation. Our rich knowledge of Greece's rural history based on regional surveys has posited the notion of a contingent countryside, of a landscape continuously responding to global pressures (Sutton 2000). Greece has experienced influxes of refugees and internally displaced persons through its entire history, with references to forced migration as early as the seventh century (Charanis 1948); revolution, failed or successful military offensives, invasion, civil war, political incarceration, ethnic cleansing, genocide, dictatorship, internal displacement, and forced population exchange have contributed to the establishment of thousands of refugee camps and settlements in modern Greece. Those figures include 12 refugee camps from the Greek War of Independence, 2089 refugee settlements from the Asia Minor Crisis of 1922, and 1600 settlements destroyed in the Second World War (Karamouzi 1999; Doxiadis 1947). The Greek landscape is saturated with refugee settlements like no other European country. Many are fully deserted and prone to archaeological investigation; however, Greek archaeological culture has shied away from an archaeology of the recent past, while camp excavations have been developing in Europe and the USA (Skiles and Clark 2010; Persson 2014). The proliferation of camps constructed during the most recent influx of refugees and undocumented migrants underscores the need for archaeology to respond to migration with disciplinary rigor and coherence. With 65.3 million people – one in every 113 citizens of the world – listed by the United Nations as refugees or internally displaced, we must bring into greater focus an archaeology of care.

The Migrant and Refugee Crisis in Greece

In March 2016, Greece's northern neighbors closed their borders to refugees and migrants. Approximately 57,000 individuals could not reach their intended destinations in northern Europe and were effectively stuck in a country they did not want to be in, and which was not prepared to host them. A situation that had already escalated into a humanitarian crisis took an unusual turn towards long-term settlement rather than temporary passage, while the closing of borders, an exclusionary foreign policy, and a deal struck between the EU and Turkey on 18 March, 2016 changed the spatial character of Greece's migrants and refugee management. Before this date, the humanitarian crisis had been concentrated on the islands of the Aegean; the treaty with Turkey gave control over points of arrival to Frontex (the European Border and Coast Guard Agency) and mandated that no refugees be moved beyond the islands. The refugees and migrants already trapped in Greece became *de facto* a Greek internal affair.

Initially, the landlocked refugees created *ad hoc* camps, with a large concentration at the rail depot and northern border control at Idomeni and at the port of Piraeus. Greece's inability to process even the minimum number of asylum seekers in the early 2000s had been compounded by the 2009 debt crisis. Without the bureaucratic, logistical, or financial infrastructure to solve the humanitarian crisis, the Greek government initiated a decentralization plan of dispersing its new migrant population across the provinces in newly erected camps. Starting in March 2016 with 26 camps, by August that number had grown to 69. The United Nations recognized the geographic fragmentation and lack of accountability in the management of Greece's refugee crisis during the summer, and established an online digital mapping service that tabulates camp data provided by Greek governmental agencies in real time (United Nations High Commissioner for Refugees 2016).

The central government approached regional authorities and requested feasible locations to station camps within each territory. Although not clearly formalized, the process necessitated an informal assessment of real estate assets that was closed to the public. Proximity to pre-existing infrastructure was a central consideration, but at the same time, the prospective sites had to be unclaimed by pre-existing private or public stakeholders. Neither fully rejecting nor fully welcoming the refugees, each local administration sought installations of no public or private value but with access to amenities (water, food, electricity, sewage). The site selection was determined by the availability of pre-existing assets that required minimum investment and were far enough from inhabited areas to avoid political upheaval.

Although related to earlier manifestations of forced migration, the 50 camps on the Greek mainland resulting from the 2015–2016 escalation represent a single historical episode. Also, while spread throughout Greece, all the camps share the common feature of occupying abandoned sites, namely decommissioned army bases, deserted factories, inactive airports, bankrupt resorts, vacant supermarkets, and sports arenas from the 2004 Olympics. The refugees were forced into an archaeological environment of modern ruins from recent economic or military decline. These edge cities have become organic appendages to a failed supermodernity (González-Ruibal 2008). They form microcosmic borderlands between the global, the local, and the national, or compressed proxies of global conflict.

The recent arrival of large numbers of migrants and refugees from Africa, Asia, and the Middle East to Europe has created a diversity of solutions on how and where to manage their housing. The legal obligation to process asylum applications at the point of entry has contributed to the centralization of containment, and clustering at urban points of passage. Greece has opted for a policy of dispersing the burden across the country. Dispersed camps accomplish a paradoxical effect: on the one hand, they embed newcomers into an expanded social fabric, but, on the other, they decentralize their political presence and render them invisible. Scholarship on the spatial character and distribution of camps has informed humanitarian activism (Migreurop 2012), while geographical analysis of spreading the burden has created the foundations for better policy implementation (Robinson *et al.* 2003). Greece's policy of dispersing its refugee and migrant population across the mainland has been criticized in retrospect as economically wasteful. Multiplying the provision of services and infrastructure by 50 has led to an estimated annual cost of $14,088 per beneficiary (Howden 2017).

Methodology

Archaeology responds to materiality at varying scales. An archaeology of forced and undocumented migration can focus on the micro-scale of objects that participate in complex networks of use and exchange (De León 2015; Papataxiarchis 2016), but it can also explore the macro-scale of cultural landscapes and consider camps as the latest episode in an ongoing sequence of inhabitation. Archaeologists study the Greek countryside as a dynamic system. There have been 24 pedestrian regional surveys since the pioneering 1961 Minnesota Messenia Expedition (McDonald and Rapp 1972), and the sophisticated methodology of landscape archaeology developed in Greece from that time should encourage the archaeological community to apply tools developed for the study of ancient settlements towards the contemporary landscape.

This landscape approach turns migrants and refugees into subjects of a historical experience unfolding in particular places, rather than being abstract bodies with acute biopolitical needs in universal space. The focus on place, moreover, avoids violating the proximities of individual human experiences or the tropes of suffering dominant in photographic coverage. It also integrates the contemporary camps into the *longue durée* of forced migrations in Greece. Recent studies of political detention camps at Makronissos and Ai Stratis and of militarized border zones at Prespa Lakes are beginning to establish the twentieth century as a legitimate period of archaeological investigation (Hamilakis 2002; Pantzou 2011; Papadopoulos 2016). In the Second World War, 1600 Greek villages (a quarter of the total 6500 inhabited villages) were destroyed by the Nazis, with their populations internally displaced (Doxiadis 1947). The Lidoriki Project in Phocis has surveyed one such village (Brenningmeyer *et al.* 2015); it was the last season of survey at the village of Strouza/Aigition that offered the possibility of fieldwork in contemporary camps in June 2016.

A close archaeology inside Greek camps is difficult, as the authorities heavily restrict entry. Short of carrying out clandestine documentation, remote sensing provides a legal but subversive strategy of what photographer Allan Sekula defined as counter-surveillance (Keenan 2014). This approach has entered archaeological pedagogy in academic programs, such as the Penn Cultural Heritage Center at Penn Museum, Philadelphia and the Forensic Architecture program at Goldsmiths, University of London. It has been successfully applied to the documentation of archaeological looting in Syria, the drift of migrants' boats in the central Mediterranean, drone strikes in the Middle East, and the archaeology of Guantanamo Bay (Myers 2010; Forensic Architecture 2014, 411–433, 657-684; Casana 2016). Since 1999, remote sensing via satellite images has created new forms of human rights documentation during ethnic cleansing in Kosovo, slum clearance in Zimbabwe, and the Darfur crisis (Herscher 2011).

Koutsochero: A Case Study

A case study from the region of Thessaly illustrates the potential for a remote archaeology of place. The refugee camp known as Koutsochero is a decommissioned army base next to a rock quarry and near a refugee settlement from 1926. The tent camp was vacated in summer 2016 in order to install permanent trailers funded by the United Arab Emirates (UAE). Online media coverage allowed for a complete reconstruction of the extended biography of the site from the construction of the tent camp in March 2016 and the completion of the trailer camp in November 2016. A quick and unauthorized visual survey was carried out by Todd Brenningmeyer, Kostis Kourelis, and undergraduate students from Franklin & Marshall College in June 2016. The terrestrial and aerial data gathered onsite and was remotely processed by undergraduate students in Brenningmeyer's "Introduction to GIS" course at Maryville University in Fall Term 2016.

The administrative region of Thessaly initially proposed two abandoned supermarkets along the Larissa–Trikala and Karditsa–Trikala roads. When those two retail spaces did not work out because of private ownership complications, Trikala turned to a national property, namely the archaeological site of its medieval citadel. A tourist pavilion built on the castle in 1960 was not operative and offered housing. On 10 March, 2016, the first 180 Syrian refugees arrived at Trikala Castle. They received a warm welcome by locals, which caught the attention of the international press. The *New York Times* reported how refugees were placed "even in a castle" at Trikala (Yardley 2016).

The placement of Syrians inside Trikala's most important historical locus highlights the coexistence of a shared cultural heritage between host and guest that received no attention in the news or from the archaeological community. With the exception of some Justinianic sections, the walls of the fortress date to the Ottoman period. The old town of Aleppo, before its wholesale destruction, shared similarities with Trikala, including a medieval citadel and an important mosque right below it. As in many provincial towns in continental Greece, the citadel offers a monumental testimony to architectural variety, multiculturalism, and continuity, in contrast to the purified national narrative fabricated in sites where all post-classical buildings have been removed. Thanks to its provinciality, the medieval and post-medieval heritage of Trikala is better preserved than that of Athens, where the Acropolis has been stripped of its rich post-classical monuments.

Also, unlike sites of antiquity, which are fenced off, medieval citadels are integrated into the social life of Greek towns. They are leisure destinations in the summer, containing theaters, playgrounds, promenades, coffee shops, and gardens. Many citadels entered modern life negatively as prisons. Akronauplia in Nauplion and Heptapyrgion (Yedikule) in Thessaloniki incarcerated political dissenters within their walls as late as the 1960s; surviving political prisoners from the Heptapyrgion have protested archaeological plans to demolish the modern prison to highlight the medieval masonry below. For their first nights in Thessaly, the Syrian refugees slept under the city's iconic tower, dating from the seventeenth century and celebrating Pax Ottomanica. Having been bombed by the Germans in 1941, the clock tower represents resilience and resistance. Below the walls of the castle, Trikala contains the Osman Shah Mosque built in the 1550s, which is the only work of the architect Mimar Sinan that survives intact in Greece. Sinan, born in an Armenian or Cappadocian Christian family, is considered the Michelangelo of Ottoman architecture; he was the builder of the Suleiman Mosque in Istanbul and Selimiye Mosque in Edirne. Sinan's earliest masterpiece is the 1536 Hüsrey Pasha Mosque in Aleppo, which was razed in the summer of 2014 during the Syrian Civil War. Surreptitiously, the experience at Trikala triggers a moment of common global history shared by both Greeks and Syrians. Hüsrey Pasha Mosque in Aleppo cannot be recovered, but its experience can be shared by proxy in the Osman Shah Mosque at Trikala.

The reception at the castle of Trikala was conceived as a temporary measure, while the Hellenic Army prepared a more extensive camp on the abandoned Euthymiopoulos army base near the villages of Mandra and Koutsochero, 47 km east of Trikala. The camp's proximity to Larissa, home to the First Army, guaranteed convenient military control. Work at the site began on 9 March, 2016, with the first refugees arriving ten days later. Multiple Google Earth satellite images show the site between 2004 and the present: the camp is surrounded by fertile agricultural land, but located on an aggressively quarried rocky outcropping.

After leaving Trikala, 1000 refugees were accommodated in 300 army tents. Although closed to the public, the tents can be mapped with great detail by analyzing Google's coverage on 22 April, 2016. The archaeology of the original army camp is traceable through the surviving vegetation visible from the earliest satellite images available. Six buildings date to the original phase of the camp, and they were deserted (with collapsing roofs) already in 2004. Upon entering the camp today, the viewer encounters a decommissioned line of defense, a deserted guard post, and a religious shrine. During the clearing of the camp for the refugees, the army ruins were left intact. The camp was organized around a dozen parallel bays, c. 50 m long. The tent city was built within those pre-existing compartments. A plan produced by the students maps the precise number and location of the tents (Figure 8.1).

Immediately to the southwest of the camp, across a busy road, was an older refugee town named Mandra. Interviews with its residents revealed an extraordinary awareness of shared experience. Mandra was constructed in 1924 to resettle refugees from Cappadocia, specifically from one village, Misti. Mandra's residents keep the memory of their village alive through Cappadocian folk customs and festivals, while their church of St Basil replicates St Basil of Misti. When planned, Mandra was strategically positioned by the Venizelos government to break up a landlord monopoly that had resulted from the privatization of Ottoman farmland after Thessaly's annexation in 1881 (Knight 2015). Satellite analysis of Mandra illustrates the structure of the original refugee town. Much has changed architecturally in the intervening 92 years of continuous inhabitation, but the original fabric is traceable. The town was planned along a grid of nine square insulae (108 × 94 m), with a narrow axis in the middle containing civic spaces and the Church of St Basil, and extending north to the cemetery. Each block is divided into 12 equal rectangular lots (47 × 18 m each), with a house placed at each corner facing the street. Mandra represents the construction of refugee housing as executed by the Refugee Settlement Commission (RSC) founded by the League of Nations in 1924 to facilitate the relocation of

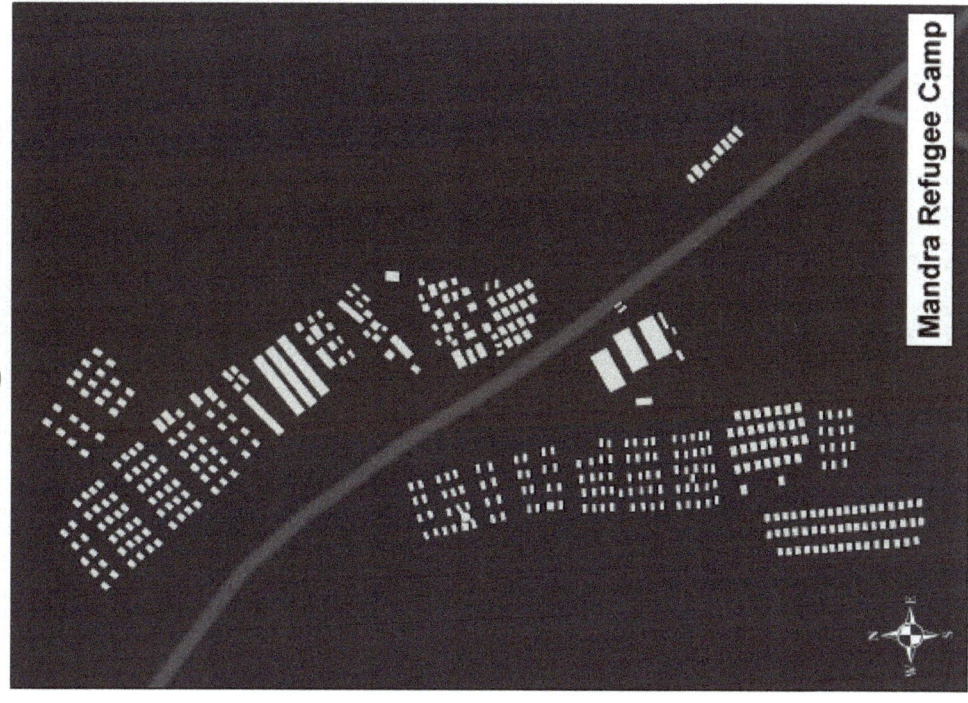

Figure 8.1. Remote sensing of tents at Mandra/Koutsochero Camp, Thessaly, Greece, on 30 May, 2016, by Adam Rork, Joseph Schmitz, and Todd Brenningmeyer, Maryville University.

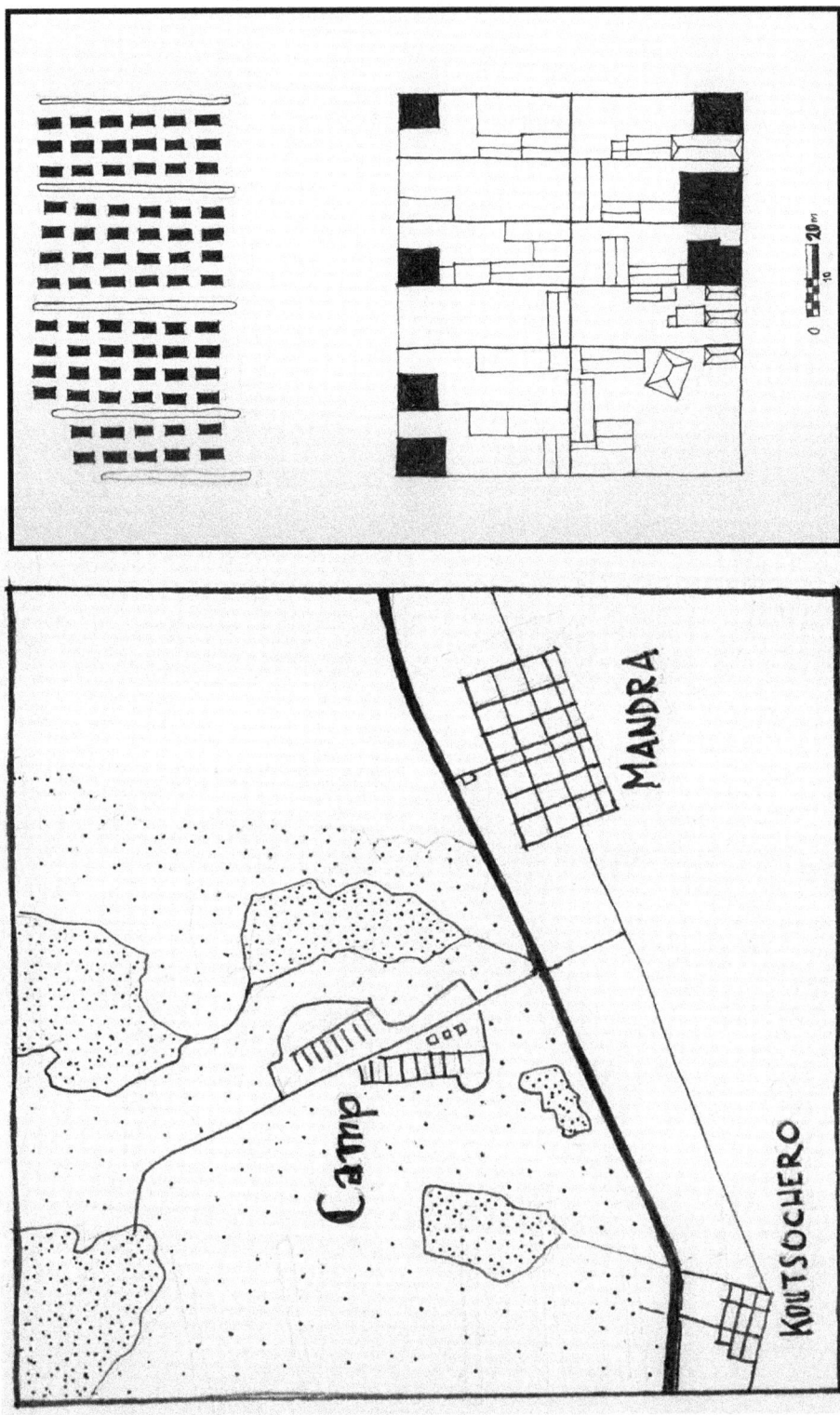

Figure 8.2. Left: proximity between 2016 refugee site camp and 1924 refugee settlement (Mandra). Right: Housing comparison (in black) between 2016 refugee camp (above) and 1924 refugee settlement (below) at Mandra/Koutsochero (by author).

1.3 million Greeks from Asia Minor. Unlike the *ad hoc* solutions of the current state, the RSC employed 1700 dedicated staff members and was funded by special loans granted by the US Congress. The RSC employed a similarly decentralized approach, utilizing local contractors and not specifying a strict typology. Interestingly enough, the RSC repeatedly complained about resistance by the Greek government to creating maps (even in cases where the RSC provided the expertise for their execution). In the northern regions of Macedonia and Thrace, the cartographic data produced by the RSC remains the most reliable urban mapping of the area. The graphic comparison of residential units between Koutsochero Camp and Mandra highlights a striking difference: in Mandra, a modest house (c. 8 × 8 m) in a lot (47 × 18 m) accommodates one family, while the same area in Koutsochero accommodates 18 families in tents (Figure 8.2).

The fate of Koutsochero Camp changed in early June 2016, after the UAE and the Red Crescent made an economic commitment to finance 200 permanent trailers with modern amenities. On 9 June, the camp began a process of closing for a projected two-month period of construction. The 700 residents had to be evacuated to new sites, which generated another round of site assessments and negotiations. Unlike the peaceful relocation from Lesvos to Trikala and from Trikala to Koutsochero, the evacuation of the camps three months later became violent and contested. The decision was made to relocate the refugees to another abandoned military camp, the Anargyros Zogas base near the village of Kypselochori. The army began making installations by setting up tents, but these were damaged by members of the Neo-Nazi Golden Dawn party who entered the camp on 11 June, 2016. Reports also emerged about a scarcity of water and the need to drill wells for water provisioning. The camp at Kyspelochori was put on hold while alternative sites were investigated. The proposed UAE camp would be limited to Syrians, which meant that it was necessary to ethnically differentiate Syrians and others during the process of evacuation. Eventually, it was decided to take the Syrians to a camp in Thessaloniki and to move them back to Koutsochero after the construction was completed. Afghan residents of Koutsochero, meanwhile, would be relocated to Kypselochori, where they would remain. News reports indicate that the residents of the camp resisted this segregation; they also pleaded with the authorities to wait for two more weeks for the relocation, until the end of Ramadan in early July. Despite this, the first group of 130 Afghans was transported to Kypselochori by bus on 22 June. After seeing the site, the migrants refused to disembark. They argued that the accommodation was worse than at Koutsochero, with no electricity and questionable water sources. When forced to enter the camp they protested violently by burning mattresses. They also asked the bus drivers to take them back to Koutsochero, but the drivers refused. They were forced to spend the night in Kypselochori (according to some reports, by use of force and tear gas). The following morning, the refugees evacuated the camp by foot, walking towards Larissa or Athens (their destination after this dispersal is unclear). The new plan, at this point, shifted to busing the Syrian population to Kypselochori instead.

In the midst of this controversy, the administration in Thessaly began exploring alternatives beyond Kypselochori. The Demetrios Ziogas military camp in Kalampaka was investigated, but there were protests about its proximity to Meteora – not just a tourist site, but a center of Orthodox monasticism. As such, anti-immigration groups turned this site into a nationalist battleground. A descendent of Demetrios Ziogas appeared at the site and declared that his grandfather's heroic death at the Albanian front in 1941 would be marred by transforming the military camp dedicated to his honor into a settlement for foreign nationals. Two alternatives were suggested: the ruins of the Thessaly Paper Making Industry, which was a factory constructed in 1965 but deserted in 1991, and an abandoned lot next to a Mercedes Benz car dealership closer to Larissa. Neither plan materialized. In July 2016, our team visited the site of Koutsochero, hoping to enter the site during the interim phase of construction. A quick record of extant structures was made in the three minutes it took for the police to arrive and expel us. By 17 August, 144 out of the planned 200 housing units had been completed, with a projected reopening of the camp on 20 September. The camp in fact opened on 23 November, with great fanfare. Many dignitaries from the Greek government, the UAE, the Red Cross, and the Red Crescent attended the inauguration. Koutsochero served as the poster child of governmental success, including a visit by Santa Claus on 29 December.

The Koutsochero case study illustrates the multi-period complexities in the foundation of refugee and migrant camps in Greece. However, each of the current 69 camps has its own story evolving in the limited horizon of 2016. We investigated two additional camps, Elaionas in Attica and Katsikas in Ioannina. The collected data include a comparative study of trailers and the investigation of the industrial economy that surrounds the sites. Elaionas, for example, is situated along an old axis that segregated the management of disease and horticultural training. The trailers in Elaionas are recycled from the disaster relief camps from the 1999 Athens earthquake. Although intended to be temporary, some of the earthquake relief camps have resisted eviction. Resembling a favela, the earthquake camp of Kapota continues to house 5000 residents. Moving trailers from 1999 earthquake camps to 2016 refugee camps reveals a continuous use of architectural culture in the management of conflict across time. For the study of Elaionas, we are collaborating with a team of undergraduate students from other universities who have served as humanitarian volunteers with the Swedish NGO Lighthouse Relief.

Towards a Comprehensive Humanitarian Archaeology in Greece

With one in every 122 humans classified as a refugee or internally displaced person, scholars of material culture must face a growing body of evidence in global inhabitation. The fluidity of capital, labor, and natural resources has escalated transience and transient housing (Madden and Marcuse 2016). Favelas in Latin America (Perlman 2010) or the cities "yet to come" in Africa (Simone 2004) point to an urban future lacking traditional structures associated with the cities of modernity. Sociologists argue that modes of informality associated with the developing world are also becoming the norm in the cities of the developed world, from taco trucks to border colonias and man camps (Mukhija and Loukaitou-Sideris 2014).

Greece offers a fertile ground to embark on a diachronic and transnational archaeology that situates the most recent migration in a long comparative perspective. This archaeology would have to embrace the documentation, survey, and excavation of nineteenth- and twentieth-century sites, while also devising methodological strategies for the more difficult sites that are constructed, lived in, and abandoned in real time. If the refugee challenges the very notions of state sovereignty, Greece's response to the current crisis will offer a valuable test case because of its own indeterminate status as crypto-colonial, compromised, failed, contingent, mixed, or supermodern (some of the many terms used to describe Greek exceptionalism).

Although Greece has had a vibrant archaeological culture, very little of its attention has been directed to the recent past, which has been violent, traumatic, and politically contested. Invested with the task of constructing a hegemonic national identity, archaeology has consistently purified sites of complex chronologies into the monolithic narrative of a classical golden age. Paradoxically, archaeology has traditionally aligned itself with the destruction rather than the documentation of impermanent housing, serving the state apparatus for the clearing of slums, shantytowns, and refugee settlements and thus placing it in an adversarial relationship with humanitarianism. As early as the 1860s, archaeologists sought to displace a neighbourhood of squatters that had formed on the hills of the Acropolis, which had in turn displaced the "Black Rocks" neighbourhood of African slaves (Caftantzoglou 2000). Similarly, the granting of the Athenian Agora to the American School of Classical Studies at Athens in 1932 was intended to eradicate the settlement of refugees and displace a working-class slum (Sakka 2008; Hamilakis 2013).

From another vantage point, archaeology in Greece has played a catalytic role in modern humanitarianism via an Anglo-American intellectual tradition with deep Protestant missionary roots. After serving as a doctor in the Greek War of Independence, the Boston humanitarian Samuel G. Howe received permission from President Kapodistrias to erect a refugee town in Corinthia, which he named Washingtonia. It housed 200 internally displaced individuals and 29 refugees from Asia Minor (Howe 1906, 354). By the time that American archaeologists began the excavations of ancient Corinth in 1876, the traces of the Washingtonia refugee town had disappeared. Washingtonia has since been identified by the Eastern Korinthia Archaeological Survey, and there are hopes of embarking on an excavation in the near future (Gregory 2007, 180; Sanders 2013, 111–114). American archaeologists were central participants in the resettlement of refugees in 1922, either through the RSC (which included an American archaeologist on its board), the American Red Cross, or Near East Relief. The excavations at Olynthus had a refugee field director, employed 350 refugees on its staff, and even resided in a refugee camp (Robinson 1930, 113). Although embroiled in controversial negotiations of concerning eminent domain, the Agora excavations sustained refugee camps, and recycled demolished building material to nearby shantytowns (Dumont forthcoming). Archaeologists of the British School at Athens were similarly invested in the refugee crisis, particularly in Euboea's Noel-Baker estate, or in new Macedonian towns designed by Piet de Jong (Noel-Baker 2000, 281; Kourelis 2007, 420–422).

For Greece, an archaeology of forced and undocumented migrants must take a number of tactics. First, it must focus on the documentation of current camps; second, it must embrace the archaeology of historical camps, including the 1829 Washingtonia or any of the 2089 villages built by the RSC in 1923–1930. Thirdly, it must acknowledge historiographical traditions, such as the deployment of archaeological capital as an instrument to evacuate refugees, and Anglo-American proclivities towards humanitarianism (Davis and Vogeikoff-Brogan 2013).

In his typology of camps, Charlie Hailey has shown that the EU's migrant camps oscillate between open and closed, between centralized control and local contingencies: "The camps, complex and diverse as they are both in name and in formulation, illustrate spatially the bordering process of a continually emergent Union and a developing system of multiple statehoods" (Hailey 2009, 243). Greece has been a state of constant migration, whether inward or outward. The sharp tools in archaeology's arsenal can create a fact-based material record to complement the ever-growing theoretical discourse of contemporary archaeology.

References

Brenningmeyer, T., K. Kourelis, and M. Katsaros. 2015. "The Lidoriki Project: Low Altitude Aerial Photography, GIS, and Traditional Survey in Rural Greece." In *CAA 2015: Keep the Revolution Going*, edited by S. Campana, R. Scopigno, G. Carpentiero, and M. Cirillo, 979–988. Oxford: Archeopress.

Caftanzoglou, R. 2000. "The Sacred Rock and the Profane Settlement: Place, Memory and Identity under the Acropolis." *Oral History* 28 (1): 43–51.

Casana, J. 2016. "Using Satellite Imagery to Monitor Syria's Cultural Heritage." *Anthropology News*, 7 April. Available online: http://onlinelibrary.wiley.com/doi/10.1111/j.1556-3502.2016.570402.x/pdf

Charanis, P. 1948. "The Slavic Element in Byzantine Asia Minor in the Thirteenth Century." *Byzantion* 18: 69–83.

Davis, J. L. and N. Vogeikoff-Brogan, eds. 2013. *Philhellenism, Philanthropy, or Political Convenience? American Archaeology in Greece.* Special issue of *Hesperia* 72.

De León, J. 2015. *The Land of Open Graves: Living and Dying on the Migrant Trail.* Berkeley: University of California Press.

Doxiadis, C. A. 1947. *Destruction of Towns and Villages in Greece.* Athens: Undersecretary's Office for Reconstruction.

Dumont, S. Forthcoming. Ανασύνθεση μιας γειτονιάς στο κέντρο της Αθήνας. Η εξαφάνιση της λεγομένης συνοικίας του Βρυσακίου για την ανακάλυψη της Αρχαίας Αγοράς. Athens: Melissa.

Forensic Architecture. 2014. *Forensis: The Architecture of Public Truth.* London: Sternberg Press.

González-Ruibal, A. 2008. "Time to Destroy: An Archaeology of Supermodernity." *Current Anthropology* 49 (2): 247–279. https://doi.org/10.1086/526099

Gregory, T. E. 2007. "Contrasting Impressions of Land Use in Early Modern Greece: The Eastern Corinthia and Kythera." In *Between Venice and Istanbul: Colonial Landscapes in Early Modern Greece*, edited by S. Davies and J. Davis, 173–198. Princeton, NJ: American School of Classical Studies at Athens.

Hailey, C. 2009. *Camps: A Guide to 21st Century Space.* Cambridge, MA: MIT Press.

Hamilakis, Y. 2002. "The Other 'Parthenon': Antiquity and National Memory at Makronissos." *Journal of Modern Greek Studies* 20 (2): 307–338. https://doi.org/10.1353/mgs.2002.0025

____. 2013. "Double Colonization: The Story of the Excavations of the Athenian Agora (1924-1931)." In *Philhellenism, Philanthropy, or Political Convenience? American Archaeology in Greece.* Special issue of *Hesperia* 82, edited by J. L. Davis and N. Vogeikoff-Brogan, 153–177.

Herscher, A. 2011. "From Target to Witness: Architecture, Satellite Surveillance, Human Rights." In *Architecture and Violence*, edited by B. Kenzari, 127–148. Barcelona: Actar.

Howden, D. 2017. "How Millions in Refugee Funds Were Wasted in Greece." *Kathimerini*, 19 March. Available online: http://www.ekathimerini.com/216968/gallery/ekathimerini/community/how-millions-in-refugee-funds-were-wasted-in-greece

Howe, S. G. 1906. *Letters and Journals of Samuel Gridley Howe: The Greek Revolution.* Boston: Dunn, Estes, and Co.

Karamouzi, A. 1999. "Καταγραφή και χαρτογράφηση των προσφυγικών οικισμών στον ελληνικό χώρο από το 1821 ως σήμερα." In *Ο ξεριζωμός και η άλλη πατρίδα: Οι προσφυγουπόλεις στην Ελλάδα: Επιστημονικό συμπόσιο, 11 και 12 Απριλίου 1997*, edited by M. Stephanopoulou, 15–57. Athens: Hetaireia Spoudon Neoellenikou Politismou kai Genikes Paideias.

Keenan, T. 2014. "Counter-Forensics and Photography." *Grey Room* 55: 58–77.

Knight, D. M. 2015. *History, Time, and Economic Crisis in Central Greece*. New York: Palgrave Macmillan.

Kourelis, K. 2007. "Byzantium and the Avant-Garde: Excavations at Corinth, 1920s-1930s." *Hesperia* 76: 391–442.

Madden, D. and P. Marcuse. 2016. *In Defense of Housing*. London: Verso.

McDonald, E. and G. R. Rapp Jr, eds. 1972 *The Minnesota Messenia Expedition: Reconstructing a Bronze Age Regional Environment*. Minneapolis: University of Minnesota Press.

Migreurop. 2012. *Atlas des migrants en Europe: Géographie critique des politiques migratoires*. Paris: Armand Colin.

Mukhija, V. and A. Loukaitou-Sideris, eds. 2014. *The Informal City: Beyond Taco Trucks and Day Labor*. Cambridge, MA: MIT Press.

Myers, A. 2010. "Camp Delta, Google Earth and the Ethics of Remote Sensing in Archaeology." *World Archaeology* 42: 455–467.

Noel-Baker, B. 2000. *An Isle of Greece: The Noels in Euboea*. Procopi: Barbro Noel-Baker.

Pantzou, N. 2011. "Materialities and Traumatic Memories of a Twentieth-Century Greek Exile Island." In *Archaeologies of Internment*, edited by A. Myers and G. Moshenska, 191–206. New York: Springer.

Papadopoulos, D. C. 2016. "Ecologies of Ruin: (Re)bordering, Ruination, and Internal Colonialism in Greek Macedonia, 1913-2013." *International Journal of Historical Archaeology* 20 (3): 627–640. https://doi.org/10.1007/s10761-016-0364-3

Papataxiarchis, E. 2016. "Being 'There': At the Front Line of the 'European Refugee Crisis', Part 1." *Anthropology Today* 32 (2): 5–9. https://doi.org/10.1111/1467-8322.12237

Perlman, J. 2010. *Favela: Four Decades of Living on the Edge in Rio de Janeiro*. Oxford: Oxford University Press.

Persson, M. 2014. "Materialising Skatås: Archaeology of a Second World War Refugee Camp in Sweden." In *Ruin Memories: Materialities, Aesthetics and the Archaeology of the Recent Past*, edited by B. Olsen and Þ. Pétursdóttir, 435–461. London and New York: Routledge.

Robinson, D. 1930. *Excavations at Olynthus*. Volume 2: *Architecture and Sculpture: Houses and Other Buildings*. Baltimore: Johns Hopkins Press.

Robinson, V., R. Andersson, and S. Musterd. 2003. *Spreading the 'Burden'?: A Review of Policies to Disperse Asylum Seekers and Refugees*. Bristol, UK: Policy.

Sakka, N. 2008. "The Excavation of the Ancient Agora of Athens: The Politics of Commissioning and Managing the Project." In *A Singular Antiquity: Archaeology and the Hellenic Identity in the Twentieth Century*, edited by D. Damaskos and D. Plantzos, 111–124. Athens: Mouseio Benaki.

Sanders, G. D. R. 2013. "Landlords and Tenants: Sharecroppers and Subsistence Farming in Corinthian Historical Context." In *Corinth in Contrast: Studies in Inequality*, edited by S. J. Friesen, S. James, and D. Schowalter, 103–125, Leiden: Brill.

Simone, A. 2004. *For the City Yet to Come: Changing African Life in Four Cities*. Durham, NC: Duke University Press.

Skiles, S. A. and B. Clark. 2010. "When the Foreign is not Exotic: Colorado's WWII Japanese Internment Camp." In *Trade and Exchange: Archaeological Studies from History and Prehistory*, edited by C. D. Dillian and C. L. White, 179–192. New York: Springer.

Stefatos, K. and I. Kovras. 2015. "Buried Silences of the Greek Civil War." In *Necropolitics: Mass Graves and Exhumations in the Age of Human Rights*, edited by F. Ferrándiz and A. C. G. M. Robben, 161–184. Philadelphia: University of Pennsylvania Press.

Sutton, S. B., ed. 2000. *Contingent Countryside: Settlement, Economy, and Land Use in the Southern Argolid since 1700*. Stanford, CA: Stanford University Press.

United Nations High Commissioner for Refugees. 2016. "Sites in Greece." Available online: www.unhcr.gr/sites

Yardley, J. 2016. "A 'High Degree of Miserable' in a Refugee-Swollen Greece." *New York Times*, 17 March. Available online: https://www.nytimes.com/2016/03/18/world/europe/greece-idomeni-refugees.html

Kostis Kourelis is an Associate Professor of Art History at Franklin & Marshall College. Address for correspondence: Franklin & Marshall College P.O. Box 3003, Lancaster, PA 17604-3003, USA. Email: kkoureli@fandm.edu

Chapter 9

Orange Life Jackets: Materiality and Narration in Lesvos, One Year after the Eruption of the "Refugee Crisis"

George Tyrikos-Ergas

Many material remains of past civilizations are so great or tiny, so elusive in structure, number or location, that in order to be examined – or even be discovered – they need to be looked at from either very close or from very high above. Last summer (2015) in Lesvos, Greece, an aerial perspective was the only way for one to fully and dramatically grasp, through its striking materiality, the massive influx of more than 500,000 refugees who arrived between March and October (United Nations High Commissioner for Refugees 2016). A bird's eye view was necessary in order to visually grasp at once (just like when examining a simple yet comprehensive grapheme) the dynamics of the phenomenon during this short period of eight months. One could see from high up that the northern and eastern shores of the island of Lesvos, hundreds of kilometers of shoreline that consist of grey-brown rock and pebbles or sand, had changed colour. It had turned into a very bizarre, out of context, phosphorescent orange hue, covered by the discarded life jackets worn by the refugees. As people and objects persist in time and space, they transform each other. This chapter will focus on the way life jackets and humans have interacted on the island of Lesvos in the context of what was performed and tagged as the greatest refugee crisis since the Second World War.

Near Molyvos, a small town in the north of Lesvos, there exists the so-called "cemetery of life jackets". Thousands of them lie there, in piles that can truly be referred to as actual hills, carried there by the municipality, NGOs, or volunteers worrying about a potential large-scale pollution of the shoreline. It is difficult to find out who first named this place a "cemetery". Many say it was a volunteer's doing, one of these romantic notions of theirs, but some locals deem it a reasonable name: "Look at them lying there", says Panayiotis, a young tavern owner from Petra, "these life jackets, each one of them a person, each one of them a story, resting there as dead after a battle. No wonder this place is called a cemetery." Volunteers have no concrete answer either. They can't remember who initially told them this place is a "cemetery" and even if they do the line of informants never leads back to a single person.

Common discourse often uses symbols and representations that appear to have no parent-hood. Such a parenthood would easily reveal or even victimize a person or a social group that sometimes, for its own reasons, wishes to remain anonymous the very moment that it narrates its worldview.[1] Legends, rumors – such "stories" may lack parenthood and details that would provide concrete knowledge, but that does not mean that they are not valued as true, that they do not reveal the "truth", or that such conflicting structural elements deem them without interest and debate for a given community (Dégh 2001, 30–31). And indeed, there has been a great deal of heated conflict and fervent debate in recent years between locals and volunteers or NGOs in Molyvos, which has spread more widely. In this chapter, we examine common discourse, a narrative that is collective and yet reveals two distinct representation of the "truth" around the very existence of life jackets, and also two conflicting worldviews that are equally hidden or revealed, performed publicly or spoken in lower tones. Such things may be expressed in more than one language: they may involve locals from Lesvos, volunteers from around the world, or far-away spectators or readers, but here they are, utilizing the materiality, fabric, colour, structure, and location of life jackets as their elements. The life jackets, their orange hue, their abandonment on the shore and their piling up in a "resting place", in a "cemetery", have become something of an optic narrative, distinctive symbol, representation, in a common tongue: orange fabric now stands for the voyage of the refugees. Matter, language, object, symbol, locals, and strangers mutually implicate and perform "reality".[2]

Everyone involved in any degree with the refugee issue in Lesvos reacts similarly to the materiality and symbolism of orange life jackets: the connotations involve two kinds of movements and furthermore two kinds of worldviews concerning refugees. The two kinds of movements are either a successful passage through sea towards safe land, or an attempted passage that failed and that has ended in the direst of ways, by drowning; thus the orange colour echoes in narratives of every kind around the refugee issue as a colour of both hope and despair. The two worldviews, meanwhile, are a pro-refugee orientation or one that tends to demonize them. For some, the life jackets stand for "invasion": it is their quantity that stands out, not their colour, not their location, not their very reason for existing, which is to be used by people trying to avoid drowning in a trafficker's dinghy after having barely escaped death from war, terrorism, or starvation back home. For some people, and for some politics and media, the refugee movement is an invasion of "otherness" into Europe. The very number of the life jackets on the shores of Lesvos or in the "cemetery" in Molyvos has, for them, become a representation of a very concrete threat. "All this filth entered Europe", said a local official in Molyvos, pointing to a pile of life jackets thrown in a municipal rubbish bin. A woman of the conservative left wrote fervently to the local press against "volunteers and refugees destroying our homeland", warning that "all these life jackets hide stories of hundreds of jihadists that are now here, somewhere hidden threatening us. Look at the life jackets. They are proof of what I say."

The life jackets are used by members of the local community and beyond as representations of an ominous local, national, and even global threat that has been initiated by the great

---

1. See Scott's (1990) study on Burma, which focuses on points of conflict between social groups and their largely performative way of representing and communicating their relations publicly and in private.

2. As for this relation between mater and language, object and identity in a posthumanist materialist account of performativity perspective see Barad (2003).

refugee movement of summer 2015. They have become a symbol of an invasive, corrosive evil that threatens sanity, locality, common identity in Lesvos, in Greece, and in the western world in general – a symbol that is perhaps part of a neo-Orientalist representation of otherness (Tuastad 2003). Unlike refugees now contained around the capital city of Mytilene in the camps of Moria and Kara-Tepe, life jackets are still to be found everywhere in the island. Scattered, they continue to be used as reminder of the evil done and as its narrative fabric.

However, life jackets have also become the fabric of pro-refugee representations that aspire to humanitarianism and solidarity: a reminder of the very fact of refugee movement and of the necessity for an official response based on these principles. Many activist groups and individuals in Lesvos in recent years have worn life jackets while protesting in the streets, while Greenpeace activists used numerous life jackets from the "life jacket cemetery" of Molyvos to form a peace symbol on the outskirts of a nearby hill, intending to raise global awareness of the need for safe passage and asylum for the refugees (Gray-Block 2016). Life jackets have also been worn or carried as tokens of a pro-refugee campaign during the visits of officials to Lesvos, such as that of the UN Secretary General Ban Ki Moon, the Italian President of Parliament Laura Boldrini, and the European Parliament President Martin Shultz. Movie stars known for activism such as Angelina Jolie have also used orange life jackets as a visual element of their humanitarian portfolio.

As refugees have moved out of Lesvos and into Europe, so have life jackets. They have moved out as souvenirs, and as converted bags and wallets and tents by people who had the inspiration to create new things out of them, both handy and densely symbolic.[3] They have moved out in matter and in narration: "These life jackets have become the symbol of perilous refugee movement from the coasts of Turkey onto European soil through the sea, and of the need for refugees to be treated with respect and humanity", said the mayor of Lesvos, Spyros Galinos, in a public announcement in Strasbourg in one of his many attempts to raise European awareness of what was happening in Lesvos. The famous artist Ai Wei Wei, on the occasion of the Cinema for Peace gala, carried 14,000 life jackets from Lesvos to Berlin, which he wrapped around the five pillars of the façade of the Wiener Korzerthaus (Al Jazeera and Associated Press 2016). Another artist, Arabella Dorman, installed a capsized refugee dinghy into St James's Church in Piccadilly, London, for Christmas 2015 (Jones 2015), as an art installation called "Flight". The dinghy was suspended from the church's ceiling, along with three life jackets – two for adults and one for a minor – in a clear allusion to the Holy Family and their story of persecution and seeking refuge from Judea in Egypt.

One may walk the shorelines of Lesvos a year after the great refugee surge of the summer of 2015: the life jackets no longer cover kilometres of the ground but they are still there, hidden in mossy crevices, squeezed by the waves between rocks, surrealistically hung on top of trees, and used as raw material by seagulls for nests. Some of them are even used by locals to dress up their scarecrows in fields and vegetable gardens. Their formerly vivid orange colour has turned into a washed-out pink. A walk to the distant beaches in the north reveals the remnants of an arrival on the island – perhaps successful or a failure, who can

---

3. A giant chessboard was created in the grounds of the University of the Aegean campus (Sideridis 2016). For life-jackets turning into bags see Wilding (2016).

really tell? Clothes, shoes, broken piles of medicine bottles, used diapers, pages from a torn passport, family photographs, a tiny booklet that contains suras from the Qur'an and in the back pages some phone numbers, some names. Have these people arrived safely, or did only their belongings? Where are they now?

Refugees have left things behind on the shores of Lesvos which have turned into stories. Sometimes refugees leave their very bodies on the shore. At one time, I visited a hard-to-reach but well-known fishing spot in northern Lesvos. The year before, ever so often one would see an orange life vest in the distance, being carried by the waves. I had friends asking aloud about such a spectacle: "Is it inhabited? Is it empty?" An eerie feeling about the distant life jacket which was approaching, stories about the drowned refugees being washed ashore, still deter many fishermen from visiting the place. This year I decided to fish there, even if nobody cared to join me. I caught a fish and brought it back to the village for dinner. A local fisherman asked me where I caught it and I said "at the Rooster Shore [Peteinos], at that edge of it we call The Seal [Fokia]." "That's not what it's called now", he answered. "Now it's called Yeros [Old Man]." Silent, I listened to the story of how that name had changed since the previous year: they say that fishermen had found a drowned old man there, a refugee. The waves had set him up on the rock as if he were just sitting there, gazing at the open sea. From a distance you'd think he was resting. He was still wearing his life jacket.

Many days later I found the fisherman again. I told him that after what he told me, at nights before going to bed, I cringe while thinking of all that time I spent fishing by myself in the dark on that rock that unbeknownst to me now belongs to the Old Man – the Yero. Another fisherman who was standing nearby was apparently vexed: "The rock is not called the Old Man. It is the Seal. The illegal immigrants [*lathrometanastes*, a pejorative term] will not make us change the names of our place." And turning to his fellow fisherman he added, "You must not speak such nonsense." "That's what everyone says, it's not just me", shrugged the other.

Stories that use tangible materials from the refugee odyssey or even the very bodies of refugees also spread into common discourse in what can be termed, urban legends (Brunvard 1993). While the two fishermen were arguing whether the rock should be named "Yeros" or remain known as "the Seal", a tavern owner came closer: "You should not eat fish from the north", he told me while patting me on the back. "These fish are fed from the corpses of drowned immigrants. You eat them, and you eat human flesh." The tavern owner insisted: "Even if the fish have not eaten immigrants, think of the thousands of tons of plastic in the sea, all these dinghies and life jackets. They are ripped into extremely tiny pieces by the sea and enter the organism of fish just like that. And then, you eat them."

Working on the local community of the small island of Lipsi in southern Greece, Marilena Papachristophorou has studied the community's very own *narrative maps* (Papachristophorou 2013). More than often the very existence of the human body, its movements, its interaction with matter, its movement through space and time, and its relations with the surrounding materiality give meaning and identity to the place and ultimately to the very community. The refugees came by the thousands to Lesvos. Their coming, their very bodies existing on the spot, their number, their pressing needs as persecuted human beings, their "otherness", their vast number, was for everyone on the island – even for Europe as a whole, pro-refugee or otherwise – something unprecedented. The life jackets are shaped so much like a human torso. They are designed to fit one. They were worn – each one of them – by one refugee. And they were discarded on arrival. Their bodily relation to their bearers, their materiality, their persistence on the spot or their continued journey through their converted new forms are "oral material" for the representation of the refugees themselves and of how Europeans tend to think about their arrival. This persistent contact with the life jackets as objects and as symbols of the "refugee crisis" serves as a means to construct and communicate the refugee's identity universally and by all agents involved, pro-refugee or otherwise.

I was mentioning my thoughts and explaining my findings around life jackets to Nashrim, a young Syrian girl who had made the crossing from Turkey to Lesvos and had had to wear one. Nashrim was one of the 65 people on a death-trap dinghy, one of the thousands used by smugglers. What I tried to communicate in addition to the above was the idea that objects are sometimes linked by people "to processes of homemaking", and that this "functions to counter emotions of homelessness" (Digby 2015, 170). This way the "life jacket" can symbolically stand not only as reminder of the right of refugees to a safe passage towards safe haven, but also as a symbol of a beginning towards a long-sought-after new "home". Nasrim remembers how small and crowded the dinghy was. She remembers how full of water it was when it finally reached the shore after a plunging into the darkness and into the waves. She remembers how cold she was and how lucky she was to have barely escaped being capsized. "These things you tell me are very interesting", she said,

> and they seem natural to me. Each one will support his view and will use materials to communicate it. For some people life jackets prove we are the devil in their houses, and for some they stand for humanity and the right to live in dignity. As for myself I don't want to see a life jacket in my life. Even when I see this vivid orange colour somewhere else, my mouth turns bitter like I have swallowed sea water. My breathing becomes heavy like I am drowning. No more life jackets, ever again, I hope.

References

Al Jazeera and Associated Press. 2016. "Ai Weiwei Covers Berlin Venue with 14,000 Life Jackets." *Al Jazeera*, 13 February. Available online: http://www.aljazeera.com/news/2016/02/ai-weiwei-covers-berlin-venue-14000-life-jackets-160213190435403.html

Barad, K. 2003. "Posthumanist Performativity: Toward an Understanding of How Matter Comes to Matter." *Signs* 28 (3): 801–831. https://doi.org/10.1086/345321

Brunvard, J. H. 1993. *The Baby Train & Other Lusty Urban Legends*. New York: W. W. Norton.

Dégh, L. 2001. *Legend and Belief: Dialectics of a Folklore Genre*. Bloomington: Indiana University Press.

Digby, S. 2015. "The Casket of Magic: Home and Identity from Salvaged Objects." *Home Cultures* 3 (2): 169–190. https://doi.org/10.2752/174063106778053219

Gray-Block, A. 2016. "Peace and #safepassage for Refugees in 2016." Greenpeace blogpost, 1 January. Available online: http://www.greenpeace.org/international/en/news/Blogs/makingwaves/refugee-lifejacket-peace-sign/blog/55221/

Jones, J. 2015. "Flight by Arabella Dorman Review: Relic of a Rough Crossing Illustrates Refugee Crisis." *The Guardian*, 20 December. Available online: https://www.theguardian.com/artanddesign/2015/dec/20/flight-by-arabella-dorman-review-relic-of-a-rough-crossing-illustrates-refugee-crisis

Papachristophorou, M. 2013. *Myth, Representation, and Identity: An Ethnography of Memory in Lipsi, Greece*. New York: Palgrave Macmillan. https://doi.org/10.1057/9781137362759

Scott, J. 1990. *Domination and the Arts of Resistance: Hidden Transcripts*. New Haven, CT: Yale University Press.

Sideridis, D. 2016. "Making a Giant Chessboard from Refugee Life Jackets." *Al Jazeera*, 7 June. Available online: http://www.aljazeera.com/indepth/inpictures/2016/06/making-giant-chess-board-refugee-life-jackets-160605103440023.html

Tuastad, D. H. 2003. "Neo-Orientalism and the New Barbarism Thesis: Aspects of Symbolic Violence in the Middle East Conflict(s)." *Third World Quarterly* 24 (4): 591–599. https://doi.org/10.1080/0143659032000105768

United Nations High Commissioner for Refugees. 2016. "Operations Portal: Refugee Situation." Available online: http://data.unhcr.org/mediterranean/country.php?id=83

Wilding, M. 2016. "The Volunteers Turning Refugee Lifejackets into Symbols of Hope." *The Guardian*, 6 May. Available online: https://www.theguardian.com/global-development-professionals-network/2016/may/06/the-volunteers-turning-refugee-lifejackets-into-symbols-of-hope

George Tyrikos-Ergas holds a PhD in Folkore (University of Ioannina). He is currently Research Associate at Durham University's Anthropology Department in "Transitory Lives", an ESRC-funded comparative study of the migration crisis in the Mediterranean. He is a co-founder and frontline activist of the "Agkalia" team in Lesvos, Greece (Raul Wallenberg Prize of the Council of Europe for 2016). Address for correspondence: Department of Anthropology, Durham University, Dawson Building, South Road, Durham, DH1 3LE, UK. Email: tyrikos@hotmail.com

Chapter 10

Interrupted Journeys: Drawings by Refugees at the Kara Tepe Camp, Lesvos, Greece

Angela María Arbeláez Arbeláez and Edward Mulholland

On the very shores now interspersed with refugee camps, Plato spoke, millennia ago, of man living in the *metaxy*—that is, in between, wandering between origin and destiny (*Symposium* 202d13–e1).[1] Much later, Dante began his pilgrimage by realizing that he was lost *in mezzo del cammin*, "in the middle of the path" (*Inferno* 1.1). After years and millions of displaced refugees paddling dinghies across our nightly news screens, we can become numb to the plight of countless individual lives uprooted; but what we are witnessing is a constant in human existence as chronicled by human history: the drama of the interrupted journey.

Perhaps the most direct way to record, explore, and understand the materiality of the experience of forced and undocumented migration today, and a particularly dramatic way to communicate such experience, is to let refugees speak for themselves. Platforms like Vimeo and YouTube are full of interviews, subtitled to overcome the inevitable barrier of language; but in the camps themselves, with paper and simple art supplies, forced migrants are telling their story visually, with nothing beyond a bit of contextual background and no subtitles necessary.

The current essay presents some of these artworks[2] with the minimum context needed to enter into the experience of the interrupted journeys they represent. The artworks themselves are the work of displaced, forced migrants, at different camps and sites on the Greek island of Lesvos. Art is a powerful advocacy tool to communicate stories, and can also provide a vehicle for self-development and personal expression. Art provides a platform to raise awareness and encourage displaced persons to realize their own potential. It also has undeniable cathartic and healing value.

Kara Tepe camp was established by the municipality of Lesvos, on the outskirts of the city of Mytilene. Today it offers hospitality to approximately 900 persons, mostly families and women for the most part from Afghanistan, Cameroon, Eritrea, Iraq, and Syria. Although every resident has called Lesvos home for part of their interrupted journey, each story is as

---

1. For a more complete discussion of *metaxy* in Plato, see Rhodes (2003).
2. All photos © Angels Relief Team (ART) and Ángela María Arbeláez Arbeláez. The artwork is kept by ART.

unique as its protagonist. What they all have tragically in common are their antagonists: persecution, war, loss, racism, and marginalization.

Collective Work by Children Given to UN Secretary General Ban Ki-moon during his Visit to Lesvos, 18 June, 2016[3]

Figure 10.1. A collective work by children in the refugee camp.

Six children (ages 6 to 12) were asked to draw pictures to be given to the UN secretary general (Figures 10.1–10.3). They were free to express whatever they wished; the descriptions here go clockwise from top left.

Zahra (aged 12, a Kurdish girl from Baghdad) at first didn't know what to draw. She at last decided to draw a garden, expressing confused feelings. Elmira (from Afghanistan) chose to paint a multicoloured flag with an "A" in the middle. Nour (aged 12, a Syrian Kurd from a family of eight children) painted an aerial view of a small inflatable boat with 20 or so occupants on its way to Greece (the Greek flag representing hope) surrounded by floating bodies. Halima (aged 6, from Cameroon) painted her own name over a figurative scene. Anoar (aged 11, a Yazidi boy from Shingal in Iraq with seven siblings) brought to life a gruesome current headline: the burning to death of Yazidi women, enclosed in a cage, by ISIS. He was the clearest in his message, painting the words "Help Yazidi" and identifying with a common message and hashtag for her persecuted ethnic group. In stark contrast, Gardenia (two years younger than her sister Nour) painted a blonde girl in a long blue dress standing in a field of flowers.

---

3. The moment when this picture was given to Ban Ki-moon received attention from multiple media outlets, thus fulfilling the desire of many displaced persons to get their message out.

Figure 10.2. Refugee children with their collective work.

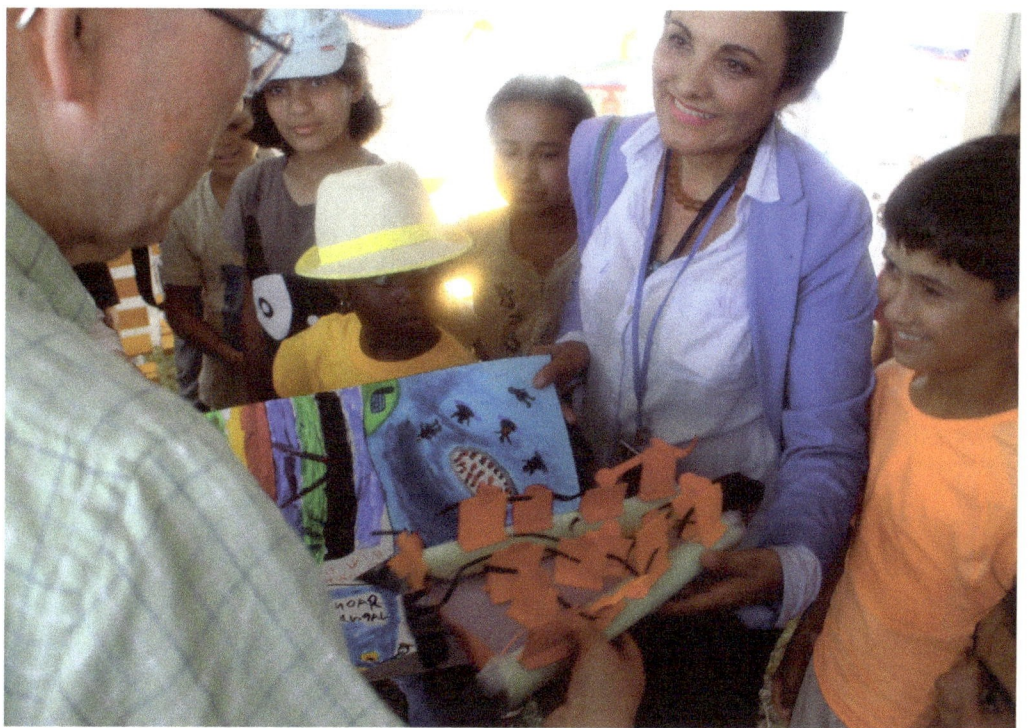

Figure 10.3. The children's work presented to Ban Ki-moon, 18 June, 2016.

The world community, in the person of Ban Ki-moon, received this varied message from these displaced children. Visions of beauty and visions of horror, symbols of home and symbols of exile, the thoughts of innocent victims whose life journey has been interrupted.

Series of Drawings by Shaima, a 45-Year-Old Mother of Two

Shaima, from Afghanistan, had worked as a tailor. She approached one day and said, in clear and correct English, "I want to paint, I want to express how I feel." As the children had an art workshop, she joined in and made drawings with markers and a watercolour self-portrait (Figure 10.4). The self-portrait, all in black, is a veiled woman weeping. The drawings reveal the source of the tears. Birds fly above a paradisiacal beach scene in softly muted colours, with the words "Fredom Birts" (sic). An interior vision of freedom and peace. Her other drawings (Figure 10.5) show peace shattered: murdered bodies, a central focus as if it were an explosive. "This is what the Taliban did", she said. The sequence ends with a boat adrift, two passengers reflected in the waves, besides the brown of the boat and its cargo, the only color the blue of water and rain.

Figure 10.4. Self-portrait by Shaima, a 45-year old mother of two.

Figure 10.5. Drawings by Shaima, a 45-year old mother of two.

Moria Jail, by Shaima's 19-Year-Old Daughter

Shaima's family was brought to Kara Tepe from Moria, a camp that has been functioning as an overcrowded registration/detention centre, often experienced by the detained refugees as a prison. Her daughter's drawing (Figure 10.6) shows a punishing sun and a ship that promises to bring them someday to Athens to continue their journey. The bottom portrays the fence of Moria detention centre, captives looking helplessly at the boat, under the sun, luggage in hand. The words say: "She cry. It is Moria. Jail. People came for comfortable life. We escape from war fight study improve not cruel jail." Here reign the contrast and frustration of an interrupted, unfinished journey. Their Ithaca is still very far away.

Figure 10.6. *Moria Jail*, by Shaima's 19-year-old daughter.

Drawing by Mesa, an 11-Year-Old Girl

Mesa's father is a doctor, her mother a housewife. Four of her six siblings have already realized their dream and are settled in Germany. She has been in Kara Tepe since March (2016). Like all her companions of the same age, she is very aware of the pain and persecution to which her Yazidi people have been subjected by ISIS. Shingal, her native town, is a distant memory, as is the home she left behind. Her drawings depict time and again the moment of rescue and arrival in Greece. In Figure 10.7 she, like Onar, asks for help for her Yazidi people.

Figure 10.7. Drawing by Mesa, an 11-year-old girl.

Pencil Drawing by Hassan Zaheda, a Father Aged 31

The artist's name jumped into the headlines when he was one of those chosen by Pope Francis to be brought to Italy from Lesvos in April 2016. When he was making the sketch in Figure 10.8 (also detail in Figure 10.9), he, with his wife and son, would enjoy a cup of tea alongside the noisy group of children and young people who took part in the artistic expression workshop. They liked to come close and say hello, to recount how they had escaped terrorism, to explain who they were before their escape and the life they led. His wife pointed to him and said, "He's an artist, you know. He draws very well."

"Please give me a pencil", he said. A few minutes later, he had finished this sketch. Eight human faces are superimposed on a horse, all with eyes closed. Today Hassan Zaheda, his wife Nour Essa (aged 30), and their son are in Rome, and Kara Tepe and Greece are a stepping stone that has been left behind on their journey.

Figure 10.8. Pencil drawing by Hassan Zaheda, a father aged 31.

Figure 10.9. Pencil drawing by Hassan Zaheda, a father aged 31 (detail).

Drawing by Gardenia, a 9-Year-Old Girl

For Gardenia, to draw young people taken from fairy tales is as easy as capturing the trauma of a stormy journey undertaken with her family, the crossing from Turkey to reach the coast of the island of Lesvos. In her expressive drawings she recalls again and again the details of the trip and the time of redemption at the hands of "Greece". Gardenia concentrates on creating. She feels calm and recovers the peace she felt the day she was shipped off. Since she doesn't write well, she asked her Palestinian friend Sheima (aged 13) to jot down her explanation of her drawing (Figure 10.10), written on the back of it (Figure 10.11):

> When we were on the baloon boat [sic] a ship saw us and they threw the ropes to us. We were scared because we thought the ship would take us back to Turkey but eventually we knew that this ship would take us to Greece and we were super pleased.

Figure 10.10. Drawing by Gardenia, a 9-year-old girl.

Figure 10.11. Note written on the back of Gardenia's drawing.

Birthday, by Sirin, a 12-Year-Old Girl

What better epilogue than this representation (Figure 10.12) of a family group together, and a birthday celebration amidst the warmth of a home, a house that long ago ceased to exist? Sirin, aged 12, like her sisters Nour and Gardenia and the rest of her six siblings, yearns for the Promised Land of Germany. In the meantime their agony grows. No birthday cake or a table. Remembrances, dreams, and hopes of reuniting with their maternal grandparents and aunt. Their grandparents managed to reach the shores of Greece recently, but were removed

Figure 10.12. *Birthday*, by Sirin, a 12-year-old girl.

by the authorities to the Greek island of Chios rather than Lesvos, and interned in a camp at Souda. They still have not fulfilled their dream of embracing and reuniting with their daughter and grandchildren, who are living in Kara Tepe.

Final Thoughts

All of these drawings bring before us the traumatic experience of being uprooted, and the interruption of lives. There is a real sense of existing neither here nor there, in a daily insecurity which at least offers an improvement over persecution at the hands of ISIS or ill treatment by Turkish smugglers. These are images of a journey, a journey for now, which was interrupted by art classes, for some only hours after they had disembarked onto the shores of Lesvos and for others during the daily camp routine.

The documentary as well as artistic value of these aesthetic expressions is immense, and they ought therefore to be collected by an educational organization such as a university or museum. They can thus be preserved and serve as an instrument of study and as a way to increase awareness of these forced migrations and the humanitarian crisis. Another objective of this work in the camps which was begun in 2015 by Angela Maria Arbeláez Arbeláez is the creation of a travelling exhibition, starting from Lesvos to continue in other cities such as London and Berlin.

Reference

Rhodes, J., 2003. *What is Metaxy? Diotima and Voegelin.* Available online: http://sites01.lsu.edu/ faculty/voegelin/wp-content/uploads/sites/80/2015/09/J-Rhodes.pdf

Ángela María Arbeláez Arbeláez has a PhD in Art History from Lomonosov University of Moscow. She is the founder of the Angels Relief Team (ART), a curator and an interfaith activist who has been volunteering in Kara Tepe and other Greek camps for displaced persons since September 2015. Address for correspondence: "ART Bridges", Damofili 5, Mytilene, Lesvos Island, TK.81100, Greece. Email: angela.arbelaeza@gmail.com

Edward Mulholland is an Associate Professor in World Languages and Cultures at Benedictine College, Atchison, Kansas. He volunteered at Kara Tepe, Lesvos in July 2016. Address for correspondence: Benedictine College, 1020 North 2nd Street Atchison, KS 66002, USA. Email: emulholland@benedictine.edu

Chapter 11

Abandoned Refugee Vehicles "In the Middle of Nowhere": Reflections on the Global Refugee Crisis from the Northern Margins of Europe

Oula Ilari Seitsonen, Vesa-Pekka Herva, and Mika Kunnari

In June 2016, when conducting our fieldwork on Second World War heritage in Finnish Lapland, we had an opportunity to document refugee vehicles abandoned at a Finno-Russian border checkpoint only some months earlier. These vehicles are associated with the ongoing "refugee crisis" that has shaken Europe, North Africa, and the Middle East in diverse ways in recent years. More specifically, the vehicles abandoned in Salla and discussed in this photo essay are associated with the so-called "Arctic Route" of refugees (Nilsen 2016a) across Russia into Finland and the European Union. Finland is but a backwater of the worldwide refugee crisis – indeed, the refugees entering Finland via the Arctic route were welcomed by Salla municipality promotional posters which declared that they had arrived "in the middle of nowhere" (Salla Municipality 2016a) (Figure 11.1). This is likely what the refugees felt when travelling in the gloomy polar night across the snow-clad taiga wilderness, where the temperature could drop to −40°C, in search of a sanctuary in Finland. While the scale of the refugee crisis in this northeastern corner of the European Union is not even remotely comparable to the situation in, for instance, the Mediterranean, the year 2015 nonetheless witnessed an unpreceded surge of refugees to Finland, with over 32,000 asylum seekers arriving in the country – almost ten times more than the previous year (Ministry of Interior, Finland 2016a).

Although the northern offshoot of the refugee crisis and the abandoned cars connected to it may, at first, appear somewhat unrelated to what was the primary subject of our field-work – the material heritage of the German military presence in Finnish Lapland during the Second World War – we also felt that there are various resonances between the two cases, and mirroring the two cases could ultimately produce useful perspectives on both. After all, similar themes are central to both cases, including modern conflict and its consequences, different forms of mobility and dislocation of people and things, and questions of camps and confinement. Yet the decision (and permission, granted by the Finnish Border Guard) to document the said refugee vehicles also stirred up concerns of relevance and ethical aspects of this work.

Historical archaeologies nowadays commonly address a variety of "big issues", such as capitalism and colonialism, which have radically shaped the world over the last several centuries and continue to play a significant role in the present, which at least potentially makes historical-archaeological research socially relevant in the twenty-first-century world. But what does archaeology have to offer when it comes to the study and understanding of more specific and acute – but also more fleeing or short-term – phenomena in contemporary society, such as the current refugee crisis? A wide range of contemporary topics and topics related to recent past can certainly be studied from an archaeological point of view (as for instance the studies published in this very journal amply demonstrate), so present-day refugees should be no exception. However, rather than pondering whether or not refugees and the refugee crisis can be archaeologically studied in principle, we were mainly concerned with relevance – what could, would, or should be the point of such an endeavour? In other words, what relevant and useful things could be said about refugee issues by looking at refugees' abandoned vehicles – left behind by some 2000 asylum seekers who crossed the border from Russia into Lapland in 2015–2016 and representing 32 nationalities from the Near East, Central Asia, and Africa (Finnish Border Guard 2016; Kärki 2016; Mäkinen 2016; Ministry of Interior, Finland 2016b)?

The refugee traffic across the Finno-Russian border in Lapland commenced quite unexpectedly in September 2015, and the Finnish border checkpoints became the northernmost gateway to the Schengen area after refugees' entry to Norway in Storskog was barred in November 2015 (Nilsen 2016a). The reason for taking the long Arctic route to the European Union was to avoid the well-known dangers of the sea route across the Mediterranean (Konttinen 2016), although the harsh northern conditions, too, posed difficulties to the refugees, and the very crossing of the Finno-Russian border required quite a bit of manoeuvring. The refugees were first driven to the border by Russians who, however, risked having their cars confiscated by facilitating an illegal entry into Finland. As crossing the border on foot is prohibited, refugees started arriving by bicycle in October, which in turn became banned "on grounds of safety" due to the icy roads (*Finland Times* 2015). After this, refugees resorted to ramshackle vehicles, apparently supplied by Russian-organized crime syndicates (Kärki 2016; Konttinen 2016; Nilsen 2016a). If human trafficking was suspected, the Finnish Border Guard confiscated the cars, whereas other asylum seekers were given the option of leaving their vehicles at the border checkpoint and being transported by bus to a hastily established refugee registration centre in Tornio (Interview M1). The vehicles that the refugees chose to abandon were first left at the checkpoint, and when it started filling up, they were towed to the Salla waste station (Interview M2).

The flow of refugees across the Finno-Russian border into Lapland ended in March 2016 as abruptly as it had started a few months earlier, reportedly because the Russian officials had denied refugees' access to the border and had also expelled them from the town of Kandalaksha, where they had been waiting for a chance to travel to Finland (Eerola 2016). The asylum seekers who made it to Finland have been moved on to refugee centres, and we have not had a chance to talk to them; as of mid-2016, only some 100 vehicles in the waste station and 25 more cars on the border zone (Figure 11.2–11.5) remain as the material memory of this episodic mass mobility in Salla on a northern fringe of Europe, and this memory, too, will have been eradicated by now, as the abandoned vehicles were scheduled to be towed to the centre of Salla and auctioned by the municipality in July 2016 as a touristic performance (Interview M2) – some of the bicycles seized from the refugees have already been auctioned by Lapland's police (Interview M1). The auction quickly attracted public attention, especially among enthusiasts of so-called "eastern cars" (Harju 2016; Kärki 2016), and the Salla municipality advertised the event by announcing that the "[a]uction of the abandoned cars in the middle of the wilderness is becoming a spectacle which will be discussed for decades afterwards" (Salla Municipality 2016b). Similarly, the Finnish Customs announced that in September they would also be auctioning the 36 vehicles abandoned by refugees at the northernmost Raja-Jooseppi border point (Tynkkynen 2016).

There is a striking banality to these events, as they effectively turn an offshoot of the global refugee crisis into a show for promoting Lapland tourism. On the other hand, however, tourism is vitally important to the economy of Lapland (e.g. Saarinen 2001), and sparsely populated peripheral municipalities like Salla (with its fewer than 4000 inhabitants) in particular are struggling to survive in the contemporary world, and keen to seize every feasible opportunity to improve their current socio-economic conditions. The abandoned refugee vehicles are thus linked to at least two very different types of mobility – forced and recreational – both of which are nonetheless characteristic of the contemporary world. Paradoxes, contradictions, and ambiguities of diverse kinds would indeed appear to be at the heart of refugee issues today, both in general and in regard to the specific case discussed here. For instance, the automobile, a symbol of western freedom and individuality (Redshaw 2008), emerges in this context as a symbol of dislocated and desperate people in search of a better future in Europe.

Yet we are still left with the question of what the abandoned vehicles are about – what do they "mean"? – from an archaeological or heritage point of view. Or more specifically: how could the attention given to the refugee cars, as material things, contribute to the understanding of, or facilitate dealing with, any aspect of the refugee crisis and refugee experience? Granted, a plethora of specific observations can be made about the vehicles and their latest users when taking a close look with a keen multi-sensorial eye. For instance, the registration information of some Ladas (Ru. Жигули) show that they had originally been imported from the Soviet Union to Finland in the 1980s, then transported from Finland to Russia after the collapse of the Soviet Union, and were now being driven back by the refugees on their one-way trip. Likewise, the personal items left in the cars (Figures 11.6–11.10) can potentially provide all kinds of insights into refugees' lives during their desperate voyage, but such a focus may also run the ethical risk of trivializing refugee issues, which, after all, are intertwined with a host of larger-scale matters. Refugee camps, for example, are arguably but one expression of the much broader phenomenon of "the twentieth century [as] the era of camps" (Löfgren 2003, 245, quoted in Minca 2015, 75), while the "refugee is today a key figure to understand the crisis of the state [...] and the camp is all too often the state's response to this uncertainty", caused by "the increasing number of stateless people and their uncertain status as well as the difficulty in assigning them a fixed and spatially stable identity" (Minca 2015, 79).

Archaeology and heritage studies are, or should be, in a position to say something meaningful about these broader issues entangled with refugees, and not least because recent research in both fields has addressed themes that are more or less directly related to refugee issues on the one hand, and materialities similar to the abandoned cars on the other. For example, refugee issues represent a natural extension of the flourishing interest in twentieth- to twenty-first-century conflicts, while the abandoned refugee vehicles strike a resonance with themes such as "dark tourism" and ruins, or "ruin porn".

The attraction to modern ruins and abandoned places and things, as exemplified by the hobby known as "urban exploration", is a mirror that reflects the significance of the very materiality of the abandoned refugee vehicles. That is, the interest in urban exploration and related practices would appear to denote a desire or need to encounter the world and the past in an unmediated, "raw" form, "face to face", and in one's own terms. For better or worse, the interpretation and understanding of the past and its material remains have traditionally been dominated by experts who have told the public why this or that thing surviving from the past is important, hence distancing non-experts from the valuation of heritage. The same applies to refugee issues, which are governed by the state in a faceless and bureaucratic manner, which in turn distances the public from the lived experience and distress of the refugees. Direct encounters with the material realities of the refugees, however, could be employed to spark personal, first-hand reflections about, and connections with, refugee issues (cf. Burström 2009).

Our photographs illustrate some of the manifold aspects connected to the flow of refugees into the EU via the Arctic route. The abandoned vehicles and items left or forgotten inside them illustrate well, for instance, the refugee life-experiences on their perilous journey through the frozen wilderness, yet as heritage professionals we need to try and find ways of avoiding the ethical risk of banalizing refugee issues. In our upcoming research we aim to assess this northern offshoot of the global refugee crisis and its material expressions, particularly the abandoned vehicles and the wider, large-scale issues associated with them, from multiple perspectives, including "new mobilities" (Sheller and Urry 2006), the relationship between refugee mobilities and "non-places" (Augé 1995), and vehicles as a means of place-making (Seamon 2000) and as manifestation of mobile cultures (Vannini 2010). We will also discuss further the ethically disquieting and paradoxical question of these abandoned vehicles being used for promoting tourism in these peripheral regions, and combine the study of migrant materialities with refugee interview materials, in order to detail the experiential perspectives of their journey through this strange, dark land of snow and ice.

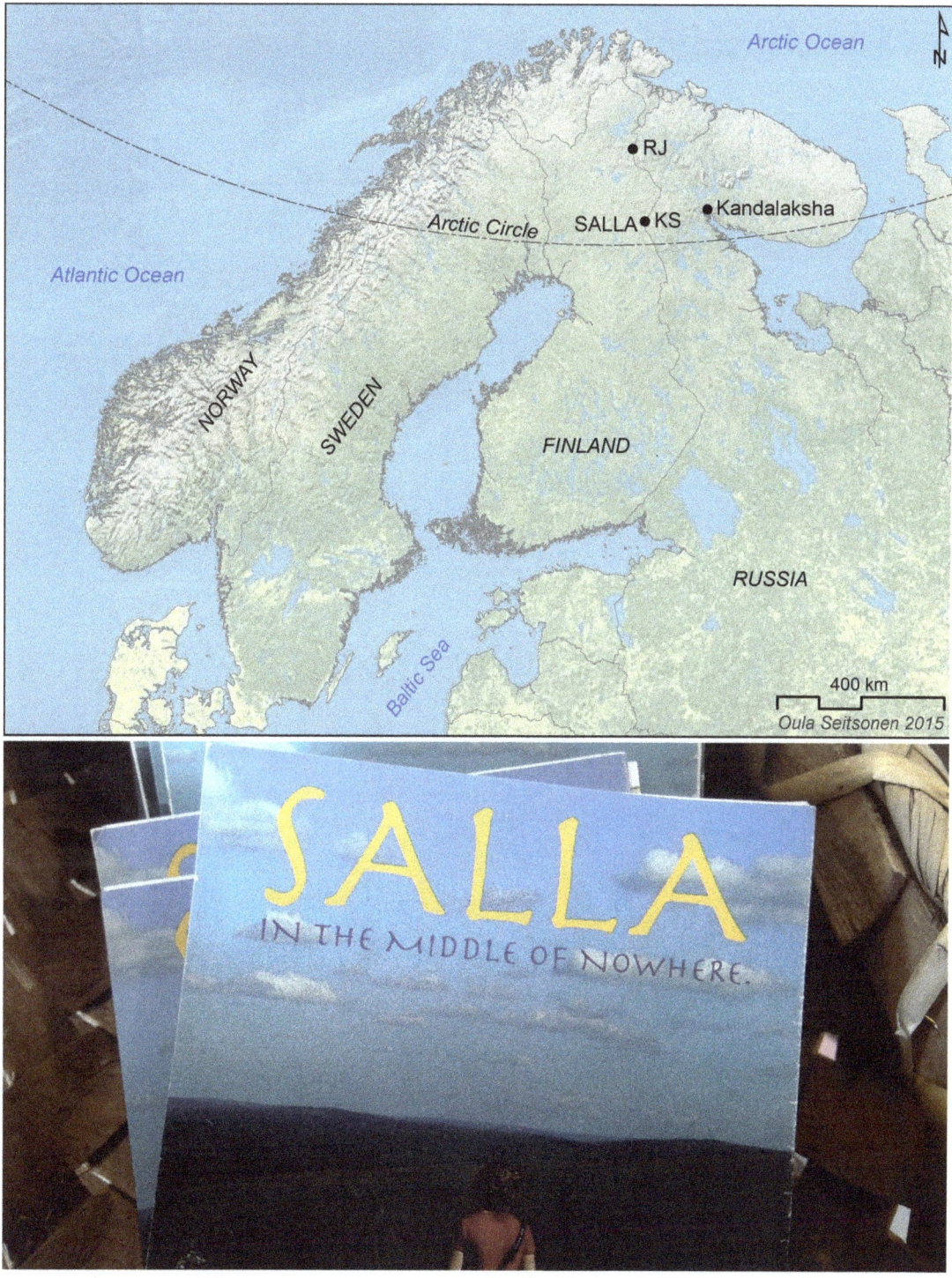

Figure 11.1. Top: Location of Salla, border checkpoints at Kelloselkä (KS) and Raja-Jooseppi (RJ), and at Kandalaksha, Russia. Bottom: Tourist hiking maps of Salla municipality on sale at a local shop (photograph by Oula Seitsonen).

Figure 11.2. Top: Abandoned vehicles on the border zone: when the refugees arrived, the long polar night made the landscape dark and gloomy, frost was extreme, and forests were covered by nearly a metre of snow. Bottom: Vehicles towed to the Salla waste station from the border (photographs by Oula Seitsonen).

Figure 11.3. Vehicles of every kind and condition were used in the refugee traffic. The majority are decades old, rusty, derelict, and barely running cars which in the West appeal only to automobile enthusiasts. The refugees, however, typically had to pay over a thousand euros to acquire a ramshackle vehicle (Konttinen 2016), which was then abandoned after a single one-way cross-border trip (photographs by Oula Seitsonen).

Figure 11.4. Some of the vehicles exhibit elaborate decorative designs, but these are probably completely unrelated to the preferences of the refugees, as their journeys seem to have been orchestrated by organized crime syndicates (Konttinen 2016; Nilsen 2016a) (photographs by Oula Seitsonen).

Figure 11.5. The vehicles in themselves show practically no signs of their latest owners, who were for the most part Muslim refugees. The "personalizing" elements of the cars tend to consist of Russian patriotic motifs and paraphernalia, such as orange-and-black Saint George ribbons (originally symbolizing the defeat of Nazi Germany, but lately with connotations to the ongoing Ukrainian crisis [Kunnas 2016]), "On the Victory Day" (Ru. С днем победы!) stickers, and air-fresheners of various scents. A Kalashnikov-shaped air-freshener had been taken down from its place; the refugees in the car perhaps did not want to stare at a familiar gun hanging from their rear-view mirror. In some cases, icons – typical apotropaic elements in Russian cars – were found on the floor, while in others they were still attached to the dashboards (photographs by Oula Seitsonen).

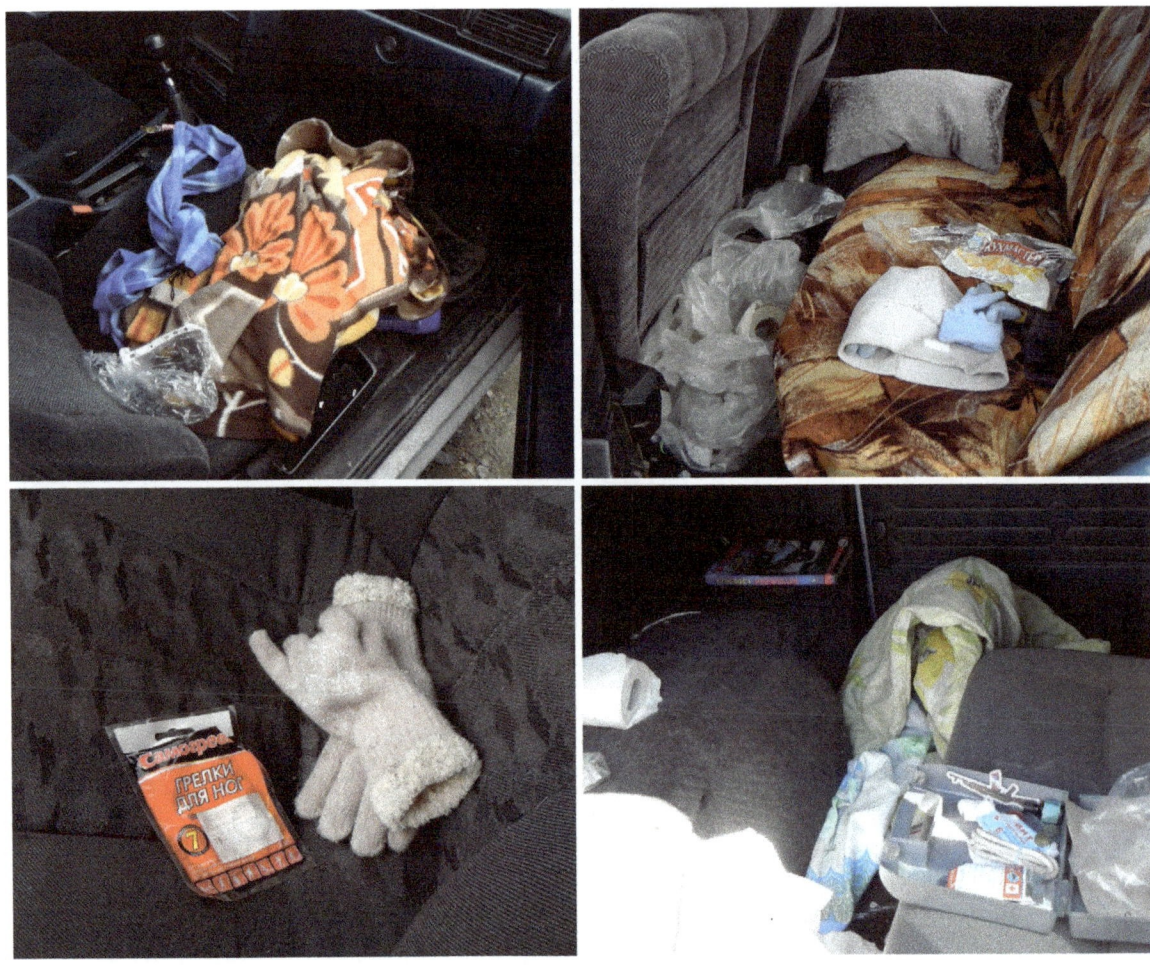

Figure 11.6. The refugees had to spend considerable time queuing and overnighting in their cars and to cope with extreme cold inside the flimsy vehicles: eventually this cost one Indian refugee his life, after which the Russian officials banned queuing in the border zone and herded the refugees back to Kandalaksha, where the conditions were not much better (Konttinen 2016; Nilsen 2016b). Warm blankets, pillows, and winter clothing such as woollen socks, gloves, scarfs, and beanies, were commonly present in the cars, and plastic sheeting had sometimes been used in an attempt to insulate vehicles better. Note the Kalashnikov-shaped air-freshener in the first-aid kit (cf. Figure 11.5): this might also have been taken down and placed inside the kit, out of sight, by the refugees using the vehicle (photographs by Oula Seitsonen).

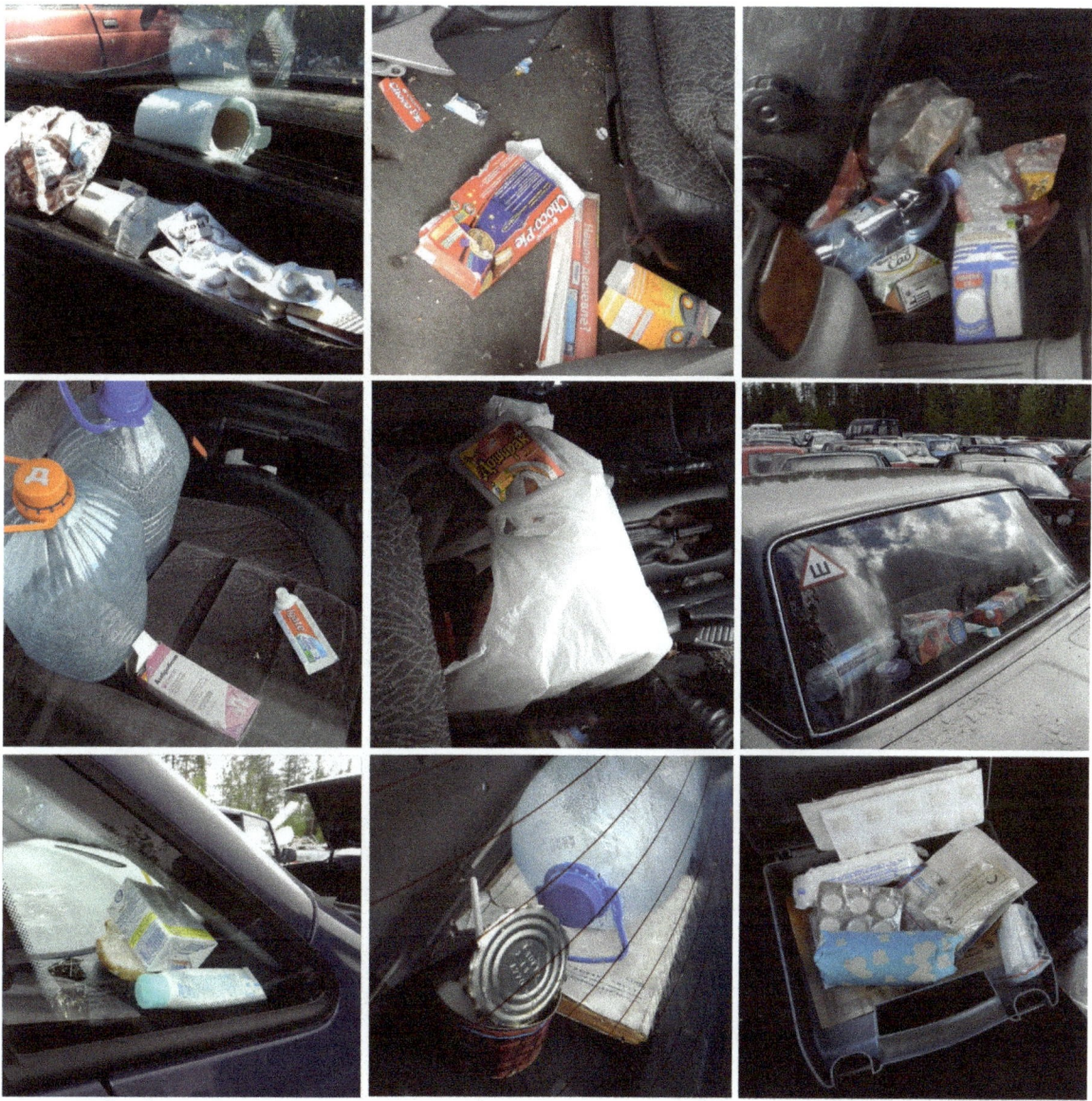

Figure 11.7. People overnighted, ate, and took care of their personal health and hygiene in the cars. Water was a vital supply and plastic water bottles abundantly present. All the consumed food supplies are typical Russian provisions, often cheap convenience-food meals, chocolate bars, and tea, and show no obvious clues about their consumers' cultural background or place of origin. Alcohol bottles were not observed. First-aid kits, typically with a plenty of antibiotics, were commonplace in many vehicles (photographs by Oula Seitsonen).

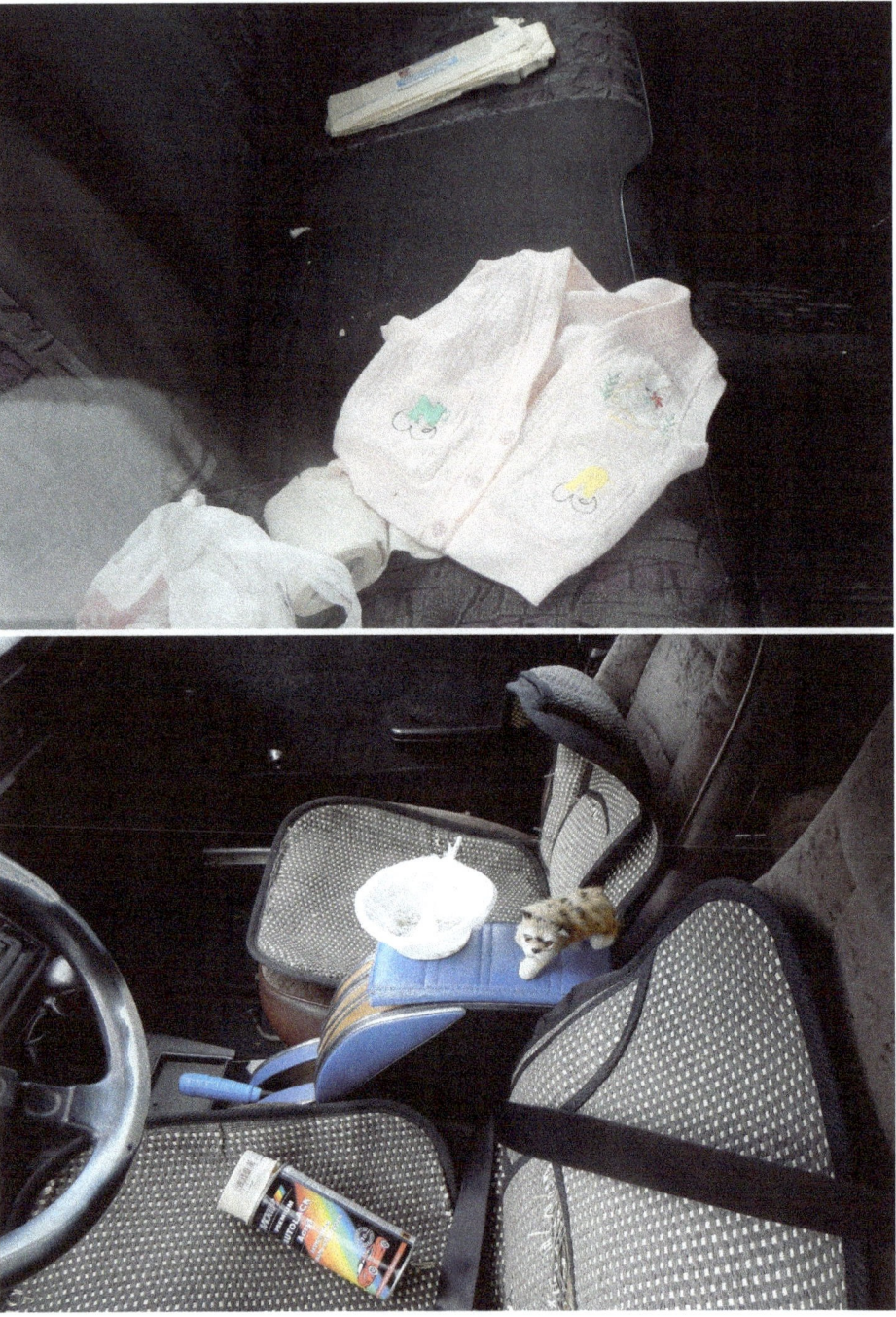

Figure 11.8. Abandoned children's and women's clothes and occasional toys are emotional reminders that whole families struggled through the snow-covered wilderness towards Finland (Nilsen 2016b). Public discussions in Finland, and also elsewhere, often tend to emphasize that a majority of the refugees are young men (Koivuranta 2015; Mykkänen 2015), yet these forgotten artefacts display a more accurate and complete picture of contemporary forced migration and the range of people affected by it. However, sending out the ablest men of a family on a long, costly, and potentially hazardous voyage has its own rationale, as they may be considered most likely to succeed (photographs by Oula Seitsonen).

Figure 11.9. We found very little evidence of recreation- or entertainment-related items in the vehicles; the refugees presumably used their money on more pressing subsistence items and if they had books or recorded music, they did not leave them behind. Recordings were observed only in one vehicle: a pile of pirate CDs that comprised an eclectic collection from classical music to Demis Roussos and the rock bands Nazareth and Iron Maiden. The only popular book that we found was a humorous detective story by the Russian author Darya Kalinina, entitled *In Pursuit of Rough Sex*. Car repair manuals, on the other hand, were commonplace, as is typical in Russian vehicles (photographs by Oula Seitsonen).

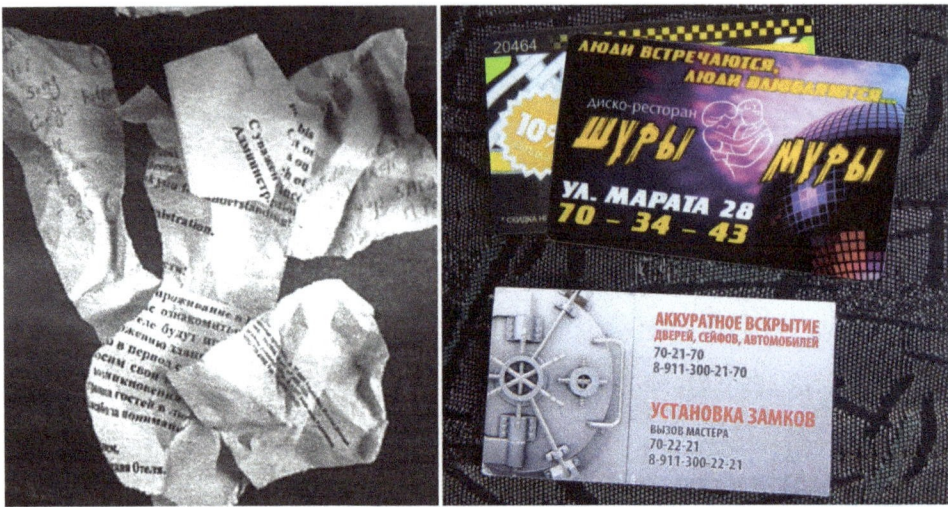

Figure 11.10. Various handwritten notes were present in the vehicles, for example basic phrases in English and Russian, as well as addresses and other contact information in Russia, Finland, and also Norway (which suggests that some refugees had tried entering Norway before Finland), including business cards of locksmiths, taxis, and discos. In one car we also found a pile of credit cards, all ascribed to the same person (photographs by Oula Seitsonen).

Figure 11.11. Local teenagers are rumoured to have been looting the vehicles, smashing windows, sucking petrol from their tanks, grabbing drugs from the first-aid kits, and stealing car radios (photographs by Oula Seitsonen).

Figure 11.12. An Egyptian-style decorative artefact in one of the cars: this could be a refugee item, but decorative pieces like this are also popular in Russia (photograph by Oula Seitsonen).

Figure 11.13. A soggy, collapsed cardboard sign next to the vehicles declares: "Confiscated. The Finnish Border Guard" (photograph by Oula Seitsonen).

Acknowledgments

Authors are grateful to the Finnish Border Guard, Finnish Customs, and the Salla municipality for granting us permission to document the abandoned vehicles before they were auctioned. This research is part of the project "Lapland's Dark Heritage" (Academy of Finland, decision no. 275497).

Interviews

M1. Male border guard at Kelloselkä border point (anonymous for professional reasons), 3 June, 2016, Salla.

M2. Male municipality official (anonymous for professional reasons), 3 June, 2016, Salla.

References

Augé, M. 1995. *Non-Places: An Introduction to an Anthropology of Supermodernity*, translated by J. Howe. London: Verso.

Burström, M. 2009. "Garbage or Heritage: The Existential Dimension of a Car Cemetery." In *Contemporary Archaeologies: Excavating Now*, edited by C. Holtorf and A. Piccini, 131–143. Frankfurt am Main: Peter Lang.

Eerola, A. 2016. "IL Kantalahdessa: Yllätyskäänne itärajan tilanteessa - pakolaiset ajettiin ulos rajakaupungista." *Iltalehti*, 6 March. Available online: http://www.iltalehti.fi/pakolaiskriisi/2016030621226199_cm.shtml

Finland Times. 2015. "Move to Control Refugee Influx from Russia thru Lapland: Finland Bans Border Crossing on Bicycle." 27 December. Available online: http://www.finlandtimes.fi/national/2015/12/27/23644/Finland-bans-border-crossing-on-bicycle

Finnish Border Guard. 2016. "Venäjän rajalta Lappiin suuntautuva laiton maahantulo ja sen hallinta." Available online: http://www.raja.fi/tietoa/tiedotteet/1/0/venajan_rajalta_lappiin_suuntautuva_laiton_maahantulo_ja_sen_hallinta_64776

Harju, J. 2016. "Sallan romu-Ladat kiinnostavat harrastajia." *Helsingin Sanomat*, 18 January. Available online: http://www.hs.fi/kotimaa/a1453003137920

Kärki, K. 2016. "Rajan hylättyjen autojen jäteasema on Lada-Jussin taivas – katso video Sallasta." *Inarilainen*. 4 June. Available online: http://www.lapinkansa.fi/lappi/rajan-hylattyjen-autojen-jateasema-on-lada-jussin-taivas-katso-video-sallasta-15562204/

Koivuranta, E. 2015. "Ylivoimainen enemmistö on miehiä – Yle kokosi tuoreimmat faktat turvapaikanhakijoista." *Yle Uutiset*, 5 October. Available online: http://yle.fi/uutiset/ylivoimainen_enemmisto_on_miehia__yle_kokosi_tuoreimmat_faktat_turvapaikanhakijoista/8354207

Konttinen, J. 2016. "HS seurasi pakolaisten piinaa Venäjällä – toive Suomeen pääsystä elää Kantalahden pakkasissa." *Helsingin Sanomat*, 26 January. Available online: http://www.hs.fi/kotimaa/a1453786224448

Kunnas, K. 2016. "Pyhän Yrjön nauha sitoo yhteen venäläisiä Moskovasta Tallinnaan ja Donetskiin." *Helsingin Sanomat*, 12 December. Available online: http://www.hs.fi/paivanlehti/12122016/art-2000005001247.html

Löfgren, O. 2003. *On Holiday*. Berkeley: University of California Press.

Mäkinen, T. 2016. "Kansainvälisen rikollisorganisaation epäillään salakuljettaneen kymmeniä Suomeen Sallan ja Raja-Joosepin kautta." *Helsingin Sanomat*, 5 May. Available online: http://www.hs.fi/kotimaa/a1462325554902

Minca, C. 2015. "Geographies of the Camp." *Political Geography* 49: 74–83. https://doi.org/10.1016/j.polgeo.2014.12.005

Ministry of Interior, Finland. 2016a. "Turvapaikanhakijoita saapui viime vuonna ennätysmäärä." Available online: http://www.intermin.fi/fi/maahanmuutto/turvapaikanhakijat

_____. 2016b. "Over 90 Per Cent of Asylum Seekers Arriving via Russia Refused." Available online: http://www.intermin.fi/en/current_issues/news/1/1/over_90_per_cent_of_asylum_seekers_arriving_via_russia_refused_64911

Mykkänen, P. 2015. "'Miksi lähes kaikki ovat nuoria miehiä?' – Eurooppaan saapuvat turvapaikan-hakijat antavat väärän kuvan pakolaiskriisistä." *Helsingin Sanomat*, 18 August. Available online: http://www.hs.fi/ulkomaat/a1305978043206

Nilsen, T. 2016a. "Asylum Stream Directed by Crime Elements." *The Independent Barents Observer*, 12 January. Available online: http://thebarentsobserver.com/borders/2016/01/asylum-stream-directed-crime-elements

_____. 2016b. "Refugees with Children Walking towards Finnish Border in Extreme Frost." *The Independent Barents Observer*, 13 January. Available online: http://thebarentsobserver.com/borders/2016/01/refugees-children-walking-towards-finnish-border-extreme-frost

Redshaw, S. 2008. *In the Company of Cars: Driving as a Social and Cultural Practice.* Aldershot, UK: Ashgate.

Saarinen, J. 2001. "The Regional Economics of Tourism: A Case Study of the Economic Impacts of Tourism in Salla, Eastern Lapland." *Nordia Geographical Publications* 30 (4): 11–18.

Salla Municipality. 2016a. Website http://www.salla.fi/

_____. 2016b. "Itäautojen tullihuutokauppa 15.–16.7." 29 June. https://web.archive.org/web/20160703190329/http://loma.salla.fi/fi/tapahtumat/1466425944

Seamon, D. 2000. "A Way of Seeing People and Place." In *Theoretical Perspectives in Environment-behavior Research*, edited by S. Wapner, J. Demick, T. Yamamoto, and H. Minami, 157–178. New York: Plenum. https://doi.org/10.1007/978-1-4615-4701-3_13

Sheller, M. and J. Urry, 2006. "The New Mobilities Paradigm." *Environment and Planning A* 38 (2): 207–226. https://doi.org/10.1068/a37268

Tynkkynen, J. 2016. "Tulli järjestää uuden itäautojen huutokaupan Raja-Jooseppissa." *Yle uutiset*, August. Available online: http://yle.fi/uutiset/tulli_jarjestaa_uuden_itaautojen_huutokaupan_raja-joosepissa/9068666

Vannini, P. 2010. "Mobile Cultures: From the Sociology of Transportation to the Study of Mobilities." *Sociology Compass* 4 (2): 111–121. https://doi.org/10.1111/j.1751-9020.2009.00268.x

Oula Seitsonen is an archaeologist and geographer, and a project coordinator in the project "Lapland's Dark Heritage". Address for correspondence: University Of Helsinki P.O. Box 33 (Yliopistonkatu 4), 00014 University of Helsinki, Finland. Email: oula.seitsonen@helsinki.fi

Vesa-Pekka Herva is Professor of Archaeology, University of Oulu, Finland, and the principal investigator of the project "Lapland's Dark Heritage". Address for correspondence: Pentti Kaiteran katu 1, 90014 Oulu, Finland. Email: vesa-pekka.herva@oulu.fi

Mika Kunnari is an archaeologist and artist at the University of Lapland, Finland, and he works in the project "Lapland's Dark Heritage". Address for correspondence: Yliopistonkatu 8, 96300 Rovaniemi, Finland. Email: mikkunnari@ulapland.fi

Chapter 12

The Garden of Refugees

Rui Gomes Coelho

> A little garden,
> Fragrant and full of roses.
> The path is narrow
> And a little boy walks along it.
>
> A little boy, a sweet boy,
> Like that growing blossom.
> When the blossom comes to bloom,
> The little boy will be no more.
>
> —Franta Bass, "The Garden" (written at Terezín, c. 1943)[1]

Every garden needs to be tended, and needs a caretaker who knows about the cycles and moods of nature. It is hard to conceive that refugees may have anything to do with gardens, as they are always on the move, but in this essay I will show how there is a connection. First, I will evoke the manifold, conflictive character of the garden as a trope of modernity, an evocation of agency and freedom that is also a site of entrapment and violence. Second, I will show how the garden can be used as a focal point to observe the articulation of forced displacement and labour, an intersection that is the crux of modernity. Finally, I will briefly discuss the potential role of archaeology in contemporary phenomena of forced displacement.

Scholars have assumed gardens to be not only ecological phenomena but also the articulation of ideas, places, and action. Mark Francis and Randolph Hester (1990, 8) called the garden "a complex ecology of spatial reality, cognitive process, and real work." They can be places that express the power of humanity over natural circumstances, the projection of an idealized order, or a place of seclusion and escape. That is the reason why gardens are such a powerful trope, and that is also why they are sites of entrapment in societies that simultaneously incite and estrange the refugee.

However, as a trope gardens are also ambiguous, and as such they help us articulate various scales of ambivalence towards contemporary refugees. In what follows I show that gardens are places in which refugees define some control over their lives, but also

---

1. Published in Volavková (1993 [1959], 70), translated into English by Jeanne Nemcová.

where they are rejected. I argue that the conflictive encounters that take place in gardens are better understood when we see them as workplaces, sites in which people produce goods to provide for themselves and their families, and to supply the market. Further, the ambiguity of the garden conjures an invitation to us archaeologists to glance beyond the narratives of victimhood that reinforce the estrangement of the refugees, and to see the transitory materialities of their lives as mirrors of our own societies.

Very few of us would notice gardens amidst the virulent imagery that accompanies news of suffering in the journeys of refugees and other migrants. There is a good reason for that: we tend to believe that gardens mean home, and that gardens are part of a predictable world in which suffering is moderated by the certainties of our quotidian life. Refugees cannot return home, and they do not expect a routine to comfort them. Indeed, to nurture a garden has been a sign of place-making, and of social integration. In the early twentieth-century USA, immigrants were encouraged to keep neat gardens and lawns as tokens of social order (Alanen 1990, 161).

We might be surprised, then. In October 2014, a journalist named Rosie-Lyse Thompson documented gardens and their makers in Zaatari Camp, Jordan. The Syrian refugees who live there created a variety of gardens with multiple purposes (either vegetable patches, or elaborate decorative flowerbeds – Figure 12.1). Save the Children, an NGO operating in the camp, provides "gardening and landscaping" lessons to its dwellers. For the refugees, to keep a garden is a way of reminding them of home, but also a way of transforming the harsh conditions in which they are forced to live: "Even if we are to have little joys, [gardens] would make a great difference" (quoted in Thomson 2014). Similarly, it was reported in March 2015 that a Mauritanian migrant living at the makeshift camp near Calais, northern France, popularly known as "the Jungle", had built a hen house and a small vegetable garden while waiting to find a place to settle in and start a new life: "You'll never be stressed with the garden and the animals", he explained (*Franceinfo* 2015). Gardens become sites in which people seclude themselves from their surroundings and conjure alternatives (Francis and Hester 1990, 11). Refugees are also nurturing gardens in the camp of Kara Tepe, in the Greek island of Lesvos. The NGO Humanitarian Support Agency seeks to engage the camp's temporary dwellers in the production of agricultural goods, to be entirely distributed among Lesvos' "impoverished families": the NGO sees the gesture as a symbolic reciprocation for the hospitality of the local municipality. In this case, gardening becomes a way of stressing common hardships and lowering barriers (Germain 2016).

In extreme circumstances, such as in the case of enslaved communities, designing and pursuing a garden was a form of resistance (Pulsipher 1994, 217–218). The inmates of concentration camps also nurtured, or imagined, gardens as a way of coping with violence. Korbinian Aigner, a German Catholic priest and opponent of the Nazi regime, was assigned to forced agricultural labour while imprisoned in Dachau from 1941. In spite of the camp's conditions he nurtured a small apple orchard, and by the end of the war he had bred five new varieties (Larsen 2012). Franta Bass's poem, used as the epigraph at the start of this essay, shows that Aigner's and Bass's sensibilities converged under similar circumstances. Bass, who was born in 1930, wrote his poem while interned at the camp of Terezín (Theresienstadt) between December 1942 and 1944, and he died at Auschwitz in October 1944 aged 14 (Volavková 1993 [1959], 96).

Figure 12.1. Zaatari Camp, Jordan, 2014 (photograph by Rosie-Lyse Thompson).

Figure 12.2. Greenhouse in Demre, Antalya, Turkey, 2015 (photograph by author).

Whether in refugee camps, plantations, or concentration camps, gardening is far from those who garden in freedom, at home. It is a way of remembering what it means to be human, of growing through nature in times of privation and suffering (Irigaray and Marder 2016).

Zygmunt Bauman (1989) saw in the garden a powerful metaphor of modernity; the production of a fully regulated and bureaucratized order was similar to the gardener's work. Like the gardener, the state and other crafters of modernity pursued a series of procedures to keep the garden free of weeds, organized according to a series of rational principles and exclusionary of those forces that could constitute a threat. In this sense, the Holocaust was a by-product of the gardener's work while working towards a perfect, idealized garden free of undesirable plants. The gardener's effort in clearing off the weeds is as important as his or her role in organizing the garden: laying out the flowerbeds, selecting the right plants, and watering them at the right times. A garden is the pride of the gardener when it grows and its plants prosper, but also when it is clean.

Bauman's gardener is not only theoretical; the creation of gardens is also a practical element in the construction of modernity. In the eighteenth century, elites wanted their gardens to represent the world that they ruled, with shaped boxwood and carefully maintained parterres, as at the archaeologically documented gardens of William Paca in Annapolis, Maryland (Leone 2005, 63–83). Some elites encouraged the construction of gardens as a way of attaching their subjects to the land in which they were forced to live: planters across the Americas throughout the nineteenth century, especially coffee planters in the province of Rio de Janeiro, encouraged their slaves to create gardens and grow vegetables (Werneck 1985 [1847], 63–64).

Gardens are more than a "technology of ideology", as Mark Leone has put it (2005, 67). They were integral to two of the foundational institutions of modernity: slavery plantations and concentration camps. Gardens were complementary to the plantation economies by making slaves generate a significant portion of their own food, and by encouraging them to pursue local trade networks through which they could exchange goods or make some cash. Gardens were also a part of twentieth-century experiences of concentration camps. There were greenhouses in the complex of Auschwitz, where the inmates grew vegetables and flowers for the camp's consumption and to supply the war economy. Coincidentally, in 2015, Syrian refugees were being accommodated at the former agricultural units of the Dachau concentration camp in Germany, to the astonishment of Holocaust survivors who had worked in the camp's herb gardens (Hardach 2015).

Again, the garden metaphor is important for understanding the ambivalence towards refugees. Host states and NGOs are trying to manage the current refugee crisis by organizing refugee camps; the European Union is also trying to cope with the recent events in its southern borders via an agreement with Turkey that is supposed to rearrange the migration routes and minimize the influence of human traffickers (European Council 2016). However, the initiatives of many of these institutions go beyond humanitarian reasons and follow the racist and xenophobic rationale of the modern nation-states. They bureaucratize refugees in a way that is similar to gardeners taking pride in growing vegetables and their neat beds. Camps generate new subjectivities. They can also produce new political and economic arrangements: the states eventually end up using the relocation of refugees within their own borders as a token of humanitarian prestige. But the camp is, as Michel Agier has put it, a site of desocialization, and of submission to a new social arrangement in which refugees will be identifiable either as a threat or as a group to be pitied (Agier 2011, 148). The refugee will always be a stranger once he or she enters the camp.

Bauman defined the stranger as the radical other that concurrently charms and defies the order of modernity. Indeed, the stranger does not oppose the order, but challenges it, by being undecided and by blurring its limits (Bauman 1991, 53–56). Bauman further suggests that refugees are, in the modern world, "human waste": undesired humans with no place in society, no possible assimilation, no future other than to be confined to dumping sites. Like with other types of waste, its management is a social device (Bauman 2004, 76–82). However, it seems to me that the refugees occupy an important economic function.

Claude Meillassoux's explanation of how people become slaves may help us to articulate Bauman's notions of strangehood with the economic functions of the refugee. For Meillassoux, slaves are unable to socially reproduce themselves. Slaves are desocialized, depersonalized, desexualized, and decivilized during the process of enslavement. As a consequence, they are inscribed as strangers (*étrangers*), and are assigned to economic functions (Meillassoux 1986, 99–116).

The same could be said of those incarcerated in concentration camps, particularly in the case of forced labour camps. The Nuremberg Trial prosecutor Benjamin Ferencz (2002 [1979], 17–30), significantly, defined forced labour in the Nazi camps as a process of "extermination by labour". This is not to mean that slavery and the Nazi Holocaust are synonyms. Rather, they are both modern and dehumanizing experiences defined by labour. In a capitalist society like ours, in which personhood is expressed by the exchange and ownership of commodities, workers are defined as those who possess their labour. Its ultimate effect is that of transforming workers into commodities (cf. Arendt 1998 [1958], 161–163), people who become things while doing things for others. Slaves, prisoners, and refugees: they are seen as deprived of political agency by those who have the power to determine the rules, and their bodies are detached from their subjectivities so as to match an economic order (cf. Agamben 1998; Starzmann 2015a). Could we talk about a similar process of dehumanization by labour in the case of contemporary refugees?

The stories of Syrian refugees being chased out of Turkish towns are particularly evocative of the stranger's ambivalence, and how that ambivalence intersects with labour practices. The Doğan News Agency reported that, on 23 December, 2014, the inhabitants of Antalya Province attacked the houses of Syrian agricultural workers in what seemed to be a conflict over jobs. The governor of Antalya tried to reassure the locals that public order would be kept by sending the Syrians away: "We are sending notices to leave the city. But our food producers are demanding to hire Syrians because of cheap labor and that they are trusty people" (quoted in Doğan News Agency 2014). In 2015, the people of a town in the same province spotted a group of about 100 Syrians camping in the woods while looking for work in greenhouses. The locals called the police, who forced them to leave for Antalya (*Sun Express* 2015). In spite of the economic crisis that is shaking most of the continent, some of the narratives we see in the European media in support of accommodation for refugees are indeed based on refugees' economic potential in a continent with a pessimistic demographic outlook (Dettmer *et al.* 2015). This narrative matches the EU's ambiguous relationship with seasonal workers from the southern side of the Mediterranean, who are allowed to cross the sea to engage in agricultural labour under special arrangements (Mésini 2009).

When interviewed about the concentration of refugees near their homes, the distressed neighbors of the Calais "Jungle" mentioned undesired intrusions into private gardens. The locals accused refugees of taking their gardens' fences and trashcans, materials that seem to be of use at the camp (Baer 2015; *Ouest-France.* 2015). As Christopher Tilley (2008) has shown, the nation can be imagined and reproduced through the routine of gardening. In this way, gardens are locales of exclusion, and the strangers' incursions can be seen as invasions. The mayor pointed out alternatives: planned "gardens, playgrounds, and bike paths" that are supposed to replace the temporary tents of another makeshift camp near Dunkirk (Boitiaux 2016). Of course, what the local authorities mean by "gardens" are the monotonous public spaces full of "roadside garnish" (Burckhardt 2006, 288–289) that are now typical of most European suburban towns. They may be as dull as a highway, but for the distressed locals these so-called gardens will be more comforting than a landscape occupied by passing strangers.

These stances regarding refugees are only superficially paradoxical. Bauman's garden is comprised of "cultured plants" and weeds that wait to be eradicated (Bauman 1989, 17–18). Refugees are political and cultural others in the current migratory crisis, vegetation that needs to be domesticated into the proper garden arrangement. That domestication, I argue, happens through labour. The refugees are trapped in the machine of modernity, and the garden symbolizes the intersection of two of its operative modes: social estrangement and economic exploitation. Refugees build temporary gardens in the camps they are compelled to live in as attempts to ameliorate their transitory condition; they are also forced to sell their labour in difficult situations, in greenhouses (Figure 12.2) and other places from where we will get our food. Meanwhile, far-right groups such as the National Front in France accuse Germany's government of accepting the arrival of refugees in order to enslave them (Faye 2016). When international law complicates the formal estrangement of refugees, extremists turn their cultural anxieties to labour standards.

The garden, as we see, is a multifarious site with conflictive meanings: one in which refugees are domesticated and confronted with their strangehood, but also a space of dissent and resistance. Gardens convey the affective traces of refugees' experience: displacement, estrangement, violence, determination, invention, emotion (cf. Hamilakis, this volume).

Like most people, archaeologists are overwhelmed by what they see of the refugee crisis. The violence of the mediated image makes our societies for the most part unable to witness the suffering of the refugees. Journalism may not be enough to portray the suffering, to create empathy, and to outline what needs to change; the photographs and videos that enter our lives every day are meant to document the perilous journeys and hardships of those who try to escape, move away, and build new lives; but the effect of those images is to act as a filter that estranges the refugees by producing simply victimhood.

Archaeologists have a different approach to violence and the variety of its effects. They investigate material traces left by humans in an attempt to understand and signify realities that are, or have been, forgotten. In many cases those material traces are the only evidence left from an event, or from someone's life. Sometimes, when there are attempts to erase or disrupt the existence of individuals or entire groups, only archaeology can make sense of those traces (González-Ruibal 2016, 34–37). Archaeologists do this through methodical documentation, and by organizing the evidence. The results of these methods are reassembled in a set of products – images, texts, relationships – that themselves become another material layer of what they seek to study; a more profound, nuanced layer of understanding. In relation to photographs of "the most solemn or heartrending subject matter", Susan Sontag argued that their "weight and seriousness [...] survive better in a book, where one can look privately, linger over the pictures, without talking." This applies to the products of archaeologists' work as much as to photographs. Sontag adds, however, that

> [s]till, at some moment the book will be closed. The strong emotion will become a transient one. Eventually the specificity of the photographs' accusations will fade; the denunciation of a particular conflict and attribution of specific crimes will become a denunciation of human cruelty, human savagery as such. (Sontag 2003, 121–122)

To do archaeology becomes an act of witnessing (cf. Starzmann 2015b).

Raffaella Puggioni (2014, 954–956), in her analysis of migrant detention in Italy, proposed that testifying to violence is a form of resistance against dehumanizing agents, and a way of reasserting a sense of humanity. I would like to suggest that our responsibility as archaeologists is to actively witness and highlight testimonies triggered by refugees' journeys and the material traces they leave behind (Starzmann 2015a). Activists face the temptation of assuming the role of translating experiences of violence and suffering, thus directing and politically determining what violence is, and how the other suffers (Fassin 2008). The challenge is to look at the temporary materialities of refugees and disclose what they embody, either in their oppressive potential or in the alternatives they conjure. And then we have to write about it, and make others feel it:

> [D]iscursive forms of dissent have the potential to transgress boundaries and engender human agency, not by directly causing particular events, but by creating a language that provides us with different eyes, with the opportunity to reassess anew the spatial and political dimensions of global life.
>
> (Bleiker 2000, 45, in Puggioni 2014, 953)

Roland Bleiker was thinking of dissidents' poetry when he wrote this passage, but we can extend it to our work.

The role of the contemporary archaeologist as witness is crucial here. The archaeological gaze, Gabriel Moshenska (2013) has argued, thrives in modern societies due to its uncanny character. Just like the anatomical theatres in early modern Europe, archaeology is a performance through which the hidden is disclosed and exposed to public scrutiny. Referring to the uncanny in the Freudian sense, Moshenska maintains that the process of disclosure of what was supposed to be hidden can be simultaneously compelling and repulsive. It is from this tension that our perception emerges, as well as its relevance to discussing refugees' lives.

We need a multi-sensorial engagement with their suffering (*sensu* Hamilakis 2013). Not that we should seek to replicate their experiences – as if it would ever be possible – but we need to encounter them in their camps and shelters, acknowledge and confront their material circumstances. In doing so, archaeologists may reveal what the pursuit of ever-increasing wealth by global elites actually entails.

On the other hand, archaeologists also have the option of uncovering the social and economic devices that estrange human beings and alienate them from dignity; and here I see the usual products of archaeological research (i.e. books, flyers, papers, and brochures) as a cause for rebuke, particularly for scholars who see themselves as activists. What makes our work different from that of anthropologists, as well as from sociologists or NGO workers, is that we look at material culture as socially constitutive, and we deal with material culture through a particular craft that is a bundle of theory and technique, skill, and creativity (McGuire 2008, 85–86). Hence, a politically coherent archaeology can help connect the scales involved: the gardens in refugees' camps and the greenhouses where they are compelled to work, the invaded gardens in the vicinity of refugees' camps, and the metaphorical garden of the EU and other host states. Our role as archaeologist-witnesses is to reveal the sharp gradations of a complex context that goes far beyond the narratives of victimhood and rescue normally portrayed by the media. As Yannis Hamilakis has suggested (this volume), migrants show and reclaim their agency in the move, or even when they are forced into camps. It is our duty to engage with them in a politically consequent way.

The garden-making trope then becomes part of a revelatory landscape. The creation of a garden is a disguised way of accepting its organic condition, and the ways it will escape human control. Plants will grow and die in spite of all human efforts to train life (Betsky 2001, 9). According to Bleiker, the

> potential of agency, its ability to open up new ways of perceiving global politics, can be appreciated once we accept, with Rilke, and as a permanent condition of life, that we always "stand in the middle of a transition, where we cannot remain standing".
>
> (Bleiker 2000, 281)

By the same token, the transitory gardeners of Zaatari, the "Jungle", and Kara Tepe will keep moving until they finally find a safe place to settle, and to create new gardens.

As I conclude, I watch again the young man talking about his garden at the "Jungle" of Calais. He is certainly not there anymore, as the camp was dismantled while this essay was being reviewed. I hear his words with hope, however. The paths taken by refugees to move through the gardens of modernity are almost as narrow as the little boy's in the epigraph. But their ability to transform and thrive in the landscapes they navigate is an opportunity for us to question narratives of victimhood that reinforce their estrangement. For Luce Irigaray, the myriad of sensorial signals elicited by the vegetal world may help people make sense of their own existence and become different, organic beings (Irigaray and Marder 2016, 99–102). In this sense, gardens are a double opportunity: to think about the institutions and the material circumstances refugees face, and to think of ourselves – scholars and activists – as part of the same ecology of dissent and resistance.

Acknowledgments

These cogitations are the result of many conversations, and I wish to thank Alfredo González-Ruibal, Hande Sarikuzu, Lúcio Menezes Ferreira, Maria Theresia Starzmann, Yannis Hamilakis, and the anonymous reviewers.

References

Agamben, G. 1998. *Homo Sacer: Sovereign Power and Bare Life*. Stanford, CA: Meridian.

Agier, M. 2011. *Managing the Undesirables: Refugee Camps and Humanitarian Government*. Cambridge: Polity.

Alanen, A. R. 1990. "Immigrant Gardens on a Mining Frontier." In *The Meaning of Gardens: Idea, Place, and Action*, edited by M. Francis and R. T. Hester Jr, 160–165. Cambridge, MA: MIT Press.

Arendt, H. 1998 [1958]. *The Human Condition*. Chicago: University of Chicago Press. https://doi.org/10.7208/chicago/9780226924571.001.0001

Baer, S. 2015. "Migrants: les riverains de la 'jungle' de Calais traumatisés." *Franceinfo*, 11 November. Available online. http://www.franceinfo.fr/actu/societe/article/migrants-les-riverains-de-la-jungle-de-calais-traumatises-744865

Bauman, Z. 1989. *Modernity and the Holocaust*. Ithaca, NY: Cornell University Press.

____. 1991. *Modernity and Ambivalence*. Ithaca, NY: Cornell University Press.

____. 2004. *Wasted Lives: Modernity and its Outcasts*. Cambridge: Polity.

Betsky, A. 2001. "Dig We Must: An Argument for Revelatory Landscapes." In *Revelatory Landscapes / Aaron Betsky, Leah Levy, Dean MacCannell*, edited by A. Betsky, 8–17. San Francisco: San Francisco Museum of Modern Art.

Bleiker, R. 2000. *Popular Dissent, Human Agency and Global Politics*. Cambridge: Cambridge University Press. https://doi.org/10.1017/CBO9780511491245

Boitiaux, C. 2016. "La boue au ventre. Dans le premier camp humanitaire de France." *France 24*, 15–16 March. Available online: Part 1: http://webdoc.france24.com/grande-synthe-migrants-camp-insalubrite-calais-dunkerque-humanitaire-msf-mdm/ Part 2: http://webdoc.france24.com/migrants-camp-humanitaire-grande-synthe/

Burckhardt, L. 2006. *Why Is Landscape Beautiful? The Science of Strollology*. Basel: Birkhäuser.

Dettmer, M., C. Katschak, and G. Ruppert. 2015. "German Companies see Refugees as Opportunity." *Spiegel Online*, 27 August. Available online: http://www.spiegel.de/international/germany/refugees-are-an-opportunity-for-the-german-economy-a-1050102.html

Doğan News Agency. 2014. "Syrian Refugees Attacked, Urged to Leave in Antalya." *Hürriyet Daily News*, 24 December. Available online: http://www.hurriyetdailynews.com/syrian-refugees-attacked-urged-to-leave-in-antalya.aspx?pageID=238&nID=76056&NewsCatID=341

European Council. 2016. "EU-Turkey Statement, 18 March 2016". Available online: http://www.consilium.europa.eu/en/press/press-releases/2016/03/18-eu-turkey-statement/

Fassin, D. 2008. "The Humanitarian Politics of Testimony: Subjectification Through Trauma in the Israeli-Palestinian Conflict". *Cultural Anthropology* 23 (3): 531–558. https://doi.org/10.1111/j.1548-1360.2008.00017.x

Faye, O. 2016. "Crise des migrants: le FN tient Angela Merkel pour responsable." *Le Monde*, 24 September. Available online: http://www.lemonde.fr/politique/article/2015/09/24/l-allemagne-nouveau-bouc-emissaire-de-marine-le-pen_4770239_823448.html#HDr2sBzMQA1BazKJ.99

Ferencz, B. B. 2002 [1979]. *Less than Slaves: Jewish Forced Labor and the Quest for Compensation*. Bloomington: Indiana University Press.

Franceinfo. 2015. "Migrants à Calais: la jungle est devenue une véritable petite ville." 7 August. Available online: http://www.francetvinfo.fr/france/nord-pas-de-calais/migrants-a-calais/migrants-a-calais-la-jungle-est-devenue-une-veritable-petite-ville_1033081.html

Francis, M. and R. T. Hester Jr. 1990. "The Garden as Idea, Place, and Action." In *The Meaning of Gardens. Idea, Place, and Action*, edited by M. Francis and R. T. Hester Jr, 2–19. Cambridge, MA: MIT Press.

Germain, B. 2016. "A Garden That Outgrows Its Fence." *The Lyceum*, 14 August. Available online https://learninglyceum.org/2016/08/14/a-garden-that-outgrows-its-fence/

González-Ruibal, A. 2016. *Volver a las Trincheras: Una Arqueología de la Guerra Civil Española*. Madrid: Alianza Editorial.

Hamilakis, Y. 2013. *Archaeology and the Senses: Human Experience, Memory, and Affect*. Cambridge: Cambridge University Press. https://doi.org/10.1017/CBO9781139024655

Hardach, S. 2015. "The Refugees Housed at Dachau: 'Where Else Should I Live?'" *The Guardian*, 19 September. Available online: http://www.theguardian.com/world/2015/sep/19/the-refugees-who-live-at-dachau

Irigaray, L. and M. Marder. 2016. *Through Vegetal Being: Two Philosophical Perspectives*. New York: Columbia University Press.

Larsen, L. B. 2012. "Korbinian Aigner." In *Documenta (13): The Guidebook. Catalog 3/3*, 34–35. Ostfildern, Germany: Hatje Cantz.

Leone, M. 2005. *The Archaeology of Liberty in an American Capital: Excavations in Annapolis*. Berkeley: University of California Press. https://doi.org/10.1525/california/9780520244504.001.0001

McGuire, R. 2008. *Archaeology as Political Action*. Berkeley: University of California Press.

Meillassoux, C. 1986. *Anthropologie de l'Esclavage*. Paris: Presses Universitaires de France.

Mésini, B. 2009. "Enjeux des mobilités circulaires de maind'œuvre: l'exemple des saisonniers étrangers dans l'agriculture méditerranéenne." *Méditerranée* 113: 105–112. https://doi.org/10.4000/mediterranee.3753

Moshenska, G. 2013. "The Archaeological Gaze." In *Reclaiming Archaeology: Beyond the Tropes of Modernity*, edited by A. González-Ruibal, 211–219. London and New York: Routledge. https://doi.org/10.4324/9780203068632.ch16

Ouest-France. 2015 "Réfugiés. Nouveaux heurts aux abords de la 'Jungle' de Calais." 11 November. Available online: http://www.ouest-france.fr/monde/refugies-nouveaux-heurts-aux-abords-de-la-jungle-de-calais-3832298

Puggioni, R. 2014. "Against Camps' Violence: Some Voices on Italian Holding Centres." *Political Studies* 62 (4): 945–960. https://doi.org/10.1111/1467-9248.12051

Pulsipher, L. M. 1994. "The Landscapes and Ideational Roles of Caribbean Slave Gardens." In *The Archaeology of Garden and Field*, edited by N. F. Miller and K. L. Gleason, 202–222. Philadelphia: University of Pennsylvania Press.

Sontag, S. 2003. *Regarding the Pain of Others*. New York: Farrar, Straus and Giroux.

Starzmann, M. T. 2015a. "The Materiality of Forced Labor: An Archaeological Exploration of Punishment in Nazi Germany." *International Journal of Historical Archaeology* 19 (3): 647–663. https://doi.org/10.1007/s10761-015-0302-9

_____. 2015b. "Zeitschichten/Bedeutungsschichten: Archäologische Untersuchungen zur NS-Zwangsarbeit in Berlin-Tempelhof." *Historische Archäologie* 2015, Article 2. Available online: http://www.histarch.uni-kiel.de/2015_Starzmann_low.pdf

Sun Express. 2015. "130 Syrian Refugees in Seydikemer Sent to Antalya." No date. Available online: http://www.sunexpressnews.com/130-syrian-refugees-in-seydikemer-sent-to-antalya/

Thomson, R. 2014. "When We Garden, We Feel Happy." *Al Jazeera*, 27 October. Available online: http://www.aljazeera.com/indepth/inpictures/2014/10/pictures-when-garden-feel-happ-2014102771959578411.html

Tilley, C. 2008. "From the English Cottage Garden to the Swedish Allotment: Banal Nationalism and the Concept of the Garden." *Home Cultures* 5 (2): 219–250. https://doi.org/10.2752/174063108X333191

Volavková, Y., ed. 1993 [1959]. *I Never Saw Another Butterfly: Children's Drawings and Poems from Terezin Concentration Camp 1942-1944*. New York: Schocken Books.

Werneck, F. P. de L. 1985 [1847]. *Memória Sobre a Fundação de uma Fazenda na Província do Rio de Janeiro*. Brasília: Senado Federal.

Rui Gomes Coelho is a Postdoctoral Associate in the Cultural Heritage and Preservation Studies program at the Department of Art History, Rutgers University. Address for correspondence: Rutgers School of Arts and Sciences, Voorhees Hall 71 Hamilton Street New Brunswick, NJ, 08901, USA. Email: rui.gomescoelho@rutgers.edu

Chapter 13

Reframing the Lampedusa Cross: The British Museum's Display of the Mediterranean Migrant Crisis

Morgan Lynn Breene

Introduction: Reframing the Lampedusa Cross

Over the past 15 years, growing unrest and political instability in the Middle East and North Africa has led to unprecedented levels of forced migration into Europe: the International Organization for Migration's minimum estimates for arrivals by sea for 1 January to 7 December, 2015 is 910,563, with an additional 352,471 for the same period in 2016. During this second period, a further 4733 are estimated to have died in the attempt (International Organization for Migration 2016; *New York Times* 2016). Tension over how to receive, deal with, and place migrants and refugees fleeing persecution and terrorism has become palpable, demonstrative of the weaknesses of the EU's policies on the matter. For many migrants, the journey represents an irreversible break with their prior lives and a willingness to risk everything to build new ones. The crisis has prompted anthropological discussion considering the roles of host and guest in theories of hospitality, with Europe playing the host and African and Middle Eastern migrants as guest. Ben-Yehoyada, for example, has suggested that framing the crisis in such a way does not reflect well on Europe's response, arguing that Italy in particular has regularly broken the bonds of hospitality in failing to adequately welcome refugees and migrants, through failing to abide by the Law of Sea (whether by refusing assistance or providing it when not wanted – Ben-Yehoyada 2015, 189).

Condemnation of Italy's actions has come from sources as varied as the Pope and the European Court of Human Rights. However, the unfair burden placed on Italy and Greece by the EU's Dublin Regulation must be acknowledged (Ben-Yehoyada 2015, 189; *New York Times* 2016). This extraordinary contemporary crisis and the way in which member nations of the European Union have responded forces a reanalysis of Europe's self-perceptions and political and moral responsibilities. The way in which this process is documented and presented to the general public ought to be critically analysed to provoke both educated discussion and emotional responses. This might be achieved through an analysis of the Lampedusa Cross and its presentation in the British Museum in the spring and summer of 2016.

In October 2015, Neil MacGregor acquired his last object as director of the British Museum (British Museum 2015b). That object was the Lampedusa Cross, a wooden cross of the

Latin type (383 × 280 mm), fashioned from wood salvaged from a migrant vessel that had been wrecked on the shores of Lampedusa in 2013 with the loss of 366 of the 518 people on board (Figure 13.1). The cross-piece retains much of the boat's scuffed blue paint, while on the vertical arm several layers of paint are visible – dark green, beige, and orange. The sides and back are planed to the timber surface, there is a small hole for suspension near the top of the vertical arm, and a fragment of iron nail remains near the top of the right side of the cross-piece. The back is signed "F. Tuccio" (British Museum 2015a).

Francesco Tuccio made the piece in 2015 specifically for the British Museum after being contacted by Jill Cook, a senior curator at the museum (British Museum 2015b). He fashioned it in the same style as crosses he had been making for shipwrecked Eritrean Christians and other migrants since 2013. The press release announcing the acquisition of the cross states:

> It is essential that [the] Museum continues to collect objects that reflect contemporary culture in order to ensure the collection remains dynamic and reflects the world as it is. The Lampedusa disaster was one of the first examples of the terrible tragedies that have befallen refugees/migrants as they seek to cross from Africa into Europe.

Figure 13.1. Display location of the Lampedusa Cross, July 2016 in Room 2 of the British Museum (photograph by author).

The cross allows the Museum to represent these events in a physical object so that in 10, 50, 100 years' time this latest migration can be reflected in a collection which tells the stories of multiple migrations across millennia. (British Museum 2015b)

The object was displayed from December 2015 into the fall of 2016, but is currently not on display. It was initially displayed in an exhibit entitled "Collecting for the Future", then "Collecting for the World". As the only object displayed in 2016 referencing the Mediterranean migrant crisis, the Lampedusa Cross can be seen as representative of the event within the British Museum.

The Lampedusa Cross was originally displayed in a glass case in the middle of Room 2, a gallery off of the Enlightenment Room. In mid-June, it was lent to St Paul's Cathedral, to be displayed as part of an exhibit on the migrant crisis. (St Paul's Cathedral 2016). On its return near the end of June, it was then tucked into a corner to the left of the doorway leading from the Enlightenment Room into Room 2 and out of the line of sight of those entering the gallery from that direction (Figure 13.2). It shared the corner with inset cases displaying objects from "The Age of Curiosity", although it was still displayed in a case and could be viewed from all angles.

Figure 13.2. Display location of the Lampedusa Cross, March 2016 in Room 2 of the British Museum (photograph by author).

In its initial display location, the cross was accompanied by a text panel (Figure 13.3) that read:

> This wooden cross reflects history in the making. The wood came from a wreck carrying refugees and migrants across the Mediterranean from Africa to Europe. The cross is a symbol of the kindness of ordinary people when faced with the suffering of thousands who risk everything in search of a better life.
>
> The cross was made by Francesco Tuccio, a carpenter living in Lampedusa. Since 2011, this tiny Italian island off the southeast coast of Sicily has witnessed the deaths of many desperate people escaping war, persecution and poverty. The islanders show great charity to the survivors. After meeting Eritrean Christians in the Church of San Gerlando where he worships, Mr Tuccio wanted to do what he could to help them.
>
> [...]
>
> Mr Tuccio made and donated this cross to the British Museum where it will be a visible symbol of the suffering and hope of our times. Chosen by Neil MacGregor to represent his last acquisition as director, it is a reminder of how cultures mix and change in making the history of the world.

Upon its return to the gallery in late June, a new text panel (Figure 13.4) accompanied the cross:

> This wooden cross reflects history in the making. The wood came from the wreckage of a refugee boat that sank near the island of Lampedusa en route to Europe from Africa.
>
> Mr Tuccio made and donated this cross to the British Museum as a symbol of the suffering and hope of our times. Chosen by Neil MacGregor to represent his last acquisition as Director, it is a reminder of how cultures mix and change in making the history of the world.

However, the appropriateness of the cross as a representation of the crisis is up for debate. The object itself, its display, and the accompanying text panel might all be used to explore the role of the object as a museum exhibit, and the types of reactions it might elicit in the museum's audience.

The Lampedusa Cross as Representative Object

In choosing to acquire and display the Lampedusa Cross, MacGregor and the museum argue that it is reflective of the most recent wave of migration and its tragedies, and that it is important to collect *representative* artefacts for future study and interpretation. While this is a laudable mission, choosing to display the Lampedusa Cross as the "poster child" of such an initiative is questionable. The creation of heritage is an inherently selective process, and the choices made by heritage and museum practitioners have a major impact on the way in which the public perceive and interpret cultures and events (Atkinson *et al.* 2002, 28). The decision to display a Christian symbol is problematic. In a forced migration crisis coloured by religious intoler-

The Lampedusa Cross
Italy, 2015

This wooden cross reflects history in the making. The wood comes from a boat that was wrecked carrying refugees and migrants across the Mediterranean from Africa to Europe. The cross is a symbol of the kindness of ordinary people when faced with the suffering of thousands who risk everything in search of a better life.

The cross was made by Francesco Tuccio, a carpenter living in Lampedusa. Since 2011 this tiny Italian island off the southeast coast of Sicily has witnessed the deaths of many desperate people escaping war, persecution and poverty. The islanders show great charity to the survivors. After meeting Eritrean Christians in the church of San Gerlando where he worships, Mr Tuccio wanted to do what he could to help them.

This image captured by BBC News shows the wreckage of a refugee boat. Mr Tuccio's story came to the attention of the Museum through a BBC World Service programme made by Emma Jane Kirby.

Mr Tuccio made and donated this cross to the British Museum where it will be a visible symbol of the suffering and hope of our times. Chosen by Neil MacGregor to represent his last acquisition as Director, it is a reminder of how cultures mix and change in making the history of the world.

Figure 13.3. Original accompanying text panel, March 2016 (photograph by author).

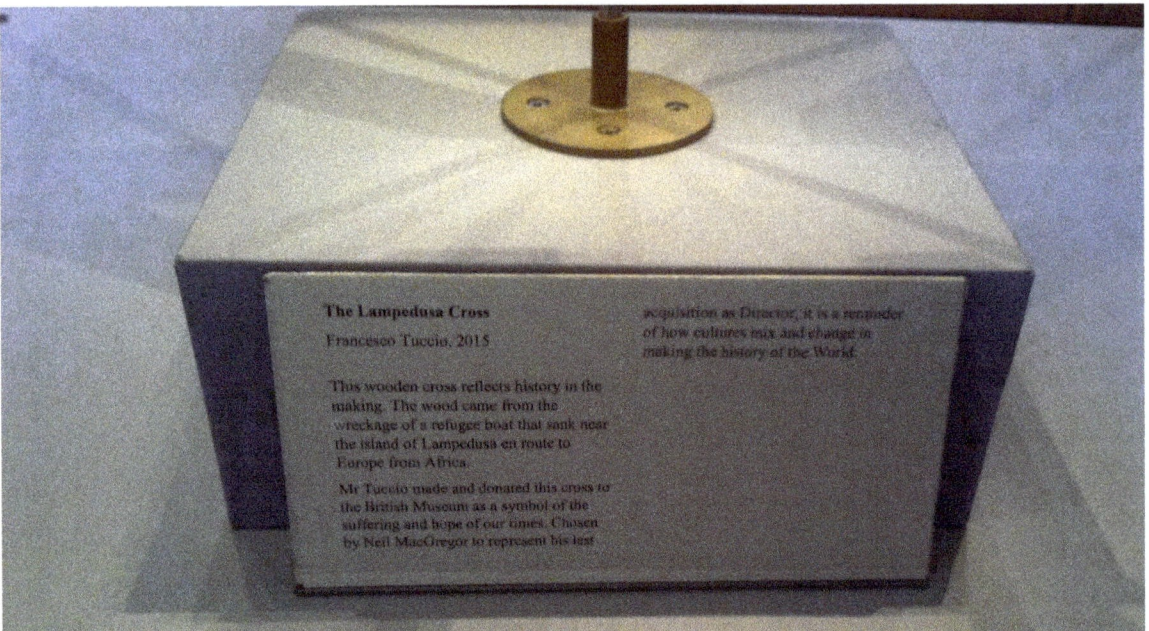

The Lampedusa Cross
Francesco Tuccio, 2015

This wooden cross reflects history in the making. The wood came from the wreckage of a refugee boat that sank near the island of Lampedusa en route to Europe from Africa.

Mr Tuccio made and donated this cross to the British Museum as a symbol of the suffering and hope of our times. Chosen by Neil MacGregor to represent his last acquisition as Director, it is a reminder of how cultures mix and change in making the history of the World.

Figure 13.4. Second accompanying text panel, July 2016 (photograph by author).

ance and animosity, the use of a religious object of any kind is a powerful statement that must be carefully considered, particularly a symbol which does not represent the belief system of a majority of those migrating. Furthermore, the Cross as a symbol of Christian compassion obscures the larger message of migrant "suffering and hope" suggested by the museum, in favour of an emphasis on "good Christian behaviour" on the part of those giving their time to help refugees. Hooper-Greenhill argues that the choice to display or not display particular objects is informed by ideas about what is and is not significant, and reveals the ideas and values of the museum in question (Hooper-Greenhill 2000, 3). The museum has chosen to represent a broad and multifaceted forced migration event with a symbol meaningful to a minority of those making the journey; it could be expected to resonate, however, with many amongst the anticipated audience. In doing this, the museum has placed significance on the attitudes of the likely audience rather than those of the population it is meant to evoke. To invoke Ben-Yehoyada's guest–host framework, choosing to represent the crisis through an object with significance to the group it represents (guest) would have been a more meaningful choice. At the very least, an object created, donated, or chosen by someone who had gone through the experience invoked would be preferable as an emblem. In this case, the cross was created and donated by a European (host) and chosen by a British Museum curator (host). The migrant (guest) experience is not inherently found in either the cross or its journey to the British Museum.

Migrant Audience versus Museum Audience

Tuccio initially began making crosses for the relatively small group of Eritrean Christians making landfall on Lampedusa, but his creations have now come to represent a much broader migrant population in a way that is not reflective of the variety in that population's beliefs or experience. While the cross may be emotive of the original audience Tuccio had in mind, it provokes contemplation on the influx of migrants from a European, rather than migrant, perspective, and as the creation of a Lampedusian islander, it represents the islander experience rather than the migrant experience. The cross represents the impact such a crisis has on small communities and their members, and the way in which Tuccio in particular felt compelled to respond. It is the gesture of a host to a guest, and Tuccio's experience and personal response to this forced migration event is reflective of the European or host experience. The cross, therefore, can be seen as representing the impact of an influx of migrants on a small community. However, while also a valid question deserving discussion, the islander community is not the community the museum is purporting to represent to the public (see, e.g., Papataxiarchis 2016). Nor should its response be represented in the museum *in lieu* of that of the migrant community.

A more evocative choice on the part of the museum might have been to display an object less culturally familiar to its expected audience, either in form, presentation in an unexpected context, or some other distinguishing feature. In displaying something produced by Tuccio, the museum perpetuates an idealized portrayal of European hospitality towards migrants, and does not provoke critical engagement or alternative points of view.

Display and Redisplay

The original location of the cross can be interpreted as a strong political statement on the museum's part; not only had they acquired an object representing an ongoing and deeply divisive crisis, but they had also chosen to display it in a prominent location. In emphasizing that the Lampedusa Cross was chosen for its contemporary and future importance for study and to "ensure the collection remains dynamic and reflects the world as it is" (British Museum 2015b), the museum implicitly recognized the impact such a migration event is having on both Europe as host and migrants as guest. The relocation of the cross to a corner of the gallery, then, weakened the efficacy of the original choice and professed motive for display. The likelihood that visitors engage with and "reflect on this significant moment in the history of Europe" (British Museum 2015b) was diminished by the move from a prominent, central position in the gallery to a corner alcove. The choice suggested a lack of willingness on the part of the museum to truly engage with and provoke discussion – a discredit to their stated mission in reference to the display of the cross. That it is currently not on display can be seen to further reinforce the lack of commitment to the original stated mission.

The Label Text

The choice of subject matter and wording of the text panel betrays a reluctance to strongly engage with or confront the reasons Tuccio was compelled to create the crosses; it also shows an unwillingness to foreground the experience of those he was seeking to comfort. If the object is meant to be representative of the migrant crisis, this is not evident in the label. The original label focuses on the experience of the islanders, Tuccio's personal desire to help those he saw as in need, and the symbolism of Neil MacGregor's last acquisition.

That the panel focuses on the islander (host) experience, rather than the migrant (guest) experience is problematic, in that it reinforces a constructed self-perception of European hospitality that is not reflective of the daily experiences of migrants trying to enter Europe, particularly across the Mediterranean. The reality of Italy's "push-back" agreements with Libya and subsequent interception of vessels not in distress contradicts the message of hospitality and welcome implied by the label. While the islanders do have a history of localized hospitality, this welcoming attitude is not reflective of overarching EU and state approaches to the crisis.

The text states that the cross is meant to serve as "a symbol of the suffering and hope of our time", but it more accurately serves as a symbol of a model European response to suffering and hope (represented by the actions of the islanders) than the reality of what is experienced by many migrants. It is a neat and uncritical choice that masks rather than illuminates the migrant experience of "suffering and hope".

Further, choosing to mention the role of the object in reference to Neil MacGregor's tenure at the museum detracts from its actual importance and ability to make a strong statement. While a meaningful moment in his tenure as director, the motivations he professed in acquiring the object are diminished by including his role on a text panel less than 100 words long (British Museum 2015b). Finally, arguing that this object is a "reminder of how cultures mix and change in making the history of the world" is an insupportably strong statement to make about an object in the shape of an established religious symbol. It is a comforting, familiar image, rather than one that provokes thought or draws attention.

Conclusion

In choosing to represent the Mediterranean migrant crisis with the Lampedusa Cross, the British Museum has perpetuated an idealized European perspective that is not necessarily representative of the experiences or emotional responses to the migration process of people who have actually made the journey. Rather than using the opportunity to provoke discussion by displaying remnant material culture of migration or an object chosen by someone who had undertaken the trans-Mediterranean journey that has claimed so many lives, the museum instead chose to obscure the narrative through an art object produced by a European. While thought-provoking in its own right as a representation of a specific response to tragedy, this does not make it an appropriate representation of the tragedy itself. The choice of the object, the nature of its display, and the accompanying text panels all reinforce an uncritical portrayal of European hospitality that does a disservice to those most impacted.

References

Atkinson, D., S. Cooke, and D. Spooner. 2002. "Tales from the Riverbank: Place-Marketing and Maritime Heritages." *International Journal of Heritage Studies* 8 (1): 25–40. https://doi.org/10.1080/13527250220119910

Ben-Yehoyada, N. 2015. "'Follow Me, and I Will Make You Fishers of Men': The Moral and Political Scales of Migration in the Central Mediterranean." *Journal of the Royal Anthropological Institute* 22 (1): 183–202. https://doi.org/10.1111/1467-9655.12340

British Museum. 2015a. "The Lampedusa Cross." *British Museum Collection Online.* Available online: http://www.britishmuseum.org/research/collection_online/collection_object_details.aspx?objectId=3691920&partId=1&searchText=lampedusa+cross&page=1

_____. 2015b. "Last Acquisition under Neil MacGregor Revealed." British Museum website: http://www.britishmuseum.org/about_us/news_and_press/press_releases/2015/macgregors_last_acquisition.aspx.

Hooper-Greenhill, E. 2000. *Museums and the Interpretation of Visual Culture.* London and New York: Routledge.

International Organization for Migration. 2016. "Mediterranean Migrant Arrivals Reach 352,471; Deaths at Sea: 4,733." IOM website: https://www.iom.int/news/mediterranean-migrant-arrivals-reach-352471-deaths-sea-4733

New York Times. 2016. "Editorial: Europe's Continuing Shame." 22 July. Available online: http://www.nytimes.com/2016/07/22/opinion/europes-continuing-shame.html

Papataxiarchis, E. 2016. "Being 'There': At the Front Line of the 'European Refugee Crisis', Part 1." *Anthropology Today* 32 (2): 5–9. https://doi.org/10.1111/1467-8322.12237

St Paul's Cathedral. 2016. "The Lampedusa Cross and Refugee Exhibition at St Paul's: Refugee and Migrant Displays Mark Refugee Week." St Paul's Cathedral website, 17 June. https://www.stpauls.co.uk/news-press/latest-news/see-the-lampedusa-cross-at-st-pauls-on-sunday-19-june

Morgan Lynn Breene is a researcher associated with the University of Rhode Island. Address for correspondence: Department of History, Washburn Hall, 80 Upper College Road, Kingston, RI 02881, USA. Email: morgan_breene@my.uri.edu

Chapter 14

What Anchors the *Tu Do*?

Denis Byrne

On the Waterfront

On 21 November, 1977 a Vietnamese fishing boat carrying 31 refugees tied up in Darwin after sailing across the South China Sea and down through the Indonesian archipelago to the northern coast of Australia (Figure 14.1). That boat, the *Tu Do*, was acquired by the Australian National Maritime Museum in 1990 and is now moored at the museum's wharves in Darling Harbour, Sydney's central business district (Sydney CBD) (Figure 14.2). The museum restored the boat in 2000, repainting its woodwork in the original colours of sky blue with red trim and furnishing it with replicas of some of the objects, such as bedding, food, utensils, and

Figure 14.1. The *Tu Do* in Darwin Harbour, Australia, in November 1977 (photograph © Michael Jensen).

Figure 14.2. The *Tu Do* (centre) at the Australian National Maritime Museum, Darling Harbour, Sydney, in 2015 (photograph by author).

clothing, that had been aboard it during the 1977 voyage and which the museum acquired from Vietnam (Thompson 2006). But the *Tu Do* also exists in the form of a black-and-white photograph taken in Darwin in 1977 by a freelance press photographer, Michael Jensen (Figure 14.2). In the photo, the *Tu Do*'s paintwork is scarred and worn – weathered, like the sunburned young men in shorts and jeans who can be seen standing and sitting aboard her, waiting while a customs official in a white shirt processes the refugees on another boat, which the *Tu Do* is tied up next to. It is a pensive scene in which the refugees on both boats are seemingly motionless, standing at the doorway to another country in a moment freighted with the alternatives of acceptance or rejection. In the event, they were among the 2059 Vietnamese asylum seekers who were permitted to settle in Australia.

On the day in 2015 when I went down to Darling Harbour to look at the *Tu Do* I took with me a copy of the 1977 photograph so that I could compare the two versions of the boat. The difference was jarring. In front of me, the meticulously restored *Tu Do* rocked on the water, its paintwork fresh and gleaming (Figure 14.3). But more than anything, the difference stemmed from the presence of the refugees on the boat in the 1977 photograph and the way their bodies and the boat seemed continuous with and habituated to each other. One of the young men standing at the boat's stern holds the boom in his arm, or is supported by the boom, depending on how you look at it. They fit into and extend each other. I spent a while looking backwards and forwards between the photo and the boat, dwelling on the gulf between them.

Figure 14.3. A copy of Michael Jensen's 1977 photograph on the gunwale of the *Tu Do*, Darling Harbour, in 2015 (photograph by author).

The juxtaposition was strange, but what mainly adsorbed me down at Darling Harbour was the strangeness of the *Tu Do*'s remoteness from those *other boats*, by which I mean those vessels, most of them also wooden fishing boats, which over the last few decades have braved similar hazards to carry asylum seekers to Australia but which failed to make it. Most have been intercepted at sea by vessels of the Australian Border Force and either turned back to Indonesia or burned and sunk at sea after the removal of their passengers (subsequently interned in detention camps). Among the boats that never made it are those that sank on the voyage to Australia, drowning hundreds of those on board.[1] What is it, I wondered, that

---

1. A total of 212 such drownings were recorded during 2013 (*Beyond Foreignness* 2015). There have been none recorded since then, a fact the current government attributes to its "Operation Sovereign Borders", which entails offshore detention of asylum seekers arriving in Australian waters by boat and offers no hope of eventual settlement in Australia, even for those accorded refugee status.

isolates the *Tu Do* from those other boats? What anchors the *Tu Do* in Darling Harbour, preventing it from drifting on a current of sympathy and similitude towards its companion objects, those abject boats of the more recent past?

I suspect the answer lies in the practices of museology and heritage conservation that brought the *Tu Do* to Darling Harbour in the first place, that conserve it there and also somehow quarantine it from present-day events on the border. This has not, I believe, been the museum's intention. Rather, it seems to be a case of a convergence of conservation practice and the exclusionary policies of the current government, policies that have consigned the "other boats" to destruction and conveyed their passengers to camps where they exist in a permanent "state of exception" (Agamben 2005). Is it that the conservator's attention to detail mesmerizes us? Does it rivet our attention on the minutiae of the boat's material surface and discourage the drift of our thoughts towards, for example, the very similar wooden boat that was smashed on the rocks of Christmas Island during a storm on 15 December, 2010, killing 48 of the mostly Iranian and Iraqi asylum seekers aboard (Sonti *et al.* 2010)? Perhaps, but I suspect there is something more at work here.

The *Tu Do*'s passengers were allowed to step off their boat in 1977 into a state of asylum and inclusion among the nation's citizenry. Similarly, the boat itself was brought across the border, and once inside Australia it could be made over and repurposed as a heritage object enlisted in the collective task of defining the inside of the nation-state in relation to its outside. Unlikely as it may seem, the *Tu Do* now helps construct the geobody of a nation whose outer edges contemporary asylum-seeker boats are now prevented from touching, let alone penetrating. Processes of incorporation and expulsion are mutually implicated in contemporary capitalism, including in the arena of human migration (Agamben 1998; Mezzadra and Neilson 2013). Similarly, the nation-building work of the Australian heritage inventory, which now harbours the *Tu Do*, is implicated in the exclusion of the material world of undocumented migrants. Another, equally valid, way of viewing the reception of the *Tu Do* in Australia stems from Jacques Derrida's proposition that acts of welcoming are grounded in acts of appropriation:

> To dare to say welcome is to insinuate that perhaps one is at home here, that one knows what it means to be at home, and that at home one receives, invites, or offers hospitality, thus appropriating for oneself a place to welcome [*accueillir*] the other, or worse, welcoming the other in order to appropriate for oneself a place.
>
> (Derrida 1999, 15)

In this view, in the act of welcoming the *Tu Do* into the fold of Australia's heritage we did not just acquire a boat, we acquired a continent as "our place", authorizing us as owner-occupiers to close the door in the face of those we do not want.

Interpretive material developed by the Maritime Museum places the *Tu Do* in the context of the aftermath of the Vietnam War and the drama of the voyage of escape. The boat is sequestered in the 1970s, moored in a seemingly gentler time prior to the "securitization" of migration (Huysmans 2006) – a time when there was broad public sympathy in Australia for "boat people". As McNevin observes, contemporary asylum seekers attempting to reach

Figure 14.4. A Nissen hut at Scheyville, Sydney, 2015 (photograph by author).

Australia by sea are "no longer termed 'boat people', an idea suggesting homelessness and genuine need" (McNevin 2007, 622). Instead, they have been reclassified as "illegal".

Detention Camps as a Subject of Theatre Archaeology

In 1994 the Australian parliament voted to introduce mandatory detention for all those arriving in the country without a visa. This has led to the establishment of migrant detention centres, mostly located in remote inland settings or on offshore islands in situations where they are isolated from the national citizenry and the press.[2] Perhaps a century from now people will see this array of sites as marking the moment when the border as a geographic line became a diffuse borderzone. The externalization of "border protection" to detention camps at locations like Manus Island, Papua New Guinea, stretches Australia's continental border outward while, simultaneously, detention camps like that at Woomera in the South Australian arid zone stretch the border inwards. Like the *Tu Do*, the Woomera internees were transported deep within the national heartland, but unlike the *Tu Do* in Darling Harbour the internees exist in these sealed-off camps in a space that is "not-Australia" (Perera 2002). Both the quasi islands like Woomera (Papastergiadis 2006) and the actual islands like Nauru and Manus capture populations in a liminal space between home and arrival (Mountz 2011, 118).

---

2. For a current list of Australian migrant detention centres see: https://www.border.gov.au/Busi/Comp/
Immigration-detention/facilities. There is also a list on Wikipedia, which includes former detention camps
since closed: https://en.wikipedia.org/wiki/List_of_Australian_immigration_detention_facilities

As in the USA, heritage policies and practices in Australia create an artificial divide between the materiality of contemporary migration and that of historical migration (Byrne 2016). As settler nations, both countries willingly acknowledge and even celebrate the fact that they have been built upon immigration. Major heritage sites, such as Ellis Island in New York and the Quarantine Station at the entry to Sydney Harbour, have been preserved to commemorate that fact.[3] In Australia, heritage designation has also been accorded to several migrant "hostels" that in the 1940s and 1950s were home to the influx of immigrants from war-torn Europe until they found jobs and their own housing. The hostels were situated in rural locations and on the urban periphery. One of the accommodation blocks at the Bonegilla Migrant Camp in Victoria, in operation between 1947 and 1971, is on Australia's peak heritage inventory, the National Heritage List (Department of the Environment and Energy, Australia, n.d.). The material fabric of these structures, like their counterparts at the Scheyville post-War migrant hostel in Sydney (NSW National Parks and Wildlife Service n.d.) (Figure 14.4), are subject to a regime of respectful care by heritage conservation experts that cannot but contrast with the kind of attention given to contemporary "irregular" migrants. Equally, the spotlight which heritage designation shines on old objects – in this case, the hostels – contrasts with the effort to keep detention camps out of the public eye (the Border Act 2015 carries a prison sentence of up to two years for anyone working within the immigration detention system who publicly discloses conditions at the camps). The heritage interpretation material developed for the mid-twentieth-century migrant hostels makes no reference to contemporary migrant detention camps. Like the *Tu Do*, the hostels are anchored in the "time of heritage".

How would it be possible to suture heritage objects like the *Tu Do* and the mid-twentieth-century migrant hostels to their companion objects in the contemporary borderzone and thus to the comparative context of contemporary asylum seeking? Given the enactment over the last two decades of laws and policies designed to prevent the arrival in Australia of undocumented asylum seekers, it is difficult to imagine any government heritage agency or any museum or heritage organization dependent upon government funding taking on this work of comparison. What may be called for is a form of "theatre archaeology", to borrow Pearson and Shanks's (2001) term, in which archaeologists and heritage experts outside the government sphere engage in the recording of contemporary migrant detention camps and asylum-seeker boats, devoting to their materiality the same minutely attentive precision and care that has been accorded to the materiality of the *Tu Do* and the hostels. While this work would be unlikely to result in official heritage designation for the boats and camps it seems quite proper that, in this context, archaeologists should perform outside the official arena and even in defiance of it. There is obvious resonance here in the work Jason De León and his coworkers have carried out in the Sonoran Desert, Arizona, on traces left by undocumented border crossers (e.g., De León 2013; see also Stewart *et al.*, this volume). Working at an intimate scale with discarded shoes and socks (among other objects), their care-full attention to the "footprint" of migrant bodies counters the effacement of migrant suffering effected by the abstractions of "trash" discourse, and, in a highly political move, reinstates the corporeal individuality of the border crosser.

3. The Quarantine Station has a website: http://www.quarantinestation.com.au/

Conclusion

In asking "What anchors the *Tu Do*?", I hope to have shed light on the way that, as a border practice, heritage has in many cases helped valorize the inside–outside distinction made by the nation-state, and also on how it has narrativized and valorized a certain narrative of migration. The exclusions from the official heritage record, discussed above, need to be seen to be implicated in those acts of *inclusion* which, for example, brought the *Tu Do* to Darling Harbour.

The kind of archaeological recording work I argue for above would aim to encourage a kind of looking that would provoke the question, why not? Why *those* ones (the mid-twentieth-century migrant hostels) and not *these* (the more recent detention camps)? Migrant detention camps have been described as "places without a place" (Papastergiadis 2006, 434). The intention would be precisely to emplace them, to encourage an acceptance of them as *our* places while simultaneously making visible the processes of exemption which currently exclude them.

References

Agamben, G. 1998. *Homo Sacer: Sovereign Power and Bare Life*, translated by D. Heller-Roazen. Stanford, CA: Stanford University Press.

_____. 2005. *State of Exemption*, translated by K. Atttell. Chicago: University of Chicago Press.

Beyond Foreignness. 2015. "Fortress Australia: Asylum Seeker and Migrant Death Statistics." *Beyond Foreignness*, last updated August 2015. Available online: http://beyondforeignness.org/fortress-australia-asylum-seeker-and-migrant-death-and-detention-statistics

Byrne, D. 2016. "Transnational Flows and the Built Environment of Migration." *Journal of Ethnic and Migration Studies* 42 (14): 2360–2378. Available online: https://doi.org/10.1080/1369183X.2016.1205805

De León, J. 2013. "Undocumented Migration, Use Wear, and the Materiality of Habitual Suffering in the Sonoran Desert." *Journal of Material Culture* 18 (4): 321–345.

Department of the Environment and Energy, Australia. n.d. "National Heritage Places - Bonegilla Migrant Camp - Block 19." Department website: http://www.environment.gov.au/heritage/places/national/bonegilla

Derrida, J. 1999. *Adieu to Emmanuel Levinas*. Translated by P.-A. Brault and M. Naas. Stanford, CA: Stanford University Press.

Huysmans, J. 2006. *The Politics of Insecurity: Fear, Migration and Asylum in the EU*. London and New York: Routledge.

McNevin, A. 2007. "The Liberal Paradox and the Politics of Asylum in Australia." *Australian Journal of Political Science* 42 (4): 611–630. https://doi.org/10.1080/10361140701595791

Mezzadra, S. and B. Neilson. 2013. *Border as Method, or, the Multiplication of Labor*. Durham, NC: Duke University Press. https://doi.org/10.1215/9780822377542

Mountz, A. 2011. "The Enforcement Archipelago: Detention, Haunting, and Asylum on Islands." *Political Geography* 30 (3): 118-128. https://doi.org/10.1016/j.polgeo.2011.01.005

NSW National Parks and Wildlife Service. n.d. "Scheyville Camp Precinct: Scheyville National Park." Service website: http://www.nationalparks.nsw.gov.au/things-to-do/historic-buildings-places/scheyville-camp-precinct

Papastergiadis, N. 2006. "The Invasion Complex: The Abject Other and Spaces of Violence." *Geografiska Annaler* 88 (4): 429–442. https://doi.org/10.1111/j.0435-3684.2006.00231.x

Pearson, M. and M. Shanks. 2001. *Theatre/Archaeology*. London and New York: Routledge.

Perera, S. 2002. "What is a Camp?" *Borderlands* 1 (1). Available online: http://www.borderlands.net.au/vol1no1_2002/perera_camp.html

Sonti, C., D. Pepper, G. Kwek, G. Robinson, T. Hunter, K. Needham, P. Tatnell, and AAP. 2010. "27 People Confirmed Dead in Christmas Island Disaster." *WA Today*, 15 December. Available online: https://www.watoday.com.au/national/western-australia/27-people-confirmed-dead-in-christmas-island-disaster-20101215-18xkm.html

Thompson, S. 2006 "Objects Through Time: 1975 Tu Do Refugee Boat." Migration Heritage Centre website: http://www.migrationheritage.nsw.gov.au/exhibition/objectsthroughtime/tudo/

Denis Byrne is a Research Fellow at the Institute of Culture and Society, Western Sydney University, Australia. Address for correspondence: Western Sydney University, Locked Bag 1797, Penrith, NSW 2751, Australia. Email: d.byrne@westernsydney.edu.au

Chapter 15

"Heritage on Exile": Reflecting on the Roles and Responsibilities of Heritage Organizations towards Those Affected by Forced Migration

John Schofield

Greece, August 2015

On a small Greek Island, during my 2015 summer break, the impact and scale of the current refugee crisis suddenly hit home. Around mid-morning of another cloudless heat-filled day, the tranquillity of the bay was filled with the noise of a fast-approaching coastguard vessel. Barely waiting to tie up alongside the tiny and rather inadequate pier, the single pilot jumped ashore and ran to the taverna, returning shortly with as many water bottles as he could carry, followed by staff doing the same. The boat sped off. An hour later it returned more sedately, packed with exhausted women and children, each with a single day-pack, the type people take on budget airlines for a weekend away. As they crossed the beach, the children from the boat waved to us, the bemused holidaymakers. The beach felt very strange after they had left. No-one knew quite how to behave, or what to do next. An hour later the boat returned, this time with men on board. The same disembarkation ritual followed, as it did several times over the next few days. And as we left the island some days later, we saw these same people, and many more, camping on the harbourside, awaiting the next inter-island ferry that would take them on to Athens and from there, in many cases, to Germany.

This short contribution is a simple reflection on the current refugee crisis, grounded in an active interest in the contributions heritage organizations can or should make towards ameliorating life-changing impacts on people directly affected by situations beyond their control. It also reflects on a career working within a UK heritage sector that can appear to me sometimes rather detached from contemporary life, or slow to respond to it. While recognizing the importance of heritage in post-war reconstruction (and recent UK government initiatives address this, in the form of, for example, the Cultural Protection Fund[1]), this chapter concerns the people themselves, forced to escape conflict and seek safe haven elsewhere at

---

1. See https://www.gov.uk/government/news/new-scheme-to-protect-cultural-sites-from-destruction

the moment of crisis, when they are at their most vulnerable: disorientated, traumatized, and isolated. They, it seems to me, are the immediate concern. Post-war reconstruction (or debates about whether this is appropriate) can follow later.

Working with homeless communities (e.g. Kiddey and Schofield 2011), and with people from socially deprived backgrounds (e.g. Lashua *et al.* 2010; Schofield and Morrissey 2013), I have seen first-hand how activism amongst archaeologists and heritage practitioners can soften the impact of unwanted change, or of becoming marginalized by or in society. (And by activism in this sense I mean being active, putting other people first, and attempting to use the subject we are most familiar with for the betterment of others. Larry Zimmerman *et al.* [2010] referred to the need sometimes for a "translational approach", in which "expertise" is given over to the participants to enhance their sense of ownership.) De León's work is an obvious example of ways in which archaeological and anthropological practices can contribute to understanding migration (Gokee and De León 2014; De León and Wells 2015; see also Stewart *et al.*, this volume), in this case across the Mexico–USA border. Such activism in these various contexts has created a sense of inclusivity and opportunity out of adversity. The 2005 Faro Convention on the Cultural Value of Heritage for Society (Council of Europe 2009) formulates a position whereby "heritage" and the rights of all people to participate in it are not only central to society, but are also an essential human right. Given the success of these previous projects, this would seem a particularly relevant contextual framework for working with Europe's refugees, as well as other minority and excluded groups.

So why is it that many heritage organizations, like Historic England to take an obvious example – established to "look after England's historic environment, [to] champion historic places, helping people understand, value and care for them" – appear reluctant to adopt such principles, and to push an agenda to which they could make such a distinctive and telling contribution? Why is this not a priority, not least given the emphasis often placed on England's diverse pasts, on the many and varied cultural contributions that have created the rich heritage which so many people now enjoy? Or should we accept, rather, that this is not an appropriate or necessary role for such organizations at all, and that projects and initiatives of this type should originate at the grassroots, not through authority?

To give some specific examples of what can be achieved by heritage organizations requires a consideration not only of the forced migrations emphasized in this collection, but also those which are unforced, where pull factors may weigh more heavily than those pushing people to new horizons. The social conditions of course are very different in these two sets of circumstances, but the examples outlined briefly above demonstrate that it can be done through conventional archaeological or heritage practice. Some 15 years ago, the Australian Heritage Commission released its *Guide to Migrant Heritage Places in Australia* (2001). In his Foreword, Peter King, the Commission's then Chairman, noted how it had recognized a problem (that the wider community was not aware of the significance attached to places by people recently arrived in Australia) and responded to it by funding a project to focus on post-World War Two immigration. The *Guide* explains what is meant by "significance" and "heritage registers" before defining a "migrant heritage place" and explaining how to assess such places. Meetings are recommended to help facilitate this process – meetings which themselves can be used to build identity and community that may previously have been lacking. Questions within the guidance included "the heritage of an immigrant group in Australia before [they] arrived" and "experiences in Australia".

There are of course critical issues to be addressed, such as whether there will always be benefits for people in participating with state-led heritage initiatives and that the stance of government agencies and heritage bodies towards present-day migrants can be very different (see Byrne, this volume). There are questions also about authority (e.g. Smith 2006), and the role of the expert (Schofield 2014), as leader or as facilitator. The "Migrant Heritage Places" example gave migrant communities in Australia the opportunity to promote the significance of those places that

> tell the history of migration in Australia. The history of migration is a valuable aspect of Australia's heritage. There are many places that are important to different migrant groups that may not be known to the wider community, such as places of worship, places of work, local shopping areas or places associated with people or events that have significance for particular migrant communities.
>
> (Australian Heritage Commission 2001, 9)

This may not be the most original or creative approach for documenting place attachment within the context of contemporary forced migration, and it does pre-date social media, but it does nonetheless demonstrate a history of good practice that may not be fully realized.

The following year, the Australian Heritage Commission extended beyond this generic guide with *Tracking the Dragon: A Guide for Finding and Assessing Chinese Australian Heritage Places* (2002). Meanwhile, the National Parks and Wildlife Service in New South Wales articulated a methodology for assessing the relationship of both Macedonian (Thomas 2001) and Vietnamese (Thomas 2002) communities to their newly familiar landscapes. The Macedonian experience is particularly relevant. Read (1996) has paid close attention to the trauma of lost places. In the case of the Macedonian community, the national parks around Sydney came to represent the "lost" and socially meaningful landscapes of rural Macedonia, into which the significance of social occasions and community building had been deeply woven. But the way Macedonian immigrants used their new environment in traditional ways was not always to the liking of the settled (including the indigenous) population. Thomas's (2001) study presents a methodology through which these tensions can be explored and resolved for mutual and long-lasting benefit. As Thomas states, this example shows how "people and the environment are inextricable", and that "maintaining cohesion was a way of ensuring some degree of continuity in a world where everything had changed." As an example, he cites parkland as having "played a unique role in consolidating the feeling of being Macedonian in Australia" (Thomas 2001, 92). This refers closely to a concept that appears prominent within contexts of upheaval and instability: that of ontological security, which Giddens (1991) referred to as the sense of order and continuity in relation to an individual's experiences, and which Grenville (2007) applied to the built environment. In short, ontological security can give heightened significance to fixed places in landscapes and social states of flux.

In Greece last summer I wondered briefly how much notice people took of the beach on which they finally and safely arrived in Europe. Listening to interviews a few weeks later of Syrian refugees at Munich railway station, I heard several talk about their journey. Most could not remember the name of the island where they came ashore, or indeed many of the countries they had passed through *en route*. Maybe the journey is always a bit of a blur, especially when it is long and traumatic. One example of this heritage of transition is Pier 21 in Halifax, Canada, where between 1928 and 1971 over a million migrants entered the country. This is now the Canadian Museum of Immigration, a popular tourist destination and archive, and a place to which many of Canada's migrant population feel a strong sense of attachment, perhaps because it is a specific and tangible point of arrival – a threshold of sorts.[2] Ellis Island in New York is another example. One thinks also of the vehicles and vessels in which journeys were made. Many of these boats now lie abandoned on Malta's shoreline. The *Tu Do*, a boat used by the so-called Vietnamese Boat People in 1977, is now part of the Australian National Maritime Museum's floating collection (see Byrne, this volume).[3]

Gard'ner's (2004) study of heritage significance in the East End of London makes a related point: here designated historic buildings in the area mean little to the c. 61% Bengalee population that has occupied the area since the 1960s. As Gard'ner describes it, this migration began with Bengali-speaking merchant seamen arriving in the docks of London's East End during the 1960s, opting to stay in Britain to escape the political tension with the Karachi government over Bangladeshi independence (Gard'ner 2004, 76). Their families joined them, and so the population grew. As with Pier 21, there appears a strong association here for these migrants with places connected with their immigration. Particular value is attached by the Bengalee community to community centres and buildings used by community groups. As Gard'ner states:

> [T]he reasons for the [importance of these buildings] to the community include providing a venue for community, cultural and musical events as well as an array of services including immigration and general advice, training and employment counselling, and day care for both the young and the elderly. (Gard'ner 2004, 79)

Returning to the examples of activist archaeology presented at the outset, the homeless heritage project is perhaps a parallel to what might be possible with displaced peoples – people lacking most of their possessions, feeling the loss of home and community, yet searching for some new sense of stability and belonging in an unfamiliar world. In the fieldwork conducted amongst homeless communities, there was crucially a translation of authority and expertise from "us" as heritage practitioners to "them" as members of the communities with whom we hoped to build relationships of trust and understanding. We gave them the methods (the tools) and taught them how to use them. The results (and the people we worked with to achieve them) were inspiring, in spite of the truly awful experiences that had shaped many of their lives. Language may be an additional barrier in cases of migration, and some

---

2. The museum maintains a designated website about the location: https://www.pier21.ca/home

3. Details of the boat's restoration can be found on the museum's website: http://stories.anmm.gov.au/tudo/restoring-tu-do/

cultural reference points may be less familiar, but with those exceptions, much of the same methodology could apply. And by heritage we can also mean its intangible manifestations, many of which have long traditions of creating unity and cohesion amongst diverse communities. One thinks immediately of music and of cooking. I recently heard of an example in Stockholm in which local women shared cookery sessions with migrant women, learning and practising each other's culinary skills together.

As an example of what might be possible, I return to Historic England, my own country's lead heritage agency and the British Government's statutory advisor on heritage matters in England. I wonder what contributions such an organization could helpfully make, and with a degree of urgency, if indeed such contributions are even appropriate. There is a question here concerning the organization's mandate to act (under the terms of the 1983 National Heritage Act), which limits its options and no doubt explains its lack of close attention to intangible heritage. That said, there do appear to be possibilities. Within the context of its mandate, Historic England currently has seven Corporate Aims:

Aim 1 Champion England's historic environment.

Aim 2 Identify and protect England's special historic buildings and places.

Aim 3 Promote change that safeguards historic buildings and places.

Aim 4 Help those who care for historic buildings and places, including owners, local authorities, communities and volunteers.

Aim 5 Engage with the whole community to foster the widest possible sense of ownership of our national inheritance of buildings and places.

Aim 6 Support the work of the English Heritage Trust in managing and safeguarding the National Heritage Collection of buildings and monuments and to achieve financial self-sufficiency.

Aim 7 Work effectively, efficiently and transparently.

(Historic England 2016, 2)

The Historic England *Action Plan 2015-2018* maps an earlier version of this list (in which just five aims were given) onto specific Objectives, and while not explicit or obvious, there are hooks onto which projects and initiatives that relate to "migrant (or refugee) heritage" could be hung. One opportunity perhaps falls under the Corporate Plan Objective 1.3, to "Use our research, archive collections and education programme to engage and enthuse people about the history of places" (Historic England 2015, 6–7). Exhibitions and publications are given as examples of how this might be achieved and have impact. But notwithstanding the dangers of being authoritative (Smith 2006), one wonders how migrants/refugees, recently arrived and feeling isolated and disorientated, would respond to any attempt to promote understanding through outputs that explicitly or otherwise promote "English" heritage, even where "non-English" heritage was clearly the focus of enquiry. This dilemma aligns closely of course with debates on nationalism, and on the idea of the nation and of national borders now challenged by the migrant/refugee (e.g. Lechte and Newman 2012, following Agamben 1995 and ultimately Arendt 1994 [1943]).

Corporate Plan Objectives 2.3 ("Improve the National Heritage List for England to make it more useful and accessible and enable others to add content") and 2.2 ("Identify, record and define the significance of heritage that is poorly understood, under-represented or most at risk") may provide further opportunities, aligned with the examples of migrant heritage described earlier from Australia. Here there could be opportunities for constructive creative interventions not unlike Gard'ner's (2004) study in the East End of London, shaping methodologies, creating toolkits, engaging community groups of all kinds and in a diversity of cultural and environmental settings to assess significance. Yet this all assumes some familiarity with and interest in the local area in which refugees find themselves. This interest takes time to develop, like a patina. Of more use initially perhaps would be initiatives that facilitate discussions amongst groups that create a sense of common heritage lost or left behind, of what really matters, both in terms of places and things, but also the things people carried on their journeys – mementoes, photographs of people and places – accepting of course that much of this material will be stored digitally, allowing a greater weight of memory to accompany people on their journeys. With the built environment in mind, one might focus on particular and familiar building types or places (e.g. mosques or markets – see Gard'ner [2004] again for examples of both), and the ways people respond to them, and the reminders they evoke (but see Mire 2007 for an alternative view). Intangible heritage is more challenging given that Historic England's mandate only extends to "ancient monuments, historic buildings and conservation areas", yet exploring associations between the built environment and associated traditions remains a possibility.

In responding to social crises it is understandable for heritage organizations to focus attention on the built environment, its security during conflict and its role in post-conflict reconstruction. Heritage is, after all, largely place- and thing-centred, at least for established heritage organizations. Yet as we have seen, the 2005 Faro Convention promotes an approach to heritage that is people-centred and focuses on the social value of heritage for "everyone in society". It also concerns the making of heritage, not just the protection of it. Maybe it will take time for heritage organizations, often established by statute and with a specific mandate, to have the capacity, skills, and the opportunity to act in response to human crises, and in the "spirit" of Faro (Schofield 2015a, 2015b). But, unfortunately, the nature of human crises is such that waiting is not an option. Or maybe this is not a matter for politically aligned or politically dependent organizations at all.

As long as politicians (and arguably also the wider public) exhibit mixed feelings about forced migration, bodies like Historic England will deliberately avoid the issue, as being too contentious. Such organizations are, after all, dependent upon politicians for their support and funding. Perhaps this is why the sector needs independent activists, to say the uncomfortable things! Equally, we should all remember what Hannah Arendt said over 70 years ago, that '[t]he comity of European peoples went to pieces when, and because, it allowed its weakest member to be excluded and persecuted' (Arendt 1994 [1943], 119) – not least in the light of Britain's recent vote to leave the European Union.

Postscript

One time, back in the eighteenth century perhaps, ancestors on my mother's side arrived in the UK on a ship. The precise journey they had taken and the reasons for it are unknown, although I intend to find out. All I know is that they had the name Davidovic, and came from

Belarus. Davidovic was translated on arrival into "Davson" (perhaps an error, as "Davidson" is the more usual translation), this being my mother's maiden name. There is also a rumour (and one wonders where it would have come from, if not true) that their journey had brought them via Papua New Guinea. Thinking about the current crisis, the migration of people – forced and otherwise – and the tensions and difficulties that movement inevitably creates (alongside opportunities of course) have caused me to think further about this story since the events and experiences witnessed last summer. I am also more determined than ever to establish the facts behind it.

Acknowledgments

I am indebted to Dan Hull, Rob Lennox, and Yannis Hamilakis for helpfully commenting on an earlier draft.

References

Agamben, G. 1995. "We Refugees." *Symposium: A Quarterly Journal in Modern Literatures* 49 (2): 114–119. https://doi.org/10.1080/00397709.1995.10733798

Arendt, H. 1994 [1943]. "We Refugees." In *Altogether Elsewhere: Writers on Exile*, edited by M. Robinson, 110–119. London: Faber and Faber.

Australian Heritage Commission. 2001. *A Guide: How to Find Your Heritage Places – Migrant Heritage Places in Australia*. Canberra: Australian Heritage Commission. Available online: https://www.environment.gov.au/resource/migrant-heritage-places-australia

_____. 2002. *Tracking the Dragon: A Guide for Finding and Assessing Chinese Australian Heritage Places*. Canberra: Australian Heritage Commission. Available online: https://www.environment.gov.au/resource/tracking-dragon

Council of Europe. 2009. *Heritage and Beyond*. Strasbourg: Council of Europe. Available online: http://www.coe.int/t/dg4/cultureheritage/heritage/identities/PatrimoineBD_en.pdf

De León, J. and M. Wells. 2015. *The Land of Open Graves: Living and Dying on the Migrant Trail*. Oakland: University of California Press.

Gard'ner, J. M. 2004. "Heritage Protection and Social Inclusion: A Case Study from the Bangladeshi Community of East London." *International Journal of Heritage Studies* 10 (1): 75–92. https://doi.org/10.1080/1352725032000194259

Giddens, A. 1991. *Modernity and Self-Identity: Self and Society in the Late Modern Age*. Cambridge: Polity.

Gokee, C. D. and J. De León. 2014. "Sites of Contention: Archaeological Classification and Political Discourse in the US-Mexican Borderlands." *Journal of Contemporary Archaeology* 1 (1): 133–163. https://doi.org/10.1558/jca.v1i1.133

Grenville, J. 2007. "Conservation as Psychology: Ontological Security and the Built Environment." *International Journal of Heritage Studies* 13 (6): 447–461. https://doi.org/10.1080/13527250701570614

Historic England. 2015. *Action Plan 2015-2018*. Available online: https://content.historicengland.org.uk/images-books/publications/he-action-plan-2015-18/he-action-plan-2015-18.pdf/

_____. 2016. *Three Year Corporate Plan 2016-19*. Available online: https://content.historicengland.org.uk/images-books/publications/he-corp-plan-2016-19/three-year-corp-plan-2016-19.pdf/

Kiddey, R. and J. Schofield, 2011. "Embrace the Margins: Adventures in Archaeology and Homelessness." *Public Archaeology* 10 (1): 4–22. https://doi.org/10.1179/175355311X12991501673140

Lashua, B., S. Cohen, and J. Schofield. 2010. "Popular Music, Mapping and the Characterization of Liverpool." *Popular Music History* 4 (2): 126–144. https://doi.org/10.1558/pomh.v4i2.126

Lechte, J. and S. Newman. 2012. "Agamben, Arendt and Human Rights: Bearing Witness to the Human." *European Journal of Social Theory* 15 (4): 522–536. https://doi.org/10.1177/1368431011432376

Mire, S. 2007. "Preserving Knowledge, Not Objects: A Somali Perspective for Heritage Management and Archaeological Research." *African Archaeological Review* 24 (3): 49–71. https://doi.org/10.1007/s10437-007-9016-7

Read, P. 1996. *Returning to Nothing: The Meaning of Lost Places*. Cambridge: Cambridge University Press. https://doi.org/10.1017/CBO9781139085069

Schofield, J., ed. 2014. Who Needs Experts? Counter-mapping Cultural Heritage. Farnham, UK: Ashgate.

_____. 2015a. "Forget about 'Heritage': Place Ethics and the Faro Convention." In *The Ethics of Cultural Heritage*, edited by T. Ireland and J. Schofield, 197–209. New York: Springer.

_____. 2015b. "'Thinkers and Feelers': A Psychological Perspective on Heritage and Society." In *The Palgrave Handbook of Contemporary Heritage Research*, edited by E. Waterton and S. Watson, 417–425. Basingstoke, UK: Palgrave. https://doi.org/10.1057/9781137293565_26

_____. and E. Morrissey. 2013. *Strait Street: Malta's "Red-light District" Revealed*. Malta: Midsea Books.

Smith, L. 2006. *Uses of Heritage*. London and New York: Routledge.

Thomas, M. 2001. *A Multicultural Landscape: National Parks and the Macedonian Experience*. Hurstville, Australia: NSW National Parks and Wildlife Service.

_____. 2002. *Moving Landscapes: National Parks and the Vietnamese Experience.* Hurstville, Australia: NSW National Parks and Wildlife Service.

Zimmerman, L., C. Singleton, and J. Welch. 2010. Activism and Creating a Translational Archaeology of Homelessness. *World Archaeology* 42 (3): 443–454. https://doi.org/10.1080/00438243.2010.497400

John Schofield is Professor and Head of Department in Archaeology at the University of York. Address for correspondence: Department of Archaeology University of York, King's Manor, York, YO1 7EP, UK. Email: john.schofield@york.ac.uk

Chapter 16

Digging Up Sounds, Images, and Words Together in Athens: Conversations with Kurosh Dadgar (Hossein Shabani) and Saeid Ghasemi on Refugee Experiences and Self-Representation through Art and Heritage Management

Christina Thomopoulos in collaboration with Kurosh Dadgar (Hossein Shabani), Esra Dogan, Saeid Ghasemi, Baba Safar, and Sophia Thomopoulos

We have met through a series of chance encounters in Athens. It is late summer 2016, early fall.

Kurosh and I met several months ago through my good friend Lauretta, who is one of the founding members of the United African Women Organization of Greece. Kurosh (a nickname; his full name is Hossein Shabani) is from Iran and has been living as a political refugee in Greece for a little less than a decade now. Recently he gave a lecture at the Silent University Athens Assembly – a platform for knowledge exchange between refugees, migrants, and locals. Together with his lecture "Contemporary Iran and its Cultural Landscape",[1] Kurosh set up a impromptu exhibition of art works, paintings, and assemblages he has begun making out of found materials and objects in Athens. Baba Safar, an English professor and poet from Iran who had studied in the UK decades ago, gave his input for the curating of the impromptu exhibition, while also assisting in the selection of Kurosh's yellow tie.

Saeid and Kurosh met in Athens three months ago. Saeid grew up in Tehran, and has been in Greece for about seven months. He and Kurosh have become good friends. Perhaps Kurosh is something like a mentor to Saeid, who is 17 and has been learning Greek in the hope of starting university in Greece to study music. Saeid writes poetry, which he hopes to perform soon with music.

Our discussion, spanning across English, Greek, and Farsi, began between friends in a coffee shop in Kipseli, one hot August day: Kurosh, Saeid, Esra, Sophia, Baba Safar, and myself started talking about ideas regarding what to contribute to the Forum on Archaeologies of Forced and Undocumented Migration Open Call. The text that follows shares parts of our shared discussions, with myself coordinating and also reflecting on this process.

---

1. Website: http://thesilentuniathens.tumblr.com. For an interesting critical response to the project see Veronica Tello's article "Performing Crisis: In critical solidarity with the Silent University" (2016).

Reading Together: An Open Call

We started our first meeting by reading in English the open call for contributions which led to the initial Journal publication and to this book, with Baba Safar translating into Farsi for Saeid (Figure 16.1). After reading aloud, we went around sharing thoughts, reactions, and ideas. I knew that sending a submission would require a collective thinking process, a time and space to understand more deeply the questions of the call, who the call is from, and who the call is for.

Mid-way through the discussion Saeid seemed worried. He asked if there were any topics off limits, if there was anything he should "avoid discussing". Saeid replied that he was an atheist, with a smile on his face.

Saeid's expression changed as he continued, telling us stories of his guitar being confiscated by the police when he was out with friends in Tehran, in Parvaz ("Flying") Park. In Iran, instruments are not meant to be seen in public, where they have the power to open people's minds, Saeid told us. After hours of pleading at the police station in Tehran, Saeid finally got his guitar back. "Next time we will kill your guitar", he remembers the police told him.

This reminded me of other histories, such as that of the Greek Rebetiko (called by many "the Blues of Greece"), which were prohibited in 1936 under the dictatorship of Metaxas. Saeid added: "The Gipsy Kings were allowed to perform in Tehran, because people would not understand their Spanish lyrics. Artists who want to make people understand more are not allowed" (Figure 16.2). In more recent memory, this reminds me of the chasing of street musicians and performers by the police in Athens in 2014. I witnessed one occurrence of this on Ermou Street near Syntagma, some years ago.

Through Saeid's question on "off-limits topics", and on hearing the story of his confiscated guitar, I understood that our group submission was more than just a discussion. It was a way to feel out the limits of speech itself, of the speakable and unspeakable in different contexts of place and time.

At various moments in our discussion we paused to discuss issues of censorship, to ensure everything was "OK".

Singing in Iran, Writing in Camps in Greece

In the midst of a bustling summer night, Saeid shared a poem he had written[2] after seeing a photograph of Aylan Kurdi (Figure 16.3); the words had been translated from Farsi into Greek. He wants to create a melody for it to be performed with music. On his cell phone Saeid showed us a video of a music performance in which he had sung and played guitar, recorded three months before leaving Tehran for Europe.

He told us a story from the camp in Athens where he had befriended a woman, a mother from Syria who each night mourned for her two lost children, killed in Syria. The memory of their lifeless bodies being brought to her haunted her through the nights at the camp. Saeid sang a song about it, telling her he would try to sing this song so that her story is not forgotten. She thanked him.

Saeid talked about the importance of having space to create, which he is missing dearly. He wants to have a space to write and make music, and, as noted above, to go to university in

---

2. The poem can be heard here: https://journals.equinoxpub.com/index.php/JCA/article/view/34227/31175

Forum: Archaeologies of forced and undocumented migration

Journal of Contemporary Archaeology

Call for contributions is now open for a special issue of the *Journal of Contemporary Archaeology*, which focuses on Archaeologies of forced and undocumented migration. Guest editor is Yannis Hamilakis. The deadline for submissions is 30 June 2016.

The political philosopher Giorgio Agamben in this 1995 article, "We refugees", elaborates on a discussion which started by Hanna Arendt in her 1943 essay with the same title; the topic is the status of the refugee today. While Arendt, however, had in mind the Jewish exiles from Nazi Germany, Agamben's thought is haunted by the contemporary migrants to the European Union and to the west in general. Both Arendt and Agamben attempt to rescue migrants and refugees from the state of victimhood, and emphasise instead their positive and even revolutionary status, as the figures that throw into disarray the status quo of the nation-state. Migrants embody, according to them, a new kind of citizen who demands to be accepted as a human being first and foremost, and not as member of a national body, not as someone who exists because s/he is inscribed by birth and descent into a national community.

Whether one agrees or not with the above thesis, it is evident that migration today is much more than a matter of regulation, law, administration, prevention and persecution on the one hand, and a matter of compassion and active solidarity, on the other. It is first and foremost a phenomenon that holds a mirror up to western societies in modernity, posing questions about their constitution as a "civilized", political community of national subjects, albeit one with a heritage of colonialism, racism, and national violence, as well as (elusive) aspirations of freedom and equality, at least of all members of the national community.

One way or another, forced and often undocumented migration is one of the key matters of concern for societies today. And while the topic is at the centre of attention and study in a wide range of scholarly fields, the materiality of the phenomenon and its sensorial and mnemonic dimensions are barely understood and analysed. Anthropological archaeologists and other material culture specialists, including specialists on museum and commemorative practices, can contribute immensely to a new understanding of the phenomenon. Forced and undocumented migration is a material and sensorial experience first and foremost: it is the lack of specific pieces of paper that results in an alien status, a status of non-existence as political beings; these people thus become 'bare lives', deprived of the right to have a 'bios', the life of a recognized citizen. The material possessions of undocumented migrants, the things they bring with them, are crucially important in the journey from the homeland to the country of destination: very few objects, the bare essentials, to make the journey as light as possible, and amongst them material things of emotional and mnemonic weight. And then, there are the material artefacts such as boats and dinkies, life vests, discarded rucksacks, which are today scattered all over, in regions such as the Mediterranean or the Arizona desert. In some cases, these artefacts become the subject of art projects or commemorative and museum exhibitions, and in others they become the raw materials for inventive initiatives, as they are transformed into useful, biographical artefacts, carrying with them the affective memory of the migration experience. Finally, there are the morbid material remnants of interrupted lives, be they shoes and clothing of those who did not make the crossing, or the anonymous and austere graves on a border island.

But even from the point of view of states and other apparatuses, it is the materialization of legality/illegality and of prevention that has become much more prominent. Borders have acquired a more visible and tactile presence than ever before in modern times; walls and fences are being erected along borderlines, and patrols are in operation in land and in sea. Furthermore, large sums of money have been devoted to creating facilities for migrants, but how does the materiality and spatial grid of these structures shape migrant experience? How do undocumented migrants maintain a sensorial and affective connection with a homeland, and how do their own things and objects, the ones they brought with them and the ones they have produced in their new home, shape their mnemonic world?

Forced and undocumented migration cannot always be expressed in words, but it can be evoked in things, in sensorial and affective experiences and gestures, in non-linguistic utterances. Or in other cases, migrants do not speak any of the languages understood in their entry or destination country, or prefer not to talk, because if they do they risk deportation to a country or region in which such language is spoken. In all these cases, materiality and sensoriality are the primary means of understanding the phenomenon.

And yet, with one or two exceptions, such as the pioneering and highly important Undocumented Migration Project in the US-Mexican border, there are still very few attempts by archaeologists and material culture specialists to engage with the phenomenon in a politically and ethically sensitive matter.

This forum will thus explore the diverse intellectual, methodological, ethical, and political frameworks for an archaeology of forced and undocumented migration in the present, through both reflective/ideas pieces and case studies. We invite short contributions from archaeologists, anthropologists, other specialists, artists, activists, including by migrants themselves, in different media (text-based essays of c. 1000-3000 words, photographic and photo-poetic essays, poetry, drawings, cartoons, sound-installations, other artwork), addressing some of the questions below:

-How can we record, explore, and understand the materiality of the experience of forced and undocumented migration today, in its diverse forms?

-How can we communicate such work to scholars and to various publics?

-What kind of theoretical and methodological stances can we deploy, avoiding the instrumentalisation of the phenomenon for purely academic purposes, and the aestheticisation of an often painful and tragic experience?

Contributions will be peer reviewed, and multi-media submissions will be publicised on the journal website. For author guidelines see: https://journals.equinoxpub.com/index.php/JCA

Send enquiries and submissions to: y.hamilakis@soton.ac.uk

Figure 16.1. Archaeologies of forced and undocumented migration: call for contributions.

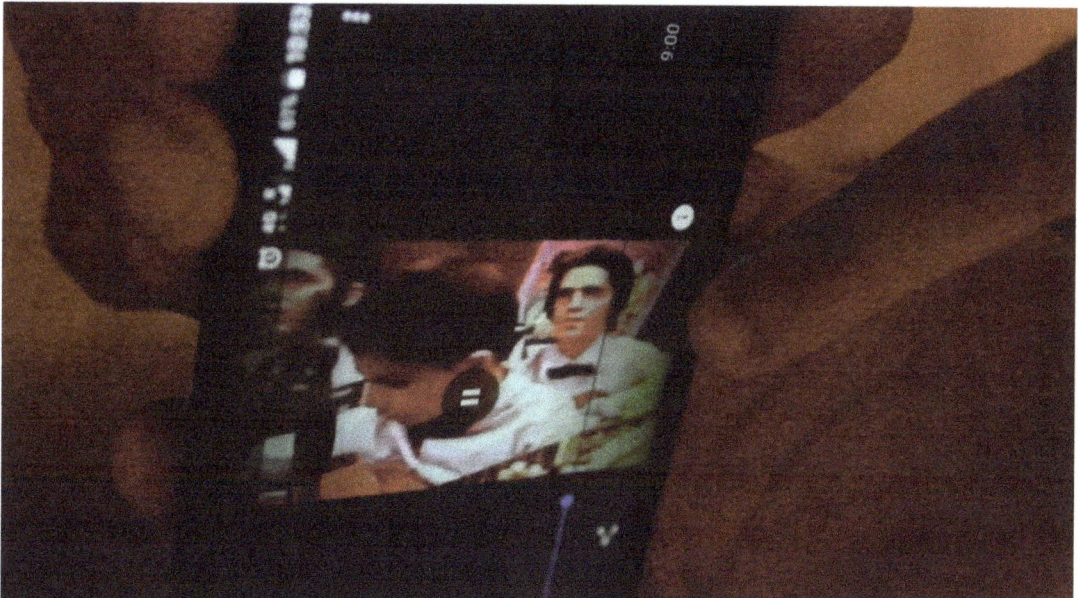

Figure 16.2. The Gipsy Kings on a mobile display (photograph by Christina Thomopoulos).

Greece. "The camps are so dark", he said, telling us he is yearning to find ways to break into local life, to meet local musicians in Athens. "You cannot be all day with refugees", he said, "you need to find the daily life of the place where you live."

But he tries to face life in the camp with humour. One night he told us he was up late writing in the cramped room he stays in at the camp. Someone in his room got up and demanded Saeid turn off the light, shouting "Turn off the light! Turn off the light now!" Saeid had replied, "I am writing. I am a prophet. I'm getting a message from God now, which I will deliver to you tomorrow morning. Silence so I can continue." The irritated roommate had responded, "Oh, OK then! Yes, in that case do keep the light on!"

Found Materials of Athens Turn into Art

Kurosh has been living in Greece for seven years, but he didn't always make art. "When you are a refugee you take care of the children", he said, suggesting the many practical matters of life which often don't allow much time and space to create for oneself. Kurosh uses found materials around Athens, forming textures and images that invite the eye and mind to wander. At Foivos Café, Kurosh shared some of his thoughts in our discussion, with Esra asking about his process:

Esra: Did you make art in Iran?

Kurosh: I was a filmmaker in Iran, working in Television Production. In Athens I began painting and designing. I started making this new work nearly two years ago.

E: When was the first time you started to paint? Do you remember?

K: For almost four years in Athens I was devoted to raising my children. But after they left to join their mothers in Sweden, I started to find my new way of working.

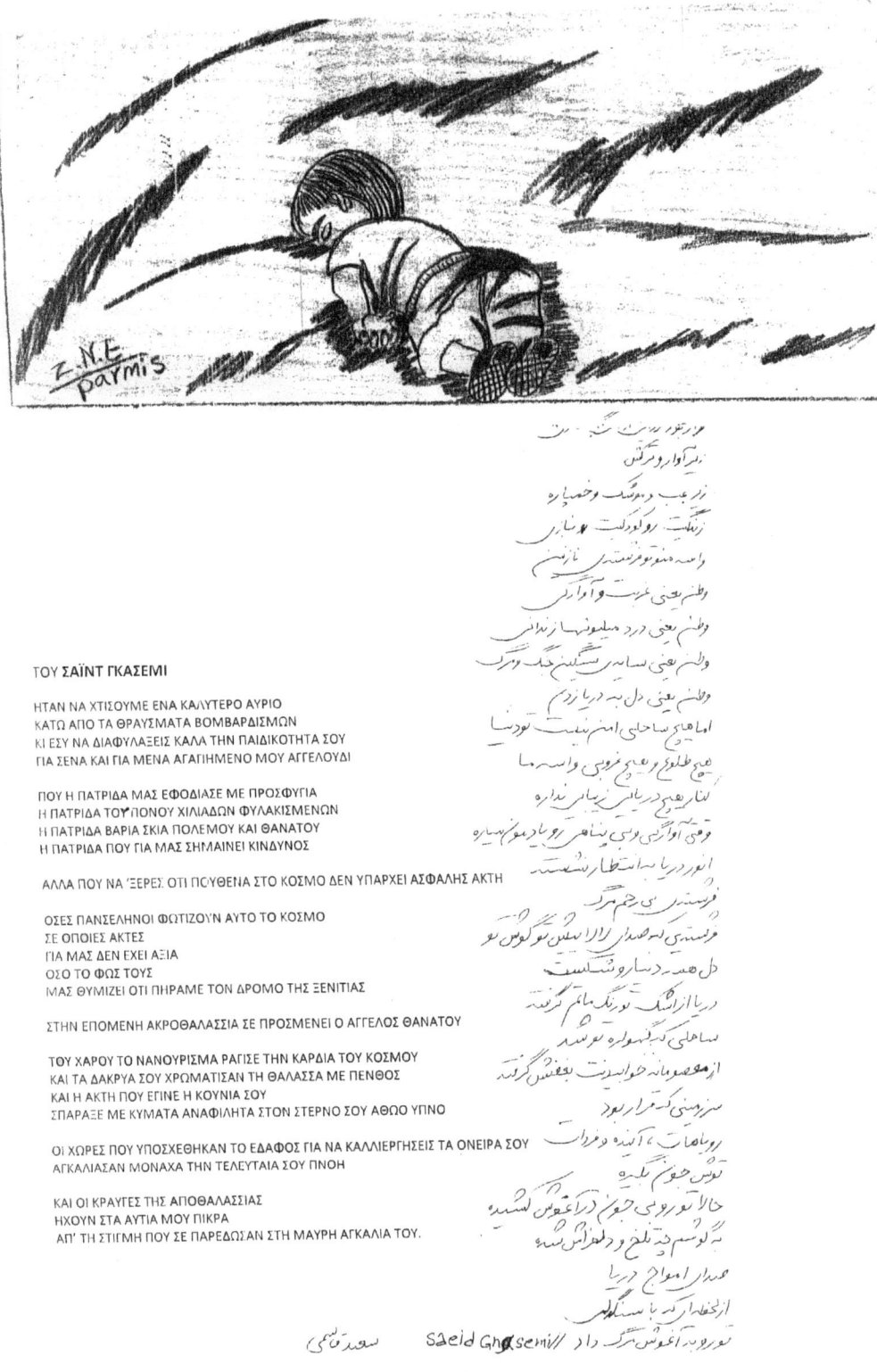

Figure 16.3. Poem by Saeid Ghasemi, with a drawing by Z. N. E. Parmis.

It is difficult to not see my family, but sometimes, this separation leads you to find yourself. It was good fortune when I started painting two years ago.

E: What triggered you to start?

K: As I was starting I found and made logos [signs/symbols], some signs and shapes I create, that repeat in all my works. Many of the logos/signs I find in Greece are similar to ones one finds in Iran. I make faces, which are also a type of logo, and which I believe are the most complete part of body. I invite people to my house to see my work and each person interprets it differently, it's surreal. According to your imagination you can receive art in many ways.

E: What feeling do you have when you make your work?

K: I enjoy creation. Art is creation. But as all artists I want to share it, to see what an audience takes from what I make. In the future I am thinking of doing an exhibition.

Baba Safar: [Theatrically tears up a napkin on the table at the coffee shop.] What do you see here? You can find many faces in there, a lion, a tiger, a… many meanings. What does the image say to you? Maybe your image, your thinking is different. It depends on your imagination, what you think you see.

K: Creation is my daily life. Sometimes I make work in five minutes, sometimes three hours and some days.
   I have the face of Lion.
   To give the sense of being free.
   I am a neo-surrealist. I am a refugee using unusual materials to make artwork [Figures 16.4–13].

As the night arrives it got louder in the café, and we headed to my house, where we all continued talking together.

In the Artist's Home Studio

The next day we met in Kurosh's home studio in Exarcheia. The space is simple, on the ground floor. In traditional Persian style, we took off our shoes. Kurosh gave me a pair of indoor slippers to wear. He said he was surprised that at my house I also adopted the "Persian style" of taking off shoes when entering the home.

To an outsider it may not be clear if it is a home first and a studio second, or a studio first and a home second. Wherever creation and life go together this hierarchy ceases to exist, and so it undoes itself here as well. A tray for cooking here is also a painting; the *akaliptos* (common courtyard between apartment buildings) becomes a temporary exhibition space; discarded finds from Athenian streets turn into surfaces of imagination and expression. Found objects from public zones are arranged into spontaneous assemblages. No surface too noble, nor unimportant. Through such a text as I am now writing, and the transmission of digital and printed data, texture and material is lost. I hope words can translate at least some feeling of space and time that afternoon in one small corner of Athens.

As we spoke Kurosh created a live exhibition, where logic and emotion go together. Expression is not explained or justified, but rather felt and shared.

Figure 16.4. Artwork by Kurosh Dadgar (Hossein Shabani).

Figure 16.5. *Another Face* (photograph by Christina Thomopoulos).

Figure 16.6. Artwork by Kurosh Dadgar (Hossein Shabani) (photograph by Christina Thomopoulos).

Figure 16.7. Artwork by Kurosh Dadgar (Hossein Shabani) (photograph by Christina Thomopoulos).

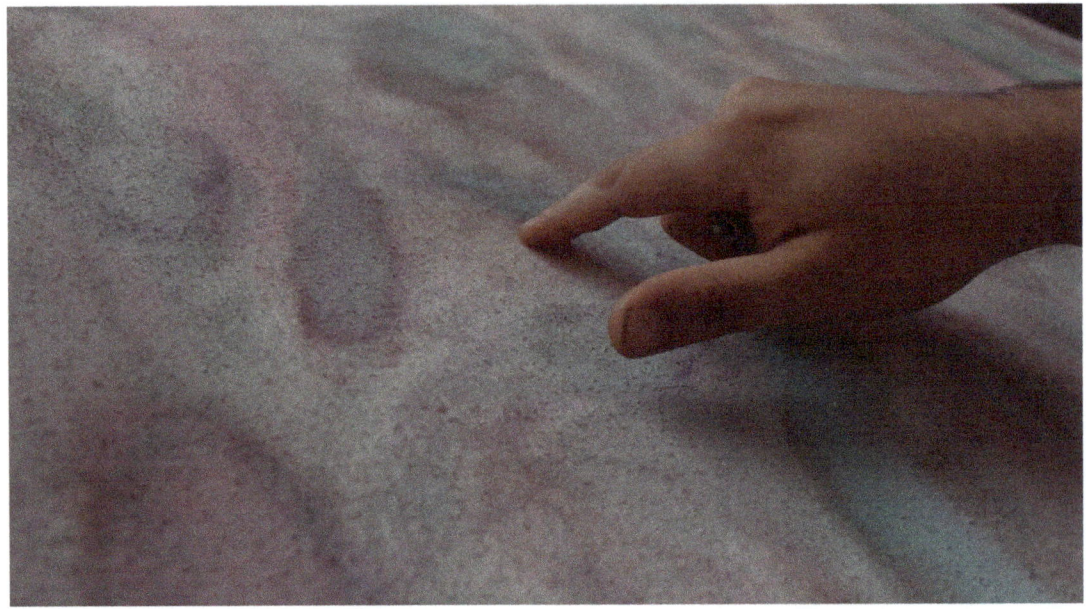

Figure 16.8. Artwork by Kurosh Dadgar (Hossein Shabani) (photograph by Christina Thomopoulos).

Figure 16.9. Artwork by Kurosh Dadgar (Hossein Shabani) (photograph by Christina Thomopoulos).

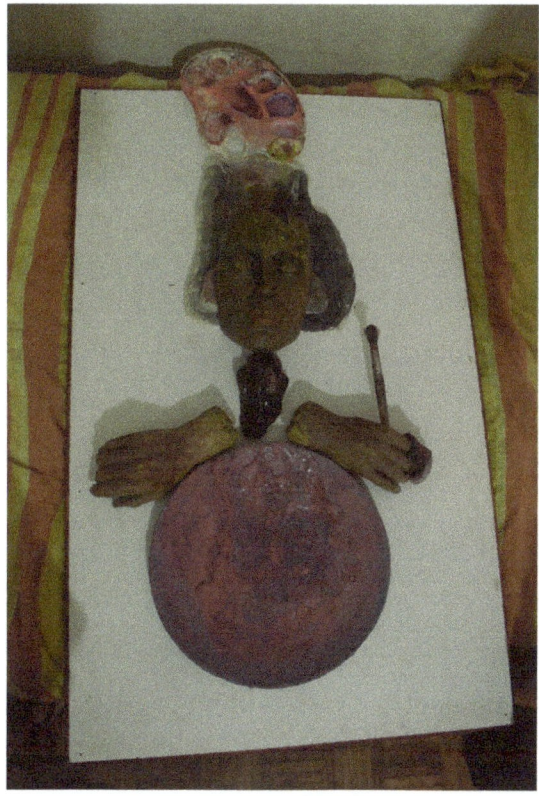

Figure 16.10. Artwork by Kurosh Dadgar (Hossein Shabani) (photograph by Christina Thomopoulos).

Figure 16.11. Artwork by Kurosh Dadgar (Hossein Shabani) (photograph by Christina Thomopoulos).

Figure 16.12. Artwork by Kurosh Dadgar (Hossein Shabani) (photograph by Christina Thomopoulos).

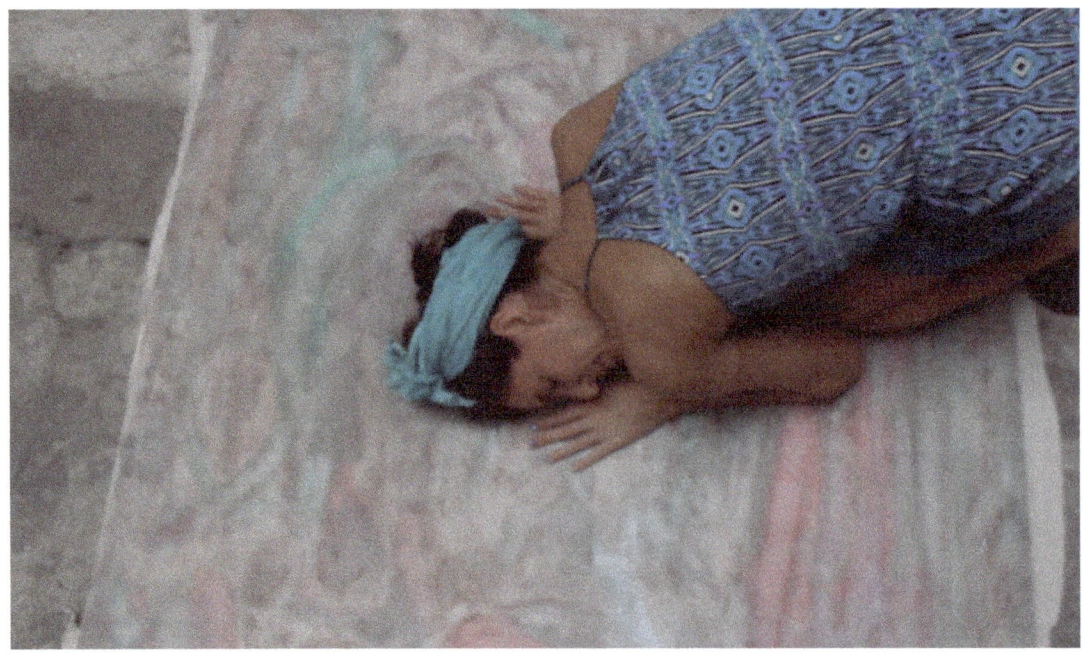

Figure 16.13. Artwork and photograph by Kurosh Dadgar (Hossein Shabani).

Here even watermelon has a face:

Kurosh: This painting makes people feel calm, some of my friends told me.

Christina: It feels like a bed, somewhere you could sleep on and have great dreams. If people's beds in the camps were like this…
  If there were no camps…

A Hard Drive and a Book

A few days after exploring the materiality of Kurosh's artwork, Saeid, Kurosh, and I met again to discuss our potential submission some more: this time exploring questions more directly about memorialization of border crossing, the materiality and immateriality of the journey and life when one has arrived at one's first destination in Europe.

Christina: What did you decide to bring with you on your journey?

Saeid: A book by Yaghma Golrouee called *Driving when Drunk* [Kurosh loosely translated the title from Farsi and spelled out *Ranandegi Dar Masti*]. Golrouee was sent to prison in Iran for singing and translating works by authors such as the Italian writer Oriana Fallaci.

C: Do you remember the first time you heard or read Yaghma Golrouee's work?

S: Some songs I remember from my childhood. Yaghma Golrouee has worked with many Iranian singers.

C: What is your favorite song of Golrouee?

S: A song called *Imagine*.

Kurosh:

  Imagine
   If the disconsideration is hard but imagine
  Meanwhile it is hard
  There is no master for the world
  The people are equal together
  And the share of any person of human kind is one wheat [bread]
  Without borders
  Without limitations
 Imagine you can be as an interpretation of this dream
And your homeland will be all the world, the homeland will be the world[3]

C: Did you bring anything else together with the book?

S: Yes. I brought two hard-drives with my favorite music in it, some books in PDF form, documentaries about social and historical issues, about world wars and the history of the 1979 revolution in Iran. I also brought notebooks with my poetry in them.

---

3. This is a loose translation made by Kurosh of some of Golrouee's lyrics. All of Saeid's words in this text are translated by Kurosh.

C: In the past year (2015–2016) there has been an intense process of documenting border crossings. A process of memorializing the so-called "refugee crisis" has begun, even in the present. If you were a historian wanting to leave something behind for people in the future about this period and your experience of it, what would you want to include?

S: I want to answer through my poetry about the Syrian woman, whose two children were killed by ISIS. Which news channel, which sentence, can show the picture, a small part of your pain? Not all of your pain. Just a small part.

As a picture. As photography.

A lot of death that happened in the sea. As a document.

But how?

Which channel? How to show it? This is the basic question. Something happened. But also some things refugees don't want to mention. Some problems you cannot mention.

When I arrived in Athens I could not get used to seeing children begging on the streets. Drugs. I thought that Iran had these problems. It makes me feel bad to see the same thing here too.

The first time I went to Monastiraki I saw children selling flowers and recalled the same bad phenomenon in Iran: children being forced to work. I thought it was only in Iran, but no. It's a common problem.

There are refugees here, I know at least ten, men who are in prostitution for 10–20 euros. They are not gay, but they have no other choice. No one talks about these things.

C: When I was in Lesvos in April there were rumors of a potential "Refugee Museum" being discussed. What do you think of this idea? Would you want a Refugee Museum to be made?

S: It depends on which view you want to show of this issue.

Maybe it is a political issue to make such a museum: To say everything is ok, and make another illusion, picture.

But maybe it will be as a reality. To show reality.

The question is: Who wants to make this museum? The Government? Activists? Who?

C: Perhaps refugees should make it?

Between Materiality and Immateriality

The dialogue we began about this publication brought with it various challenges and limitations. One could say it was a short-term research discussion we engaged in, yet at the same time it was also simply a way to discuss together more slowly on a variety of issues still reserved for "non-refugees".

With borders closed once more after the now infamous EU–Turkey deal of March 2016, many refugees in Greece experience yet another period of "waiting". A kind of waiting that affects lives, or even puts them at further risk. Journeys become more dangerous and expensive, and living trapped in Greece often becomes unbearable, as circumstances are often prohibitive of building a life there. The body itself becomes the material in question: how do we see the body? The living body? Dead bodies? Drowned bodies? Bodies on the border between life and death? There are many reports of suicides (attempted and achieved) having taken place, ample in the camps themselves – detention centre concentration camps. One of the most recent suicide attempts reported (Allileggii 2016) was on 2 August, 2016, by F, a 14-year old young girl who – underage – had/has been living in unliveable circumstances in the women's detention center in Elliniko, where many women and even children – including unaccompanied minors – are imprisoned. These events are rarely reported on by the mainstream media, but are usually publicized (with varying degrees of success) by activists, who also face their own version of bodily exhaustion (Kantor 2016). As we reflected on objects and materials of the journey and the stay, the body had many stories to tell itself. I recalled Saeid's words that "some things refugees don't want to mention. Some problems you cannot mention." It turns out that in Europe there are also taboos many do not want to openly confront too.

Materiality: yes, it is a part of contemporary forced migration. But equally, if not more so perhaps, I would argue is *immateriality*. The *lack* of objects. The *lack* of space (on the boat, in the camp, in a small bag). The *lack* of ability to move things on a long, uncertain, and expensive journey ahead. Kurosh's tiny apartment pushes his expression to be mobile, and the small space he lives in fulfills as many needs as it can: the *akaliptos* quickly becomes and un-becomes a temporary exhibition space. Saeid's mother had given him gifts to take with him, mostly clothes, some of which he had to leave behind in Turkey, on the orders of those in charge of the next step of his journey.

There is also the lack of resources (material and immaterial) once in Greece and Europe generally. Both Kurosh and Saeid talked about the lack of state support and resources to make their work. Kurosh wants to show his artwork, wants to do research, but there is a lack of organized infrastructure to make this happen. Perhaps – like in our case – work can take place on a no-budget level, but for how long?

Other friends forced into the position of "refugee" often refer to the material resources international law allocates for them, but that never reach them. The absence of resources is palpable on all levels of everyday life: food, shelter, education... Still today, even after the boom of "awareness" of the so-called "refugee crisis" during the summer of 2015 (triggered largely by the wide circulation of the photo of young Aylan washed up on the beach), basic materials of survival are still missing for those who survive the dangerous journey. Many refugees today continue to be forced to live and sleep in flimsy tents during freezing weather and snowstorms (efsyn.gr. 2017).[4]

A friend I met in Lesvos last April sent me photos (see Figure 16.14) of packed food he and others receive in Moria detention centre by hired catering companies. The image shows hundreds of packaged meals deposited immediately into the trash, as he reports it is worse

---

4. See also petitions, such as this one: "Ξενοδόχοι Λέσβου δείξτε ανθρωπιά!" (Hoteliers of Lesbos, Show Humanity!). Online: https://secure.avaaz.org/el/petition/ton_proedro_tis_Enosis_Xenodohon_Lesvoy_ Perikli_Antonioy_kai_ta_xenodoheia_Os_polites_sas_kaloyme_na_antapokritheite_sto/?aCjVxlb

Figure 16.14. Photograph taken by a young man I (Christina Thomopoulos) met in Lesvos in April 2016, who was detained in Moria detention centre, described above. The image is of hundreds of packed meals disposed immediately to trash, as they were inedible. Many people detained felt that eating them was worse for them than going hungry.

to eat it than to go hungry (which they do). The same has been confirmed by eyewitness accounts in Elaionas in Athens.

Another friend in Lesvos said to me that "people need education, things to do in the camps, to keep from going crazy." Here we see politics of deprivation, starvation, hypothermia as part of an ongoing politics of lack, absence, and indifference towards human needs for survival, of both body and mind.

Closing and Opening Thoughts: On Long-Term Engagement

I would like to conclude with some reflections this publication initiative led me to think about regarding dialogues with refugee communities in Europe today. These reflections stem from personal experiences collaborating with friends with refugee/migrant experiences since 2013, as well as self-organized refugee/migrant groups and organizations. My hope is that some of these thoughts may be useful for future initiatives – here and elsewhere – which invite submissions from refugees, with or without archaeological background, many of whom often may not speak English. While I learned so much from Saeid, Kurosh, Baba Safar, Esra, and Sophia through our collective process of co-producing this piece – and I deeply appreciate their sharing their work and thoughts with me and you – I must admit that there were times I felt frustratingly like a "middle man/woman" throughout the process: especially when it came to the issue of language, but also with regard to access and resources.

From a practical standpoint: throughout the process I became increasingly aware that if I had not been there to make this initiative known to them, but also to translate (literally and metaphorically) and to coordinate other practical matters, these voices would not have been able to reach you. And while I recognize the need for such coordination and take on this responsibility, I don't hide that I would be just as excited at the future possibility of listening to such voices on their own terms, outside the context of my (or others') narrations and even (bias) context giving. I believe *visAvis: Voices on Asylum and Migration*, based in Copenhagen, to be an inspiring example of such long-term engagement through multilingual writing, collective research, and publication of voices on asylum and migration.[5] This multilingual publication is co-produced by a multilingual editorial team of writers and editors, "with and without citizenship in Denmark" (as they write), which ensures that the group both creating and receiving this knowledge is mixed. I believe it to be important in the future to make more efforts to make similar truly open and accessible structures that can be alternatives to narratives that are mediated (with however "good intentions"). This would help us learn to listen to various forms of storytelling and narratives after having a discussion on whose terms this take place on. This could be achieved by carefully reconsidering all of the steps of the process that leads to publication, and by making space for input from voices from various backgrounds. However, this would (importantly) require building long-term relationships with people and communities, as well as rethinking set structures and processes that lead to publication – as well as the politics of language and self representation.

As an important future step, I would see it as necessary to disseminate calls for publications in the languages widely spoken by refugees, making accessible the core of the call without depending on the discretion of informal translators and "initiators" like myself. To have a link fully translated in Arabic, Farsi, Urdu, Pashtu, Bengali, and French (or even just some of these languages) would encourage a wider range of people to contribute on their own initiative, and not only by personal invitation (as happened in my case). Furthermore, resources would need to be made available in this process. Even offering access to a computer and regular access to the Internet (or lack thereof) can be a door (or barrier) to someone submitting to such an open call.

I also believe it would be important in the future to invite refugees earlier in any publication process, to co-write the open call for contributions itself, to include their questions in its scope. This would ensure that the scope reflects their needs (short and long term) more directly. Moreover, this implies that the call would already be communicating from the outset with communities such publications and their producers seek to learn from and with.[6]

To ensure that the knowledge from such a publication initiative can return to the communities it discusses, I believe it would be useful and important to to translate this book into the languages mentioned above. Public multilingual readings and events could be organized discussing the texts, inviting refugee communities.[7] These events could be a way to introduce

---

5. Website: http://www.visavis.dk

6. See here the historical call "Nothing About Us Without Us is For Us."

7. For example, visAvis holds launch parties of new issues with readings of texts it publishes in Copenhagen, for a mixed audience; for more see its Facebook page: https://www.facebook.com/events/1311332035564148/

contemporary archaeology as a discipline to non-archaeologists, and to discuss and learn from archaeologists coming from other contexts. Contemporary archaeology was not a known term for most of our group, so some of the questions of the open call were not so accessible. It was through discussion that we were able to move onto new ground.

Our process and discussions leading to this text were fragmented; much like the journey to and life in Europe often are for refugees. As is the case in all research and writing, much is lost in the dig, and edited out, regrettably for length and other reasons. In one of our meetings one evening Saeid had invited his friend Hadi, a young archaeologist from Syria who was preparing to leave Athens two days later. Despite Hadi's enthusiasm to participate in the submission this became impossible, as the link with a "middle man/woman" was being challenged. Despite emailing Hadi all the information to make an independent submission, this was not feasible. This was not a surprise, as Hadi had told me that any text would have to be written on a cell phone, amidst the challenges as moving to a new place, amongst other factors. Another example of the politics of lack, of the absence of material and immaterial resources, which institutions, big and small, might be useful in addressing, even in small ways.

Acknowledgments

I would like to thank Kurosh Dadgar and Saeid Ghasemi for sharing their work, and Esra Dogan, Baba Safar, and Sophia Thomopoulos, who contributed to the discussions which led to this text. Many thanks also to Veronica Tello, Ariel Abrahams, Vasilis Varouhakis, and Yannis Hamilakis for their feedback and suggestions on the text.

References

Allileggii, 2016. "Απόπειρα αυτοκτονίας 14χρονης στα κρατητήρια μεταναστριών στο Ελληνικό". *Αλληλέγγυες-οι Κρατουμένων στα Νότια*, 7 August. Available online: https://allilegioi-kratoumenonstanotia.wordpress.com/2016/08/07/

efsyn.gr. 2017. "Θαμμένες στο χιόνι οι σκηνές προσφύγων στη Μόρια." *efsyn.gr*, 8 January. Available online: https://www.efsyn.gr/arthro/thammenes-sto-hioni-oi-skines-prosfygon-sti-moria

Kantor, J. 2016 "The Hidden Costs of Volunteering in Greece." *Pacific Standard*, 31 August. Available online: https://psmag.com/the-hidden-costs-of-volunteering-in-greece-7fe7248b15e4

Christina Thomopoulos is an artist researcher activist. She is currently working as an Associate Researcher at the Integrated Systems Laboratory of the National Center for Scientific Research Demokritos Institute of Informatics and Telecommunications, Athens, Greece. Email: cpt012@gmail.com

Chapter 17

Commentary: Belonging and Belongings: On Migrant and Nomadic Heritages *in* and *for* the Anthropocene

Rodney Harrison, Staffan Appelgren, and Anna Bohlin

Introduction

As the introduction to this timely volume notes, there has for some time been a significant gap in the field of migration studies in relation to understandings of how the experience of forced and undocumented migration mobilizes and sets in motion different forms of material culture, and related questions of how archaeologists, anthropologists, museums, and heritage institutions can reflect upon and engage with such processes (but see, e.g. Bender 2001; Bender and Winer 2001; Byrne 2003; Basu and Coleman 2008; Dudley 2011; Soto 2016). In commenting on the issues raised within this book – which effectively begins to establish a framework for an expanded subfield of contemporary archaeology of forced dislocation and undocumented migration – for the field of critical heritage studies, we draw on current collaborative archaeological and anthropological research being undertaken across several research projects and programmes on which we are involved both individually and collectively within a European context. We engage specifically with issues arising within the UK and Swedish contexts in which we work and research, but hope to frame these issues within a broader context that will allow us to speak to the global significance of this newly emergent subfield. We close our comment by looking to the broader conditions of the "New Nomadic Age" (which the book designates) in the relations between anthropogenic climate change, conflict, food insecurity, and dislocation, and suggest an expanded role for contemporary archaeology and heritage studies in engaging these issues and their biological, discursive, ecological, material, and political conditions and consequences.

Understanding and Representing People and Things in Motion

We aim to contextualize our comments, and the book itself, by referring to three fields of academic debates and scholarship. The first relates to material culture, specifically anthropological approaches to relationships between people and things that acknowledge the propagative power of objects and the ways in which "things" and "people" are co-generative of social and material worlds. Here we take inspiration from what has been termed the "new materialism" and its relevance to the study of materials in motion. Things, in this perspective, emerge from skilful and creative engagement in the flows of materials. A thing is never fully stabilized and finished, since materials are in constant flux (Ingold 2012; 2013). Far from being closed and bounded entities, enrolled into relationships to other entities in functional networks, things are open and leaky by nature, discharging through their porous boundaries, but also perpetually absorbing from their physical and social environment. Taking material culture in motion and circulation as a point of departure we conceive of things circulating in various social contexts neither as passive objects with mere representational functions, nor as subjects endowed with agency on par with humans, but rather as embodying generative powers that move and condition people (Lee and LiPuma 2002; Bissell 2009), as constitutive forces of possible ways of being (Miller 2008), as energies that resonate with the body's capacity to be affected that goes beyond consciousness, intentions, and strategies (Massumi 1995; Thrift 2008; Mazzarella 2009; Bennett 2010), and as enacting new realities and alternative futures through contingent practices of assembling and reassembling bodies, techniques, technologies, materials, values, temporalities, and spaces (Barad 2007). Through objects in circulation the past imposes itself on the present, affectively incentivizing and entangling social subjects and institutions (Navaro-Yashin 2009; Ahmed 2010; Hornborg 2012). Approaches that highlight the affective and generative capacities of things alongside their representational politics have been shown to resonate particularly with museums (Harrison 2013; Bennett *et al.* 2014), which might be understood to operate as switchpoints within liberal governmental regimes in their production of templates for knowing, ordering, and governing populations (Bennett *et al.* 2017). Furthermore, with this vantage point we see the production of heritage in relation to objects in motion not as something which is concerned with the past as it "was", but instead as a form of future-making practice (see Harrison 2015, 2016, 2017; Harrison *et al.* 2016), a process of assembling new worlds through intimate and contingent processes of "past-presencing" (Macdonald 2013).

The second field, building on the conceptualization of things and materials as unfinished, porous, and socially engaging, concerns the role of belongings and possessions in situations of displacement and mobility, whether from the perspective of migrants or from host populations involved in exchange activities. Here we are interested in studies of how everyday classes of items can mediate sociality and memory (cf. Muntéan *et al.* 2017), and how exchange – gifting, sharing, selling, buying – of objects implies, transforms, and generates social relationships. Of particular significance are studies relating to the circulation of used and pre-owned objects, including motivations for divesting (e.g. Herrmann 1997; Gregson and Crewe 2003; Gregson 2007; Appelgren and Bohlin 2015; in a museum context see Macdonald and Morgan 2018). Discarding affectively and emotively charged belongings can strengthen or create social relationships with receivers, while also transforming the identity of the giver/seller (Herrmann 2015). Furthermore, acts of discard, gifting, "ridding", or divesting as well as acquiring can be powerful aspects of *rites de passage*, easing the transition from one life stage to the next (Herrmann 2011; Lovatt 2015). In situations of departure due to emigration, ridding may involve leaving treasured objects with relatives and friends, for temporary custody or as mementoes, and any new belongings in the new host country will be acquired in relation to those left behind (Åkesson 2004). The capacity of everyday objects to serve as mnemonic devices has further been highlighted in studies of how used and second-hand items may involve not only the transfer of affective orientation (Herrmann 2015), but also of narratives (Herrmann 1997). Traces, marks, and memories resulting from objects' trajectories and biographies (Appadurai 1986; Kopytoff 1986) cling to the items in a process akin to "growing", which lends it self to storytelling and the transmission of narratives (Appelgren and Bohlin 2015, inspired by Hallam and Ingold 2014). The fine-grained materiality of everyday life, in the form of ordinary domestic items, enables alternative heritage-like practices of narrating and remembering that tend to be beyond the reach of formal heritage management (Appelgren and Bohlin 2017; cf Byrne 2008).

In situations of displacement, personal belongings, which form part of an extended self (Belk 1988) and help anchor and narrate both individual and collective histories (Carrier 1990), take on a particular poignancy in a number of different ways, as discussed in chapters in the present volume by Butler and el-Nammari, by Tyrikos-Ergas, and by Seitsonen *et al.*, and in Byrne's discussion of preservationists' "theatre of care". Elsewhere, Parkin (1999) shows that for refugees and migrants, personal belongings may become transitional objects in redefining and re-establishing identity and home, while Burrell's work on Polish migration to Britain looks at the objects and spaces that furnish migrant journeys, exploring migrant women's experience of consumer culture following migration during socialist regime (Burrell 2008a, 2008b). Povrzanovic Frykman and Humbracht (2013) investigate this theme in the context of privileged economic migrants to Sweden, while Colomer (2013) explores tangible and intangible heritage among elderly Chilean refugees living in Sweden. By contrast, *The Undocumented Migration Project*, led by Jason De León (2012, 2013, 2015; De León *et al.* 2015; Stewart *et al.* this volume), a unique long-term empirical study of undocumented migration between Mexico and the US, using ethnography, archaeology, and forensic science to document and study the role of material culture in border crossings from Mexico to the US, highlights the often oppressive relationship between migrants and their objects. The process of undocumented migration between Mexico and the US is materially similar to that of refugees in involving legally contested border crossings, and the struggle to maintain materials for survival and flourishing during traumatic journeys. We agree with De León about the need to move beyond viewing artefacts as "simplistic metonyms for generic and de-personalized suffering" (De León 2013, 11) and to explore their multivocality through individuals' complex and embodied relationships with them.

Responses to the "Migration crisis" from the Museum and Heritage Sector

This brings us to the third field, the role of museum and heritage institutions and their relevance to understanding migration and refugee experiences. It has long been held that museums and other forms of heritage sites and organizations constitute appropriate institutions through which societies might encourage transcultural dialogue (c.f. Lévi-Strauss 1952). Since the 1980s, museums across Europe, and the world, have engaged explicitly with multiculturalism as a concept, with varying forms of success (e.g. Karp and Lavine 1991; Bennett 2006; Karp *et al.* 2006). In Sweden, for example, migration and cultural diversity has been of concern to museums since the 1970s, with a sharp rise in interest in the 2000s and the establishment of the Museum of World Culture in Gothenburg in 2004 (Aronsson 2008; Hintermann and Johansson 2010; Johansson 2014; Levitt 2015). Recently, corresponding with the massive increase in numbers of forcibly displaced people which has occurred since 2010, museums' explicit engagements with refugee history and heritage have intensified. As such, museums' engagement with refugee material culture tends to be addressed in two ways: as part of the broad context of representing global migrations (historical and contemporary), or associated with providing outreach or education programmes with or for contemporary refugee communities – although the latter does not often focus on the material culture of refugee people. An important project here is *the MeLa* (European Museums in an Age of Migration)* Project, a multidisciplinary research project that ran from 2011–2015 and produced guidance documents intended to help enhance the role of museums within the context of contemporary migrations of people(s), objects, information, and cultures (MeLa* Project 2015). *Museums, Migration and Identity in Europe: Peoples, Places and Identities* (Whitehead *et al.* 2015; see also Whitehead *et al.* 2013), one of MeLa*'s research outputs, explores museum practice case studies in Europe, as do *Museums and Migration: History, Memory and Politics* (Gouriévidis 2014), *Stories Old and New: Migration and Identity in the UK Heritage Sector* (Stevens 2009), and *Changes in Museum Practice: New Media, Refugees and Participation* (Skartveit and Goodnow 2010). The special role which city museums might assume in promoting new conceptions of European citizenship, involving more open, transcultural conceptions of belonging and more active participation in (and with) the public sphere, has been particularly highlighted in the work of the project (see Lanz 2014), which has continued and been expanded upon by the EU-funded CoHERE research project (CoHERE 2017). Labadi's recent book *Museums, Immigrants and Social Justice* (2018) comprises a detailed comparative investigation of how museums in France, Denmark, and the UK have aimed to address cultural, economic, social, and political inequalities not only through more conventional exhibitionary practices but also through a range of outreach programmes, suggesting these institutions might play a key role in intervening in questions of social justice and coherence in the future of Europe.

Within the UK and Sweden respectively, these issues have been addressed by the heritage and museum sector in different ways. In the UK, where the comparative number of dislocated peoples as a proportion of the population is extremely low, the political context of the "migration crisis" – which Hamilakis (this volume) notes following Christopoulos (2016) is actually a "*reception* crisis" – has been particularly significant, not the least in the narrow majority "Leave" vote in the 2016 referendum on the withdrawal of the UK from the EU, and the subsequent invocation of Article 50 of the Treaty of the European Union by UK Prime Minister Theresa May's administration in March 2017. The Migration Museum Project currently holds events and exhibitions intended to build toward creating the first dedicated migration museum in the UK, which will broadly explore how migration has been central to British life, past and present. Part of this is called "Keepsakes", which works with community groups, including Refugee Youth, and curates loaned, meaningful artefacts that speak to migration and identity (McAlpine 2015; Migration Museum Project 2016). The UK Museums Association (MA) has also been at the forefront in this regard, producing a series of practice guidelines for museums working with refugees that includes case studies of outreach and documentation of refugee oral histories (Bird 2013). MA case studies also profile St Fagans National Museum of Wales, which collaborated with local refugees and asylum seekers to build and furnish "Refugee House" to reflect the material and social realities of their temporary housing experiences in Cardiff and Newport (Hughes and Rhys 2012). Other examples of engagement and exhibition projects that have focused on the materiality of refugee experience have been more squarely located within the realm of the arts, such as the "Syria: Third Space" project, and various architectural conservation projects (British Council 2015; Campus in Camps 2016; HRP [Human Rights Project] Bard 2015). The language-learning, volunteering, and employment programmes developed for immigrant communities, and their imprint on the permanent and temporary exhibitions of the Manchester Museum and Manchester Art Gallery, are discussed at length by Labadi (2018).

Sweden has received the highest per capita share of refugees among the OECD countries (Ang 2017). In 2015, over 160,000 asylum seekers were registered in Sweden, followed by an additional 50,000 people over the two years 2016–2017, with the largest group being from Syria, followed by Iraq, Afghanistan, Somalia, and Eritrea (Migrationsverket 2018). Already before the steep increase in arrivals in Sweden in 2015, the topic of how the Swedish museum sector has dealt with migration and cultural diversity had received only limited scholarly attention (Johansson 2014, 123, but see Lagerkvist 2006), and the effects of the current refugee situation on the heritage sector has only just begun to be explored academically (Johansson and Bevelander 2017). Of particular interest will be to see whether the tendency – which, as Ang (2017) points out, Sweden shares with many other nations – to isolate and marginalize the story of transnational immigration from the main story of the nation, will change. The situation across the heritage and museum sector in both the UK and Sweden indicates the clear need for sustained engagements with issues arising from the present European migration situation and its place in contemporary geo(bio)politics.

New Nomadic Heritages? Towards Critical Approaches to Forced and Undocumented Migration Heritages in the Anthropocene

The title of this volume suggests we live in a "New Nomadic Age", a point which seems borne out by analyses across a range of different academic fields. Still, we think there are good reasons to be cautious before naming new epochs. One reason is that, despite numerous media reports of "unprecedented" numbers of people on the move, the statistical evidence for global levels of migration show that these have been fairly stable over a considerable period of time.[1] Here we agree with Hamilakis (this volume) about the need to critically interrogate the use of various subcategories within this broad notion of migrants, such as refugees, forcibly displaced people, or undocumented migrants, not least in order to highlight their role in the politics of representing recent migration to Europe as an extraordinary situation deviating from a prior state of affairs (including labelling it a "crisis", whether of migration or reception). Nevertheless, when considering these issues in the light of present global social

---

1. In 1960, migrants constituted 3.1% of the world's population (Czaika and de Haas 2014). In 2017, the share was 3.3% (United Nations 2017).

and climatological forecasting, it is clear that in times ahead, we are likely to see new levels of migration taking place which will have far-reaching implications for both the heritage sector and heritage studies in terms of how heritage is conceptualized, valued, and engaged in. While the archaeology of forced and undocumented migration surely constitutes a key subfield for materializing and making visible "not only [...] the selfishness and blindness of bureaucratic machines, but [...] the basic notions themselves that regulate the inscription of the *native* (that is, of life) in the legal order of the nation-state" (Agamben 1995, 116), we also suggest the need to explore these issues within a broader framework. The current international situation in forced dislocation of human populations is embedded within a series of other global ecological, political, and cultural crises which we see as inseparable from the experience of the refugee.

Climate change, conflict, dislocation/forced migration, and food security constitute a series of pernicious and interconnected challenges, the impacts of which will likely, within decades, precipitate the most dramatic forced dislocation of people the world has ever experienced:

> Climate change will affect resource scarcity placing strain on the essential resources that underpin human, national and international security – including food and water. These are likely to heighten the scale of political turmoil, state instability and mass migration in the future, particularly in regions or nations with poor governance and existing state fragility. (EJF [Environmental Justice Foundation] 2017, 17)

While they are clearly interrelated in their effects, these challenges are similarly connected by the ways in which they have and continue to arise out of both short- and long-term histories of human–ecological, –cultural, –socio-political, and –economic engagements. As Chakrabarty (2009) puts it, in this sense the spectre of climate change collapses the distinction between natural and human history. In addition to the need for the forms of focused material-cultural research outlined within this volume, this situation also calls for research which engages the interrelationships between these various issues and their long-term cultural, ecological, and historical dimensions. It calls for creative, applied, interdisciplinary approaches which will transform our understanding of these challenges by unravelling and exploring their past, present, and future inter-relationships, proposing solutions which emerge out of radical, transnational (but locally co-designed), interdisciplinary collaborations.

We take inspiration here from Colomer's (2017) discussion of the ways in which "Third Culture Kids" and global nomads provide exemplary figures of new, deterritorialized notions of transnational and mobile heritages, in the shift from an emphasis on *roots* to *routes* as a source of collective identity (Colomer 2017, 923; Appelgren 2014; see also Braidotti's 2012 discussion of Nomadic European Citizenship). It may seem flippant to consider individuals who often represent members of cultural and economic elites together with the largely forcibly displaced peoples on which this book focuses, but despite the extreme differences in experiences, if we are to designate a new age of nomadism, both constitute emblematic constituents of this era. Perhaps the most enduring heritage of the current discussion on "the migration crisis" will not be reflected in museums or the interpretation of recent and contemporary heritage sites, but in the ways in which the figure of the refugee has provided such a significant challenge to the hegemony of the nation-state (cf. Malkki 1992; Agamben 1998) and its reliance on traditional ways of understanding biological and cultural forms of rootedness and inheritance. Dominant forms of heritage have been complicit in the construction and perpetuation of this exemplary notion of the nation state based on ideologies of territorial rootedness and the stability of sedentism. Heritage has thus often been an arena for silencing other, mobile or nomadic, forms of living with and relating to the past that might now call its hegemony in question. The challenge, then, is replacing these dominant forms of heritage with new ways of understanding and engaging collective forms of identity that transcend particularism and build on the interweaving of cultural and natural heritages in (and *for*) the Anthropocene (c.f. Harrison 2015), without simply extending sedentism through a "heritagization of the nomad" (Appelgren 2014).

Acknowledgments

This chapter arises out of the authors' collaborations as part of the "Making Global Heritage Futures" Research Cluster of the joint University of Gothenburg / University College London Centre for Critical Heritage Studies, and conversations across and between several large funded research projects and programmes led by the authors. *Heritage Futures* is funded by an Arts and Humanities Research Council (AHRC) "Care for the Future: Thinking Forward through the Past" Theme Large Grant (AH/M004376/1), awarded to Rodney Harrison (principal investigator), Caitlin DeSilvey, Cornelius Holtorf, Sharon Macdonald (co-investigators), Antony Lyons (senior creative fellow), Nadia Bartolini, Sarah May, Jennie Morgan, and Sefryn Penrose (postdoctoral researchers), and assisted by Esther Breithoff (postdoctoral researcher) and Hannah Williams. It receives generous additional support from its host universities and partner organizations. See www.heritage-futures.org for further information. Work on the relationship between heritage and migration in Europe is also supported by Harrison's *AHRC Heritage Priority Area Leadership Fellowship* grant (AH/P009719/1) www.heritage-research.org and as part of Work Package 1 (led by Harrison) on "Theorising Heritage Futures in Europe" of the EU funded Marie Skłodowska-Curie Innovative Training Network CHEurope (*Critical Heritage Studies and the Future of Europe: Towards an Integrated, Interdisciplinary and Transnational Training Model in Cultural Heritage Research and Management*). *Re:heritage. Circulation and Marketization of Things with History* is funded by the Swedish Research Council (421-203-1923), and was awarded to Anna Bohlin, Staffan Appelgren, Helene Brembeck, Mike Crang, Nicky Gregson, Ingrid Martins Holmberg, Anneli Palmsköld, Niklas Sörum, and Sarah De Nardi.

The chapter draws partially on a literature review prepared for the authors by Kyle Lee-Crossett for a separate project. We thank Kyle for his assistance with preparing that review.

References

Agamben, G. 1995. "We Refugees." *Symposium: A Quarterly Journal in Modern Literatures* 49 (2): 114–119. https://doi.org/10.1080/00397709.1995.10733798
_____. 1998. *Homo Sacer: Sovereign Power and Bare Life*. Stanford, CA: Stanford University Press.
Ahmed, S. 2010. "Happy Objects." In *The Affect Theory Reader*, edited by M. Gregg and G. J. Seigworth 29–51. Durham, NC: Duke University Press. https://doi.org/10.1215/9780822392781-002

Åkesson, L. 2004. *Making a Life: Meanings of Migration in Cape Verde*. PhD Diss., University of Gothenburg.

Ang, I. 2017. "What are Museums For? The Enduring Friction between Nationalism and Cosmopolitanism." *Identities* 24 (1): 1–5. https://doi.org/10.1080/1070289X.2016.1260019

Appadurai, A. 1986. "Introduction: Commodities and the Politics of Value." In *The Social Life of Things: Commodities in Cultural Perspective*, edited by A. Appadurai, 3–63. Cambridge: Cambridge University Press. https://doi.org/10.1017/CBO9780511819582.003

Appelgren, S. 2014. "Heritage, Territory and Nomadism: Theoretical Reflections." In *Vägskälens kulturarv – kulturarv vid vägskäl. Om att skapa plats för romer och resande i kulturarvet*, edited by I. M. Holmberg, 243–256. Göteborg: Makadam Förlag.

_____. and A. Bohlin. 2015. "Growing in Motion: The Circulation of Used Things on Second-Hand Markets." *Culture Unbound: Journal of Current Cultural Research* 7 (1): 143–168. https://doi.org/10.3384/cu.2000.1525.1571143

_____. 2017. "Second-Hand as 'Living' Heritage: Intangible Dimensions of Things with History." In *Routledge Companion to Intangible Cultural Heritage*, edited by M. L. Stefano and P. Davis, 240–250. London and New York: Routledge.

Aronsson, P. 2008. "Representing Community: National Museums Negotiating Differences and Community in the Nordic Countries." In *Scandinavian Museums and Cultural Diversity*, edited by K. Goodnow and H. Akman, 195–211. New York: Berghahn.

Barad, K. 2007. *Meeting the Universe Halfway: Quantum Physics and the Entanglement of Matter and Meaning*. Durham, NC: Duke University Press. https://doi.org/10.1215/9780822388128

Basu, P. and S. Coleman. 2008. "Introduction: Migrant Worlds, Material Cultures." *Mobilities* 3 (3): 313–330. https://doi.org/10.1080/17450100802376753

Belk, R. W. 1988. "Possessions and the Extended Self." *Journal of Consumer Research* 15 (2): 139–168. https://doi.org/10.1086/209154

Bender, B. 2001. "Landscapes-on-the-Move." *Journal of Social Archaeology* 1 (1): 75–89. https://doi.org/10.1177/146960530100100106

_____. and M. Winer, eds. 2001. *Contested Landscapes: Movement, Exile and Place*. Oxford: Berg.

Bennett, J. 2010. *Vibrant Matter: A Political Ecology of Things*. Durham, NC: Duke University Press.

Bennett, T. 2006. "Culture and Differences: The Challenges of Multiculturalism." In *When Culture Makes the Difference: Heritage, Arts and Media in Multicultural Society*, edited by S. Boda and M. R. Cifarelli, 21–37. Rome: Meltemi Editore.

_____., B. Dibley, and R. Harrison. 2014. "Introduction: Anthropology, Collecting and Colonial Governmentalities." *History and Anthropology* 25 (2): 137–149. https://doi.org/10.1080/02757206.2014.882838

_____., F. Cameron, N. Dias, B. Dibley, R. Harrison, I. Jacknis and C. McCarthy. 2017. *Collecting, Ordering, Governing: Anthropology, Museums and Liberal Government*. Durham, NC: Duke University Press.

Bird, N. 2013. "Oxford University Museums and Collections." Museums Association website, 13 December. Available online: http://www.museumsassociation.org/museumpractice/museums-and-refugees/16122013-oxford-universities-museums-and-collections

Bissell, D. 2009. "Inconsequential Materialities: The Movements of Lost Effects." *Space and Culture* 12 (1): 95–115. https://doi.org/10.1177/1206331208325602

Braidotti, R. 2012. *Nomadic Theory*. New York: Columbia University Press.

British Council. 2015. "Syria: Third Space: A British Council Exhibition about Recovery and Resilience." Available online: https://www.britishcouncil.org/arts/syriathird-space/

Burrell, K. 2008a. "Managing, Learning, and Sending: The Material Lives and Journeys of Polish

Women in Britain." *Journal of Material Culture* 12 (1): 63-83. https://doi.org/10.1177/1359183507086219

_____. 2008b. "Materialising the Border: Spaces of Mobility and Material Culture in Migration from Post-Socialist Poland." *Mobilities* 3 (3): 353–373. https://doi.org/10.1080/17450100802376779

Byrne, D. 2003. "Nervous Landscapes: Race and Place in Australia." *Journal of Social Archaeology* 3 (2): 169–193. https://doi.org/10.1177/1469605303003002003

_____. 2008. "A Critique of Unfeeling Heritage." In *Intangible Heritage*, edited by L. Smith and N. Asagawa, 229–252. London and New York: Routledge

Campus in Camps. 2016. "About". Available online: http://www.campusincamps.ps/about/

Carrier, J. 1990. "Gifts in a World of Commodities: The Ideology of the Perfect Gift in American Societies." *Social Analysis* 29: 19–37.

Chakrabarty, D. 2009. "The Climate of History: Four Theses." *Critical Inquiry* 35 (2): 197–222. https://doi.org/10.1086/596640

Christopoulos, D. 2016. "Europe's Solidarity Crisis: A Perspective from Greece. Interview with G. Souvlis." *Roar*, 8 June. Available online: https://roarmag.org/essays/Europe-refugee-solidaritycrisis-greece/

CoHERE. 2017. "CoHERE. Critical Heritages: Performing and Representing Identities in Europe." Available online: https://research.ncl.ac.uk/cohere/

Colomer, L. 2013. "Managing the Heritage of Immigrants: Eldery Refugees, Homesickness, and Cultural Identities." *European Archaeologist* 39: 17–22.

_____. 2017. "Heritage on the Move. Cross-Cultural Heritage as a Response to Globalisation, Mobilities and Multiple Migrations." *International Journal of Heritage Studies* 23 (10): 913–927. https://doi.org/10.1080/13527258.2017.1347890

Czaika, M. and H. De Haas. 2014. "The Globalization of Migration: Has the World Become More Migratory?" *International Migration Review* 48 (2): 283–323. https://doi.org/10.1111/imre.12095

De León, J. 2012. "Better Hot than Caught: Excavating the Conflicting Roles of Migrant Material Culture." *American Anthropologist* 114 (3): 477-495. https://doi.org/10.1111/j.1548-1433.2012.01447.x

_____. 2013. "Undocumented Migration, Use Wear, and the Materiality of Habitual Suffering in the Sonoran Desert." *Journal of Material Culture* 18 (4): 321–345. https://doi.org/10.1177/1359183513496489

_____. 2015. *The Land of Open Graves: Living and Dying on the Migrant Trail*. Berkeley: University of California Press.

_____., C. Gokee, and A. Schubert. 2015. "'By the time I get to Arizona': Citizenship, Materiality, and Contested Identities Along the US-Mexico Border." *Anthropological Quarterly* 88 (2): 445–479. https://doi.org/10.1353/anq.2015.0022

Dudley, S. 2011. "Feeling at Home: Producing and Consuming Things in Karenni Refugee Camps on the Thai-Burma Border." *Population, Space and Place* 17 (6): 742–755. https://doi.org/10.1002/psp.639

EJF [Environmental Justice Foundation]. 2017. *Beyond Borders: Our Changing Climate – Its Role in Conflict and Displacement*. Available online: https://ejfoundation.org//resources/downloads/BeyondBorders.pdf

Gouriévidis, L., ed. 2014. *Museums and Migration: History, Memory and Politics*. London and New York: Routledge.

Gregson, N. 2007. *Living with Things: Ridding, Accommodation, Dwelling*. Wantage, UK: Sean Kingston.

Gregson, N. and L. Crewe. 2003. *Second-Hand Cultures*. Oxford: Berg. https://doi.org/10.2752/9781847888853

Hallam, E. and T. Ingold. 2014. "Making and Growing: An Introduction." In *Making and Growing: Anthropological Studies of Organisms and Artefacts*, edited by E. Hallam and T. Ingold, 1–24. Farnham, UK: Ashgate.

Harrison, R. 2013. "Reassembling Ethnographic Museum Collections." In *Reassembling the Collection: Ethnographic Museums and Indigenous Agency*, edited by R. Harrison, S. Byrne, and A. Clarke, 3–35. Santa Fe, NM: School for Advanced Research Press.

_____. 2015. "Beyond 'Natural' and 'Cultural' Heritage: Toward an Ontological Politics of Heritage in the Age of Anthropocene" *Heritage and Society* 8 (1): 24–42. https://doi.org/10.1179/2159032X15Z.00000000036

_____. 2016. "Archaeologies of Emergent Presents and Futures." *Historical Archaeology* 50 (3): 165–180. https://doi.org/10.1007/BF03377340

_____. 2017. "Freezing Seeds and Making Futures: Endangerment, Hope, Security, and Time in Agrobiodiversity Conservation Practices." *Culture, Agriculture, Food and Environment* 39 (2): 80–89. https://doi.org/10.1111/cuag.12096

_____., N. Bartolini, C. DeSilvey, C. Holtorf, A. Lyons, S. Macdonald, S. May, J. Morgan, and S. Penrose. 2016. "Heritage Futures." *Archaeology International* 19: 68–72. https://doi.org/10.5334/ai.1912

Herrmann, G. M. 1997. "Gift or Commodity: What Changes Hands in the U.S. Garage Sale?" *American Ethnologist* 24 (4): 910–930. https://doi.org/10.1525/ae.1997.24.4.910

_____. 2011. "New Lives from Used Goods: Garage Sales as Rites of Passage." *Ethnology* 50 (3): 189–207.

_____. 2015. "Valuing Affect: The Centrality of Emotion, Memory, and Identity in Garage Sale Exchange." *Anthropology of Consciousness* 26 (2): 170–181. https://doi.org/10.1111/anoc.12040

Hintermann, C. and C. Johansson (2010) "Museums, Migration and Diversity: An Introduction." In *Migration and Memory: Representations of Migration in Europe Since 1960*, edited by C. Hintermann and C. Johansson, 135–144. Innsbruck: StudienVerlag

Hornborg, A. 2012. "Submitting to Objects: Fetishism, Dissociation, and the Cultural Foundations of Capitalism." In *The Handbook of Contemporary Animism*, edited by G. Harvey, 244–259. Durham: Acumen.

HRP [Human Rights Project] Bard. 2015. "The Architecture of Exile: Palestinian Refugee Camps as World Heritage Site." Available online: http://hrp.bard.edu/event/the-architecture-of-exile-palestinian-refugee-camps-as-world-heritage-site/

Hughes, S. and O. Rhys. 2012. "St Fagans: National History Museum, Cardiff." Museums Association website, October 10. Available online: http://www.museumsassociation.org/museum-practice/your-case-studies-homelessness-and-housing/15102012-st-fagans-cardiff

Ingold, T. 2012. "Towards an Ecology of Materials." *Annual Review of Anthropology* 41: 427–42. https://doi.org/10.1146/annurev-anthro-081309-145920

_____. 2013. "Being Alive to a World without Objects." In *The Handbook of Contemporary Animism*, edited by G. Harvey, 213–225. Durham: Acumen.

Johansson, C. 2014. "The Museum in a Multicultural Setting: The Case of Malmö Museums." In *Museums and Migration: History, Memory and Politics*, edited by L. Gouriévidis, 122–137. London and New York: Routledge.

_____. and P. Bevelander, eds. 2017. *Museums in a Time of Migration: Rethinking Museums' Roles, Representations, Collections, and Collaborations*. Lund: Nordic Academic Press.

Karp, I., C. A. Kratz, L. Szwaja, and T. Ybarra-Frausto, eds. 2006. *Museum Frictions: Public Cultures /*

Global Transformations. Durham, NC: Duke University Press. https://doi.org/10.1215/9780822388296

Karp, I. and S. D. Lavine, eds. 1991. *Exhibiting Cultures: The Poetics and Politics of Museum Display*. Washington, DC: Smithsonian Institution Press.

Kopytoff, I. 1986. "The Cultural Biography of Things: Commoditization as Process." In *The Social Life of Things: Commodities in Cultural Perspective*, edited by A. Appadurai, 64–91. Cambridge: Cambridge University Press. https://doi.org/10.1017/CBO9780511819582.004

Labadi, S. 2018. *Museums, Immigrants, and Social Justice*. London and New York: Routledge.

Lagerkvist, C. 2006. "Empowerment and Anger: Learning How to Share Ownership of the Museum." *Museum and Society* 4 (2): 52–68.

Lanz, F. 2014. "City Museums in a Transcultural Europe." In *Museums and Migration: History, Memory and Politics*, edited by L. Gouriévidis, 27–43. London and New York: Routledge.

Lee, B. and E. LiPuma. 2002. "Cultures of Circulation: The Imaginations of Modernity." *Public Culture* 14 (1): 191–214. https://doi.org/10.1215/08992363-14-1-191

Lévi-Strauss, C. 1952. *Race and History*. Paris: UNESCO.

Levitt, P. 2015. *Artifacts and Allegiances: How Museums Put the Nation and the World on Display*. Oakland: University of California Press. https://doi.org/10.1525/california/9780520286061.001.0001

Lovatt, M. 2015. "Charity Shops and the Imagined Futures of Objects: How Second-Hand Markets Influence Disposal Decisions when Emptying a Parent's House." *Culture Unbound: Journal of Current Cultural Research* 7 (1): 13–29. https://doi.org/10.3384/cu.2000.1525.157113

Macdonald, S. 2013. *Memorylands: Heritage and Identity in Europe Today*. London and New York: Routledge.

_____. and J. Morgan. 2018. "What Not to Collect?: Post-Connoisseurial Dystopia and the Profusion of Things." In *Curatopia: Museums and the Future of Curatorship*, edited by P. Schorch and C. McCarthy (in press). Manchester: Manchester University Press.

Malkki, L. 1992. "National Geographic: The Rooting of Peoples and the Territorialization of National Identity among Scholars and Refugees." *Cultural Anthropology* 7 (1): 24–44. https://doi.org/10.1525/can.1992.7.1.02a00030

Massumi, B. 1995. "The Autonomy of Affect" *Cultural Critique* 31: 83–109. https://doi.org/10.2307/1354446

Mazzarella, W. 2009. "Affect: What is it Good for?" In *Enchantments of Modernity: Empire, Nation, Globalization*, edited by S. Dube, 291–309. London and New York: Routledge.

McAlpine, S. 2015. "'A Keepsake is a very special thing." Migration Museum Project website, 9 June. Available online: http://migrationmuseum.org/a-keepsake-is-a-very-special-thing/

MeLa* Project. 2015. "MeLa* Project Final Brochure". Available online: http://www.mela-project.polimi.it/upl/cms/attach/20150916/164249296_8862.pdf

Migration Museum Project. 2016. "Keepsakes." Available online: http://migrationmuseum.org/exhibition/keepsakes/

Migrationsverket. 2018. "Statistik". Available online: http://www.migrationsverket.se/Om-Migrationsverket/Statistik.html

Miller, D. 2008. *The Comfort of Things*. Cambridge: Polity.

Muntéan, L., L. Plate, and A. Smelik, eds. 2017. *Materializing Memory in Art and Popular Culture*. London and New York: Routledge.

Navaro-Yashin, Y. 2009. "Affective Spaces, Melancholic Objects: Ruination and the Production of Anthropological Knowledge." *Journal of the Royal Anthropological Institute* 15 (1): 1–18. https://doi.org/10.1111/j.1467-9655.2008.01527.x

Parkin, D. 1999. "Mementoes as Transitional Objects in Human Displacement." *Journal of Material Culture* 4 (3): 303–320. https://doi.org/10.1177/135918359900400304

Povrzanovic Frykman, M. and M. Humbracht. 2013. "Making Palpable Connections: Objects in Migrants' Transnational Lives". *Ethnologia Scandinavica* 43: 47–67.

Skartveit, H.-L. and K. J. Goodnow, eds. 2010. *Changes in Museum Practice: New Media, Refugees and Participation.* Oxford: Berghahn.

Soto, G. 2016. "Migrant Memento Mori and the Geography of Risk." *Journal of Social Archaeology* 16 (3): 335–358. https://doi.org/10.1177/1469605316673171

Stevens, M. 2009. *Stories Old and New: Migration and Identity in the UK Heritage Sector. A Report for the Migration Museum Working Group.* London: Institute for Public Policy Research.

Thrift, N. 2008. *Non-Representational Theory. Space-Politics-Affect.* London and New York: Routledge.

United Nations. 2017. "International Migrant Stock: The 2017 Revision." Available online: http://www.un.org/en/development/desa/population/migration/data/estimates2/estimates17.shtml

Whitehead, C., S. Eckersley, K. Lloyd, and R. Mason, eds. 2015. *Museums, Migration and Identity in Europe: Peoples, Places and Identities.* Farnham, UK: Ashgate.

Whitehead, C., R. Mason, S. Eckersley, and K. Lloyd, eds. 2013. *"Placing" Europe in the Museum: People(s), Places, Identities.* Milan: Politecnico di Milano.

Rodney Harrison is Professor of Heritage Studies at the UCL Institute of Archaeology at University College London, and the UK Arts and Humanities Research Council's (AHRC) Heritage Priority Area Leadership Fellow. Address for correspondence: UCL Institute of Archaeology, 31-34 Gordon Square, Kings Cross, London, WC1H 0PY, UK. Email: r.harrison@ucl.ac.uk

Staffan Appelgren is a Senior Lecturer in Social Anthropology at the University of Gothenburg. Address for correspondence: School of Global Studies, Box 700, 40530 Göteborg, Sweden. Email: staffan.appelgren@gu.se

Anna Bohlin is a Senior Lecturer in Social Anthropology at the University of Gothenburg. Address for correspondence: School of Global Studies, Box 700, 40530 Göteborg, Sweden. Email: anna.bohlin@globalstudies.gu.se

Chapter 18

Commentary: Nomadic Ethics

Elisabeth Kirtsoglou

War, conflict, failed states, and prolonged economic violence related to extractive economies and environmental damage constitute the post *cum* neo-colonial condition of our times. While certain regions and nations regard themselves as entitled to visions of perpetual peace and prosperity, the negative political, economic, and ecological consequences of this entitlement are endured elsewhere. It follows that many forms of mobility are forced, in the sense that they are propelled by inequality and the various economic, political, geopolitical, and ecological materializations of asymmetrical relations of power (cf. Reuveny and Allen 2007; Reuveny 2008; Sassen 2014). Stressing the forced aspect of mobility serves to question the validity of policy narratives that defend a strict differentiation between "refugees" who deserve international protection and "migrants" who are regarded as deportable, or used as a cheap and precarious labour force (cf. Walters 2002; Anderson 2012).

The category of the deportable economic migrant, who is criminalized and always suspected as trying to *pass as* an asylum seeker, is born directly out of the "gospel of laissez-faire" (cf. Comaroff and Comaroff 2001, 13). It is supported by a narrow and prejudiced definition of violence that disregards all forms of persecution and coercion that are not physical: in this liberal framework, the only thing that can possibly stand between a person and the attainment of her life goals is a direct threat to her physical existence. The flipside of the belief that anyone, anywhere, and no matter how punishing their circumstances, can have a fulfilling life[1] (if they try hard enough and so long as they are not killed by a bomb or an angry mob), is of course that the poor and the destitute somehow *deserve* their circumstances. The increasing restrictions placed on the mobility of certain people, but not on the mobility of capital or of the high-end professional-managerial class, are constituent factors of the modern condition of neoliberal capitalism (cf. Comaroff and Comaroff 2001; Green 2013; Kirtsoglou and Tsimouris 2016). Deportation, and policies such as Prevention Through Deterrence (Radziwinowiczówna,

---

1. My argument here should not be read as a criticism of the work of Rapport (2012), as Rapport does not claim that anyone *can*, but rather that anyone *ought to be able* (and free) to pursue their life project. In this sense, many of the conditions he sees as necessary for the safeguarding of individual freedom are compatible with my own thoughts, despite our different starting points.

this volume; Stewart *et.al.,* this volume), are, therefore, not only technologies of citizenship and manifestations of state power (Agamben 1998; De Genova 2010); they are also structures of the "thickening hegemony" of millennial capitalism (Comaroff and Comaroff 2001), which is at once global in its aspirations and sphere of influence and local in its implementation, which occurs at the level of the nation-state and its institutions (cf. Sassen 2005).

Liberal policy narratives that refuse to acknowledge the forced aspect of mobility and its relation to economic violence are, of course, not new at all, and certainly not confined to inter-national migration movements. In the UK, Margaret Thatcher's Secretary of the State of Employment, Norman Tebbit, famously gave a speech at the Conservative Party conference in Blackpool in 1981 in which he responded to riots in Brixton in London with the statement: "I grew up in the thirties with an unemployed father. He didn't riot. He got on his bike and looked for work and he kept looking till he found it."

When we focus closely on the relation between liberal/neoliberal ideologies and work-related mobility, it becomes evident that the movement of workers is both praised as the attitude of the white "self-made" individual and, at the same time, chastised as the racialized Other's capricious (and therefore criminal and punishable) violation of the territoriality of the nation-state (cf. Kirtsoglou and Tsimouris 2018). The paradoxical representations of mobility as simultaneously desirable and transgressive are far from accidental. They serve to support global economic, political, racial, and gender asymmetries. In this sense, the forced aspect of migration is not at all antithetical to its character as a social movement. Migration is indeed a movement that "enacts the conscious decision of millions of primarily poor people, mostly of the Global South, to take their future into their hands – or better onto their feet" (Hamilakis, this volume). It is both "forced" (in the sense that the root causes of migration are to be found in the "global allocation of roles determined by the world elites") and an action of agency on behalf of those who "refuse simply to become cheap and dispensable labour in the sweatshops of developing countries" (Hamilakis, this volume).

Migration is also a complex transfer point for relations between global politico-economic forces and the nation-state as the local terrain where those forces operate and materialize. The state and supra-state entities like the EU exhibit both fixing and unfixing qualities. A good number of nation-states today emerged out of large-scale, systematic displacements of populations (see Hirschon 2003; Riggs and Jat, this volume). Yet, once established, states draw their power from the construction of sedentary subjects (cf. Malkki 1992; Kirtsoglou and Tsimouris 2018). Sedentarization obviously transforms people into populations (cf. Foucault 1980) – into measurable, governable subjects and a stable workforce. The distinction between the civilized, sedentary citizen and the primitive nomad was important one in colonial scholarship and tightly connected to the construction of racialized geographies that produced political, historical, and (pseudo)scientific representations of the pre-modern subject, providing ample justification for colonial "civilizing" missions (cf. Silverstein 2005, 369). The view that migration was another form of nomadism (Silverstein 2005, 370) served to construct a specific, racialized representation of migrants, but also of non-sedentary populations like the Jews or the Roma (Malkki 1992). The "fixing" role of the state in colonial times goes beyond issues of the homogeneity of the imagined community (Anderson 1983). It is directly related to the establishment and reification of racialized geographies of inequality; it is a technology for the production of the Orient and the Occident.

The notion of "labour migration" – connecting, that is, mobility with the economic order – was developed by international bodies such as the UN, the World Bank, the International Labour Organization, and the Organisation of Economic Cooperation and Development (OECSD) (Silverstein 2005, 370–371). An entire discursive regime, connected to international economic agents and stakeholders, transformed the nomad into a labourer, and rendered her a racialized, gendered, uprooted victim of the manner in which non-Westernized countries supposedly lagged in modernization (Silverstein 2005; Kirtsoglou and Tsimouris 2016). The economic migrant, envisaged as being motivated solely from the material resources of the affluent (capitalist) West, is left to become prey to the "unfixing" powers of the state. The unfixing state deports, excludes, severs ties, creates transnational and transcontinental families; its job is to unmake lives. Much in the same manner that the fixing state produces racialized geographies, the unfixing state creates geographies of risk, equally aimed at safeguarding the global status-quo.

Refugees, asylum seekers, migrants, forcibly displaced, unemployed, victims of all kinds of violence, racialized and excluded subjects (to name only some of the positions the subaltern occupies), share something in common: they can potentially become agents of disorder by refusing to remain fixed in their preconceived position and by exhibiting immense durability to the "unfixing" of their lives. When studying subaltern expressions of political, economic, and existential disobedience we definitely need to focus on the effects of governmentality: what Hamilakis (this volume) calls the "heterogeneous assemblage of material and immaterial entities which coheres to enact legality and illegality" (p. 8). We also need to place our emphasis on the ontological vulnerability of the subaltern as this is accentuated by "controlled situations of abandonment" (Deleuze 2007 [1984], 236; Davies and Isakjee 2015; Muehlebach 2016). "Controlled abandonment", as a governmental ethos, becomes evident in the manner in which the state outsources its main responsibilities towards categories of citizens and "non-citizens" to the third sector, while at the same time it continues to exercise a tight biopolitical control over them. Across different frameworks that range from hot-spots and camps to austerity-induced poverty, modern states contract in favour of the humanitarian sector while simultaneously bureaucracies expand and become exercised, in an ever more marked fashion, through persons and things (cf. Foucault 1989 [1978], 101; Fassin 2011; Cabot 2012; Gupta 2012; Hull 2012).

A much-needed emphasis on power, vulnerability, pain, violence, and mourning, remains nevertheless incomplete without the careful exploration of those "unstable conditions that open up new fields of the possible" (Deleuze 2007 [1984], 233). The theorization of the Nomadic Age needs to take into consideration "nomadic ethics" (cf. Braidotti 2012): those "forces of immanence, relationality, duration and transmutation" (Braidotti 2012, 172) that allow the disobedient Other to carve new avenues of resistance and novel forms of the political.

My call for emphasis on the nomadic ethics of the Nomadic Age complements Hamilakis's (this volume) vision of the archaeology of migration. The concept refers to the embodied subject, regarding affectivity as a driving force of change and thus drawing on the emphasis on the sensorial/material and affective aspects of journeys (cf. Braidotti 2012, 175–179). The epistemic and counter-archival roles of archaeology are also vital in establishing a nomadic ethical analytical stance that will give prominence to the "micro-politics of resistance" and the "webs of emancipatory practices" (Braidotti 2012, 196). Alongside the assemblage of forces that focus on "unfixing" the lives of the subaltern, I propose that we also concentrate on the assemblage of affirmative forces that compel the subject and showcase her "ontological drive to become" (Braidotti 2012, 175–177), to "fix" social relations, to heal, to transform, and to create novel political figurations and new possibilities of belonging.

In 2015–2016 approximately one million asylum seekers, mostly from Syria, crossed from Turkey to Greece in the hope of continuing their journeys towards Germany, France, Sweden, and other northern European countries. The majority managed to reach their destinations, but many – too many – lost their lives while trying. As a result of the EU–Turkey deal of March 2016, some are now detained in Greece, and over two million are unable to leave Turkey.

As part of an ESRC/DFID-funded project called *Transitory Lives* I conducted fieldwork during the critical months from September 2015 to December 2016 in Lesvos and Athens and at Piraeus, the biggest port in Greece and a space historically associated with trauma and displacement. It was to Piraeus that 7000 refugees were transported from the Aegean islands – to an historical, spatiotemporal hot-spot of what Kourelis (this volume) calls "the *longue durée* of forced migrations in Greece" (p. 110). In 1922, following Greece's defeat in the Greco-Turkish war of 1919, nearly one million refugees arrived in Piraeus from Asia Minor. The end of the war was sealed by the Treaty of Lausanne, which commanded an exchange of populations between Greece and Turkey in favour of respective ethnic homogenization (cf. Hirschon 2003), in much the same way as occurred during Partition in India – although, of course, at a significantly smaller scale (see Riggs and Jat, this volume). The 1920s refugees were Greek-speaking and Christian Orthodox. In every way it mattered, they were "Greek", and yet the conditions of their reception by the Greek state were similarly punishing to those of the 2015–2016 refugees. The 1920s refugees were similarly forced to occupy abandoned sites near Piraeus, or to disperse around Greece, frequently in the very same areas that contemporary refugee camps are now being established (cf. Kourelis, this volume).

Many descendants of the Asia Minor refugees were affectively mobilized by the circumstances of the 2015–2016 displaced, identified with them, and exhibited various non-hierarchical forms of solidarity. During my fieldwork I met George and Stasa, a couple who lived in Drapetsona, near the make-shift camp at the Piraeus port. Both of refugee descent, they came to the port every other day and each weekend, and took one large family (or sometimes two small ones) back to their house. The families had a chance to have a proper bath, to wash their clothes, and to eat around the table with George and Stasa. Importantly, many of them, as far as the language barrier permitted, had the opportunity to learn from George and Stasa about the 1920s stories that slowly began to spread around the camp. More and more refugees started contextualizing themselves in the material and historical (archaeological) dimensions of the port: "*Do you mean that all those houses and blocks of flats I can see from here were once refugee shanties?*", one guest named Mustafa asked me, pointing to the surroundings with his finger. "*Yes*", I replied, and in response to popular demand I found a few videos and visual material of the 1920s refugees in Piraeus. Another guest, Nur, shook her head: "*Piraeus has always been a place for refugees*", she exclaimed. We looked at more pictures I found over the internet, some of them contemporary, of old, 1920s refugee houses that still stood in certain parts of the city as "material traces and remnants of interrupted lives" (cf. in this volume, chapters by Hamilakis, by Riggs and Jat, and by Pistrick and Bachmeier). "Look", a guest named Ahmed said, "*but they made it. This is where they started from, just like us, and look at them now. They made it. Didn't they?*"

Ahmed's question, directed to me, felt a bit like the rope of a life-ring. I spared him the ugly details: the manner in which the 1920s refugees were discriminated against, placed right next to the newly forming industrial zones and transformed into cheap labour for the 1920s factory owners. I did not tell him the *long story* of the "engines of Greek economic development" (as Greek school history books often call them in an objectifying manner), and I did not tell him about the persecution and criminalization they suffered as leftists, trade-unionists, and political dissidents in later years. *I cut the long story short*, placed half a century into a mental parenthesis, and opted for affirmation: "*Yes, they made it*", I replied. "*Most of them made it just fine.*" Ahmed downloaded some of the old photos into his mobile. He also took some photos of the tall blocks of flats and placed them in the same folder. "*I will keep this*", he said. "*Every time I feel discouraged I will turn into those photos to remind me of things that can be actually done.*"

Through his serendipitous meeting with George and Stasa, Ahmed (and other refugees in the makeshift camp) became an active part of an archaeological project of building webs of affirmative practices. Through sensorial engagement with the material surroundings, and through building important – however fleeting – affective ties of solidarity, they became witnesses and protagonists of a multi-local, multi-temporal, multi-ethnic, history of endurance. The discursive and narrative traces of 'unfixing', 'interrupting', destroying, and desocializing lives were thus transformed into a counter-archive of resilience that offered opportunities for self-affirmation. Piraeus has always been a port of refugees – as Nur pointed out – but refugees somehow managed to overcome the assemblage of life-destructive forces. The descendants of some were embodied "memory boxes" (cf. Pistrick and Bachmeier, this volume) and living proofs of the possible, the feasible, the attainable. In Piraeus, refugeeness often became a timeless space and a status of bonding; an alternative, multi-local, multi-religious, multi-ethnic homeland; a micro-vision of new political possibilities.

> We are fighters. We need to fight for ourselves. Don't sit here and wait for others to do something little for you…

Jamal is giving a speech in the middle of the makeshift camp. He is prompting fellow refugees to resist the conditions that construct them as passive victims and recipients of humanitarian care. Many listen to him carefully. Others nod affirmatively. This is almost a daily discussion. Sometimes it is more heated, sometimes statements are phrased in an "as-a-matter-of-fact" way. It always starts at lunch time, when everyone has to queue to have their papers stamped in order to get their ration of food. The food is usually the same: potatoes, rice, or pasta. Now and then there is meat, but meat gets usually thrown away out of fear it might be pork, or pork-contaminated. "*See? Queuing, just as if we were animals waiting to be fed*", Razan exclaims and continues:

> *Are we here in order to be fed? Of course not! But this is what they do. They make you queue for food in order to forget the real aim of the journey. Queuing three times a day gives everyone something to do and keeps them from thinking too much. And then, there is of course the money. Each stamp is money. This is how the catering company gets paid. I've heard somewhere that the catering company gets ten Euros per refugee a day. Why don't they give me ten Euros a day? I would eat like a king with ten Euros per day. But I suppose everyone is determined to earn something on the back of the refugees.*

Refugee camps are certainly assemblages of human and non-human entities, material and immaterial structures, which coagulate to compose states of exception, exclusion, desocialization, and institutionalization (Agamben 1998; Butler and al-Nammari, this volume). Frequently theorized through Augé's (1995) concept of non-places, camps are seen as spatial and bureaucratic technologies of "unfixing" human socialities (cf. Agier 2011). Tracing the history of camps in colonial times and subsequently in the Nazi regime (Malkki 1995; Netz 2004; Minca 2015), scholars, inspired by Agamben (1998), note that camps are "topologies of power", spaces of exception and spatial, biopolitical technologies of sovereign exclusion (Millner 2011; Minca 2015). Camps are spaces where the forcibly displaced are transformed and translated from risky and unknowable matter out of place, into knowable and governable subjects (cf. Malkki 1995; Foucault 2004; Ticktin 2011; Vaughan-Williams 2015, Tazzioli 2013).

As Agier (2011) discusses, however (cf. De Genova 2011; Butler and al-Nammari this volume), camps can also be contexts of resistance and refusal. The makeshift camp at Piraeus was a markedly political space. Refugees organized themselves and engaged in different forms of political struggle: they marched, refused to be relocated to remote camps around Greece, demanded that they remain visible, and even attempted to occupy Syntagma Square (the most central and evocative Athenian square, opposite the Greek Parliament). Most importantly, Piraeus was a space for politicization. Refugees discussed among themselves, reflected on their rights, and encouraged each other to resist. They organized rudimentary but solid committees that remained decidedly "mixed", composed of Syrians (who were prioritized in the asylum process) as well as Afghans, Kurds, and other nationalities who were regarded as largely deportable. Those committees attempted to articulate demands and to negotiate with the authorities on behalf of all the displaced, thus throwing into disarray – even temporarily – the hierarchies of eligibility imposed by the state and the EU. Some refugees, like Ali, even managed to get connected to local, Greek political parties and to push the refugee agenda through in more official fora.

My observations here – a bitesize of what the complex and rich context of Piraeus was about – are not meant to deny or downplay the cruelty of the humanitarian model. Piraeus was saturated with an ethic and an aesthetic of eligibility (cf. Cabot 2013), with hierarchies of deservingness and cruel bureaucracies enacted through persons and things (cf. Cabot 2012; Schofield, this volume). It was indeed an outgrowth of neoliberalism where rights were being displaced even faster than persons (cf. Soto, this volume). Witnessing, recording, and making others "feel" the violence of camps (cf. Gomes Coelho, this volume) is certainly an important counter-archiving endeavour (cf. Stewart *et.al.*, this volume). At the same time, however, it is also important to record all those bigger and smaller acts of resistance. This kind of counter-archive of the *minutiae of disobedience* is an essential exercise in nomadic ethics.

Analysing camps as political spaces and as spaces of politicization is not about redemption, or the romantization of some revolutionary aesthetic. It is about the conscious efforts of refugees to resist their reduction to bare life, to exist as social actors and to challenge hierarchies. These efforts were at times (proportionally) grand acts, like the short-lived attempt to occupy Syntagma Square. At other times, they were discursive manifestos of political aetiology (cf. Kirtsoglou 2006) that questioned the role of the "authorities" and the transparency of reception system processes. Yet, occasionally, they were sensorial events: impromptu dinners cooked at the side of the camp, the salad carefully served on plastic plates, instances of commensality that turned the displaced "guests" into powerful hosts. Hands that constantly invited the anthropologist to join the company of refugees inside their allocated spaces in the large UNHCR tents opened up worlds of possibilities. Carefully folded blankets and sleeping bags were transformed into low sofas; coffee boiled on small camping-gas gadgets filling the space with its distinct aroma; small plastic bottles were carefully cut and half filled with water to make perfect ashtrays. Oranges, seeds, or candy brought as gifts from visitors and served as treats from the hosts completed the atmosphere of the visit. Those visits, organized and carried out primarily – but not exclusively – by the refugee women in the camp were healing, affirmative instances of sociality, almost always seasoned with funny stories. Like that story of the middle-aged lady who had to queue for half an hour in one of the few toilets provided in Piraeus while a few young girls in front of her took their time making themselves up. "*Hurry on with that make-up you fools! I can't hold it forever!*", Rima recounted the incident laughingly to the amusement of everyone present:

> *We laugh, but there is always this time of day when pain hits you like a hot bullet alongside the realization that you are a refugee, that the chances of seeing your mother ever again are slim, alongside the knowledge that your family is dispersed all over the globe. A refugee… it feels like being a feather in a storm; going where the wind takes you, full of sorrow for the past and hope for the future, eager to make friends – they feel like family – at every step of the way.*

Ahmad, Jamal, Nariman, Rima, Abdulrahman, Amira, and the other refugees I spoke to in Piraeus kept promising me and each other "proper dinners" in "real homes" when "all this is over". Till then, however, they persistently refused to become saturated with destruction. The refugees in Piraeus endured. They resisted, fought, and remained disobedient. They mocked the forces that attempted to unmake their lives, to reduce their subjectivities, to transform them into bare bodies. The refugees in Piraeus kept their memories and their hopes carefully, at all times. They kept them in plastic, waterproof cases alongside their unusable passports and their registration papers. They kept them in their belts, inside pouches of mixed spices:"*Food tastes so awful here! Thank God for the spices I brought from home. I have them on me in the entire journey; right here. Can you believe it?*" Hopes and memories were kept in the intricate ways in which scarves were folded around heads, and in nearly everyone's wonderfully stubborn resistance to become unfixed by the state, or to remain fixed behind borders.

The Nomadic Age – so profoundly marked by violence, interruption, pain, and loss – is primarily the age of the nomadic ethics of migrants and refugees, and of the affirmative politics of social life that persists despite all odds.

References

Agamben, G. 1998. *Homo Sacer: Sovereign Power and Bare Life*. Stanford, CA: Stanford University Press.

Agier, M. 2011. *Managing the Undesirables: Refugee Camps and Humanitarian Government*. Cambridge: Polity.

Anderson, Benedict. 1983. *Imagined Communities: Reflections on the Origin and Spread of Nationalism*. London: Verso.

Anderson, Bridget. 2012. "Where's the Harm in That? Immigration, Enforcement, Trafficking and the Protection of Migrants' Rights." *American Behavioural Scientist* 56 (9): 1241–1257. https://doi.org/10.1177/0002764212443814

Augé, M. 1995. *Non-Places: An Introduction to an Anthropology of Supermodernity*. London: Verso.

Braidotti, R. 2012. "Nomadic Ethics." In *The Cambridge Companion to Deleuze*, edited by D. W. Smith and H. Somers-Hall, 170–197. Cambridge: Cambridge University Press. https://doi.org/10.1017/CCO9780511753657.009

Cabot, H. 2012 "The Governance of Things: Documenting Limbo in the Greek Asylum Procedure." *Political and Legal Anthropology Review* 35 (1): 11–29. https://doi.org/10.1111/j.1555-2934.2012.01177.x

_____. 2013. "The Social Aesthetics of Eligibility NGO Aid and Indeterminacy in the Greek Asylum Process." *American Ethnologist* 40 (3): 452–466. https://doi.org/10.1111/amet.12032

Comaroff, J. and J. Comaroff. 2001. "Millenial Capitalism: First Thoughts on a Second Coming." In *Millenial Capitalism and the Culture of Neoliberalism,* edited by J. Comaroff and J. Comaroff, 1–56. Durham, NC: Duke University Press. https://doi.org/10.1215/9780822380184-001

Davies, T. and A. Isakjee. 2015. "Geography, Migration and Abandonment in the Calais Refugee Camp." *Political Geography* 49: 93–95. https://doi.org/10.1016/j.polgeo.2015.08.003

De Genova, N. 2010. "The Deportation Regime: Sovereignty, Space, and the Freedom of Movement." In *The Deportation Regime: Sovereignty, Space, and the Freedom of Movement*, edited by N. De Genova and N. Peutz, 33–68. Durham, NC: Duke University Press. https://doi.org/10.1215/9780822391340-002

_____. 2011, "Spectacle of Security, Spectacle of Terror." In *Accumulating Insecurity: Violence and Dispossession in the Making of Everyday Life*, edited by S. Feldman and C. Geisler, 141–165. Athens, GA: University of Georgia Press.

Deleuze, G. 2007 [1984]. "May '68 Did Not Take Place." Translated by H. Weston in G. Deleuze, *Two Regimes of Madness: Texts and Interviews 1975-1995*, 233–236. Los Angeles: Semiotext(e).

Fassin, D. 2011. *Humanitarian Reason: A Moral History of the Present*. Translated by R. Gomme. Berkeley: University of California Press. https://doi.org/10.1525/california/9780520271166.001.0001

Foucault, M. 1980. *Power/Knowledge: Selected Interviews and Other Writings 1972-1977*. Edited by C. Gordon. Brighton: Harvester.

_____. 1989 [1978]. "Sécurité, territoire, et populations." In M. Foucault, *Résumé des Cours, 1970–1982*, 99–106. Paris: Julliard.

_____. 2004. *Society Must Be Defended: Lectures at the College de France 1975-6*. Translated by D. Macey. London: Penguin.

Green, S. 2013. "Borders and the Relocation of Europe." *Annual Review of Anthropology* 42: 345–361. https://doi.org/10.1146/annurev-anthro-092412-155457

Gupta, A. 2012. *Red Tape: Bureaucracy, Structural Violence, and Poverty in India*. Durham, NC: Duke University Press. https://doi.org/10.1215/9780822394709

Hirschon, R., ed. 2003. *Crossing the Aegean: An Appraisal of the 1923 Compulsory Population Exchange between Greece and Turkey*. Oxford: Berghahn. https://doi.org/10.2307/j.ctt1x76f3x

Hull, M. S. 2012. *Government of Paper: The Materiality of Bureaucracy in Urban Pakistan*. Berkeley, CA: University of California Press. https://doi.org/10.1525/california/9780520272149.001.0001

Kirtsoglou, E. 2006. "Unspeakable Crimes: Athenian Greek Perceptions of Local and International Terrorism." In *Terror and Violence: Imagination and the Unimaginable*, edited by A. Strathern, P. Stewart, and N. Whitehead, 61–88. London: Pluto.

_____. and G. Tsimouris. 2016. "'Il était un petit navire': The Refugee Crisis, Neo-Orientalism, and the Production of Radical Alterity." *Journal of Modern Greek Studies*. Occasional Paper 9. Available online: https://www.press.jhu.edu/occasional-paper-9

_____. 2018. "Migration, Crisis, Liberalism: The Cultural and Racial Politics of Islamophobia and 'Radical Alterity' in Modern Greece." *Ethnic and Racial Studies* 41 (10): 1874–1892. https://doi.org/10.1080/01419870.2018.1400681

Malkki L. 1992. "National Geographic: The Rooting of Peoples and the Territorialization of National Identity among Scholars and Refugees." *Cultural Anthropology* 7 (1): 24–44. https://doi.org/10.1525/can.1992.7.1.02a00030

_____. 1995. "Refugees and Exile: From 'Refugee Studies' to the National Order of Things." *Annual Review of Anthropology* 24: 495–523. https://doi.org/10.1146/annurev.an.24.100195.002431

Millner, N. 2011. "From 'Refugee' to 'Migrant' in Calais Solidarity Activism: Re-Staging Undocumented Migration for a Future Politics of Asylum." *Political Geography* 30 (6): 320–328. https://doi.org/10.1016/j.polgeo.2011.07.005

Minca, C. 2015. "Geographies of the Camp." *Political Geography* 49: 74–83. https://doi.org/10.1016/j.polgeo.2014.12.005

Muehlebach, A. 2016. "Camp in the City." *Hot Spots. Cultural Anthropology* website, 28 June. Available online: https://culanth.org/fieldsights/907-camp-in-the-city

Netz, R. 2004. *Barbed Wire: An Ecology of Modernity*. Middletown, CT: Wesleyan University Press.

Rapport, N. 2012. *Anyone: The Cosmopolitan Subject of Anthropology*. Oxford: Berghahn.

Reuveny, R. 2008. "Ecomigration and Violent Conflict: Case Studies and Public Policy Implications." *Human Ecology* 36 (1): 1–13. https://doi.org/10.1007/s10745-007-9142-5

_____. and A. P. Allen. 2007. "On Environmental Refugees and Implications for the Future." *Ecologia Politica* 33: 21–36.

Sassen, S. 2005. "When National Territory is Home to the Global: Old Borders to Novel Borderings." *New Political Economy* 10 (4): 523–541. https://doi.org/10.1080/13563460500344476

_____. 2014. *Expulsions: Brutality and Complexity in the Global Economy*. Cambridge, MA: Belknap Press. https://doi.org/10.4159/9780674369818

Silverstein, P. A. 2005. "Immigrant Racialization and the New Savage Slot: Race, Migration and Immigration in the New Europe." *Annual Review of Anthropology* 34: 363–384. https://doi.org/10.1146/annurev.anthro.34.081804.120338

Tazzioli, M. 2015. "Which Europe? Migrants' Uneven Geographies and Counter-Mapping at the Limits of Representation." *Movements: Journal für kritische Migrations- und Grenzregime-forschung* 1 (2): 1–20.

Ticktin, M. 2011. *Casualties of Care: Immigration and the Politics of Humanitarianism in France.* Berkeley: University of California Press. https://doi.org/10.1525/california/9780520269040.001.0001

Vaughan-Williams, N. 2015. "'We are *not* Animals!' Humanitarian Border Security and Zoopolitical Spaces in Europe." *Political Geography* 45: 1–10. https://doi.org/10.1016/j.polgeo.2014.09.009

Walters, W. 2002. "Deportation, Expulsion and the International Policing of Aliens." *Citizenship Studies* 6 (3): 265–292. https://doi.org/10.1080/1362102022000011612

Elisabeth Kirtsoglou is an Associate Professor in the Department of Anthropology at Durham University. Address for correspondence: Department of Anthropology, Durham University, South Rd, Durham, DH1 3LE, UK. Email: elisabeth.kirtsoglou@durham.ac.uk

Chapter 19

Commentary: Whither the History of Forced and Undocumented Migration? Notes for Genealogical and Comparative Approaches

Parker VanValkenburgh

Part One

In the essay that launched the *Journal of Contemporary Archaeology*, the journal's editors highlighted archaeology's ability to shed light not only on "the spectacular, violent, shocking extremes of the twentieth and twenty-first centuries" but also on the textures of ordinary life (*Journal of Contemporary Archaeology* 2014, 4). The authors of this collection of essays, which first appeared in the pages of *JCA*, manage to do both at once, training archaeological vision on the ordinary dimensions of migrants' experiences, while critiquing the production of migration as spectacle in popular discourse. Through their attention to ignored, forgotten, and deliberately concealed aspects of migrants' lives, they render visible both ordinary forms of suffering and the means by which people claim dignity and justice. Moreover, by documenting cases that span the globe, they reveal just how ordinary the conditions of forced and undocumented migration have become.

As an archaeologist whose work has focused primarily on the early modern period, I am struck by how many of the sensibilities described in these contemporary case studies resonate with ordinary elements of migration and resettlement in the sixteenth- and seventeenth-century Atlantic World – both specific tropes and signs of exclusion, such as the comparison of mobile peoples to animals and the gridded plans of camps, and also general trends, such as migrants' attempts to strategically mobilize the terms of their own marginalization in their struggles to control their futures. These historical traces, and the similarities we see in these case studies between migrant experiences in different world regions, frame an essential question for the archaeology of migration: what historical forces have made these lived experiences, and the forms of mobility and citizenship associated with them, so widespread? Or, to borrow a turn of phrase from Denis Byrne's contribution to this volume, what is it that *anchors* them in the ordinary, and how might archaeologists contribute to their study? These questions point us beyond the scope of these essays – not just to additional research sites and themes, but also towards a historically oriented archaeology of what Schiller and Salazar (2013) call "regimes of mobility" – the ways in which forms and experiences of movement are normalized, adjudicated, and enforced. In this brief commentary, I'd like to consider how this approach might complement the archaeology of contemporary migration, why it might be worth pursuing, and what it might look like.

Part Two

Anthropological archaeologists have produced a rich literature on migration and mobility, from classic studies focusing on economic and residential mobility among foragers and pastoralists (e.g. Kelly 1983; Chang and Koster 1986), to recent contributions that have explored the potential of archaeological science to trace mobile life histories (e.g. Price *et al.* 2002; Bentley 2006) and conceptual contributions that have compared experiences of movement in the ancient, early modern, and modern worlds (Burmeister 2000; Ur 2009; Beaudry and Parno 2013; Leary 2014; Lelievre and Marshall 2015). This body of scholarship has made it clear that, even if the number of migrants may be greater today than it has ever been, "mobile subjects are not a product of our globalized, neoliberal, post-Fordist world" (Lelievre and Marshall 2015, 435). Both large-scale population displacement and the marginalization of mobile subjects are trends that have histories as old as that of empire (e.g., Charanis 1961; Oded 1979; Chang 2007). The past also provides us with examples of radically different regimes of mobility – from cases in which motion and speed are associated with the moral and the just (Munn 1986), to complex polities built and maintained by mobile state agents (Honeychurch and Amertuvshin 2008), communities that sustain themselves through long-distance non-market exchanges among geographically dispersed kin groups (Murra 1972), and mobile groups that maintain rights to self-determination by fleeing attempts to appropriate their labor power (Scott 2009; Angelbeck and Grier 2012).

Yet to date, neither archaeologists nor historical anthropologists have articulated a coherent project for the historical and comparative study of migration before the modern era. As a result, it is perhaps unsurprising that scholarship on contemporary migration has tended to use the premodern as a foil for arguments about its present conditions. Anthropological surveys of forced and undocumented migration have generally treated displacement as an acute condition of modernity, identifying its origins with one or another threshold – such as the emergence of the capitalist world-system, the vesture of sovereign power in territorial nation-states, and/or the formalization of travel documents in the early twentieth century (Colson 2003).

The studies in this collection also generally avoid questions of sequence and causality – an emphasis that aligns with contemporary archaeology's critique of linear historicism and the broader skepticism among post-Medieval and Americanist historical archaeologists of predictive modeling and the search for origins (Latour 1993; Buchli and Lucas 2002; Thomas 2004; González-Ruibal 2008, 2013; Harrison and Schofield 2010; Graves-Brown *et al.* 2013). Where historical interpretation does enter the discussion in these articles, it is primarily in the authors' critiques of how heritage practices alienate migrants – for example, Riggs and Rehman's assessment of how "out-of-place" religious architecture on either side of the India–Pakistan border has been dislocated from the present to the "time of heritage", purifying ethno-national spaces and severing ties between monuments and descendant communities.

The lack of more extensive historical inquiry among these articles is appropriate for contemporary case studies, but I also read it as being somewhat indicative of the widening gap between contemporary and historical archaeologies. Harrison and Breithoff (2017; see also Harrison 2016) draw attention to this breach, which they attribute to to differences in methodologies and source materials – particularly, the fact that historical archaeologists emphasize the integration of multiple lines of evidence (material, visual, and historical sources) while archaeologists of the contemporary focus (strategically) on the material. At a deeper level, however, the divergence of these subfields may also be shaped by their distinct historicities. Archaeologists of the contemporary draw on Deleuzian and Benjaminian perspectives that emphasize the multitemporality of experience and perception (Lucas 2005; Witmore 2007; Dawdy 2010, 2016b; Olivier 2011) – and their historical work generally assumes the form of the map or the archive, rather than the genealogy. In contrast, Americanist historical archaeologists frequently adopt Marxian and Foucaultian orientations that attend to the sequences and pathways through which power relations emerge (e.g., Leone and Potter 1999; Thomas 2004; Croucher and Weiss 2011; Matthews 2012; Wurst and Mrozowski 2014; Leone and Knauf 2015).

Working through the antinomies between these distinct perspectives may be among the most dynamic (and challenging) domains of archaeological theory during the next decade, and two of the chapters in this volume point the way towards new modes of collaboration. In his reflections on migrant experiences in the Greek countryside, Kourelis (p. 116) calls for a "diachronic and transnational archaeology that situates the most recent migration in a long comparative perspective [... which] would embrace the documentation, survey, and excavation of nineteenth- and twentieth-century sites, while also devising methodological strategies for the more difficult sites that are constructed, lived in, and abandoned in real time". Similarly, in his discussion of heritage practices in contemporary Australia, Byrne (p. 181) calls for work that might "suture heritage objects [...] to their companion objects in the contemporary border zone and thus to the comparative context of contemporary asylum seeking".

Both Byrne and Kourelis envision historical work that would focus primarily on recent eras, on the study of migration in the nineteenth, twentieth, and twenty-first centuries. But their comments also suggest the potential of a more expansive project – one that would bridge migrant presents and pasts not by collapsing the historical into the contemporary but by attending to the affective sequences and citational chains through which these connections are forged. Following the critical tradition of Americanist historical archaeology (Leone *et al.* 1987), this historically oriented archaeology of migration would recognize that the past is forged in the present, while strategically employing the historical sequence as a tool for examining the underpinnings of contemporary regimes of mobility– an approach that Wurst and Mrozowski (2014) call "doing history backwards".

Part Three

In order to make a substantial contribution to the critical study of migration and mobility, the historical archaeology of forced and undocumented migration must be more than an encyclopedic exercise that pursues case studies for the sake of documenting the diversity of migrant experiences. We must set out to provincialize modern regimes of mobility and to recuperate visions of alternative futures that have been lost or silenced. But what specific scales, objects, and questions should we focus on?

One approach has already been suggested by Kourelis – to study particular zones of transition and examine their successive reconfiguration under distinct regimes of mobility, attending to the ways in which the traces of earlier regimes are incorporated into emerging political assemblages. Archaeology's methodological strengths are particularly suited to place-based research and the study of material transitions. Kourelis identifies Greece as a region in which it might be particularly fruitful to pursue such diachronic studies, due to its history as a salient link in terrestrial and maritime migration routes between Europe and Asia. Material histories of migration might also be fruitfully pursued in other highly regulated spaces of transition and movement, such as the Mexico–US border (Stewart *et al.*, this volume), the Inner Asian Mountain Corridor (Frachetti 2012), and the Caucasus (Lelievre and Marshall 2015; Smith 2015). While primarily ethnographic, Ben-Yehoyada's (2016, 2017) work on the history of migration and region-formation between Tunisia, Malta, Sicily, and the Italian peninsula provides additional inspiration.

The historically oriented archaeology of migration also need not be limited to the study of conceptually prominent borderlands and corridors. Lelievre's (2017) important work on colonial Nova Scotia examines how forms of mobility that were engendered in colonial relations between Mik'maw communities, Catholic priests, and colonial officials became mediators between political subjects and institutions and ultimately produced locally specific forms of sovereignty. Morrison's (2010) attention to how a particular material form – the dam – has been continually entailed in processes of displacement in southern India over the last thousand years provides a potent critique of the romantic notion that sustainable development might be achieved through a return to "traditional" pre-modern irrigation practices.

Beyond place-based studies, the historical study of migration might also examine the development of specific political formations and technologies, contributing to the broader archaeology of sovereignty (Smith 2011). Following Agamben (1998), this project might focus on understanding where, when, and through what affective means bare life (*zoe*) has become the object of sovereign power – a metaphorical and literal archaeology of the Camp, which is in part already outlined in this volume by Caraher *et al.* Other figures and tropes that emerge in the studies presented here might also be examined genealogically. Gomes Coelho identifies the Garden as an ambiguous figure that has been woven into the modern alongside (and occasionally within) the Camp – both a space in which regimes demonstrate mastery over nature and human subjects, and a space of resistance in contexts such as the plantation and the modern refugee camp. Perhaps most prominently, work on the materiality of borders (in this volume, Stewart *et al.*; Seitsonen *et al.*) points the way to a new historical archaeology of border crossing – focused less on questions of political strategy and social identity highlighted in earlier literature on borderlands (e.g. Lightfoot and Martinez 1995; Parker and Rodseth 2005) than on using border practices to better understand transformations in sovereign power.

Part Four

A final consideration for the historically oriented archaeology of forced and undocumented migration is raised by this volume's rich discussion of methodology, visualization, and presentation: where and how should this work be presented to generate the greatest impact? Innovative approaches to collaboration and publication lie at the heart of the archaeology of contemporary, but the discussion is particularly rich among this collection of articles. The contributors extend their concern for affect beyond their conceptualization of their objects of study to the relationship between reader and text, suggesting that archaeological scholarship on migration must be judged ultimately by work that it does outside academic journals. Many of the authors draw not only on ethnographic research, but also photography, visual ethnography, and art, reflecting the growth of collaboration between contemporary archaeologists and artists, including migrants themselves (in this volume, Butler and al Nammari; Arbelaez Arbelaez and Mullholland). Historically oriented work on forced and undocumented migration could be productively included in these collaborations and presented in school curricula, museum exhibits, theater performances, and demonstrations, producing dialectical images that help students and audiences question the "familiar, unchallenged, unconsidered modes of thought" that animate current migration policies and practices (Foucault 1988 [1981], 154; Dawdy 2016a, 2016b).

Many strong papers in this collection also demonstrate that there is still space for the methods of data collection, analysis, and visualization that have long been staples of archaeological practice. Orthographic imagery and spatial analysis can help us to understand migration patterns that are difficult to visualize through the camera lens and the ethnographic vignette (in this volume, Tyrikos-Ergas; Kourelis; Stewart *et al.*). Systematic pedestrian survey and revisiting sites in successive years can help us map how migrant materials and landscapes respond to changes in immigration regimes (in this volume, Soto; Stewart *et al.*).

Through these means, the historical archaeology of forced and undocumented migration that I envision would seek to serve fundamentally the same ends as the chapters in this volume – to understand conditions and conceptions of migration, mapping out the forces that sustain them, and to move public energies away from merely offering sympathy to migrants to efforts to deliver them justice.

References

Agamben, G. 1998. *Homo Sacer: Sovereign Power and Bare Life*. Translated by D. Heller-Roazen. Stanford, CA: Stanford University Press.

Angelbeck, B. and C. Grier. 2012. "Anarchism and the Archaeology of Anarchic Societies: Resistance to Centralization in the Coast Salish Region of the Pacific Northwest Coast. *Current Anthropology* 53 (5): 547–587. https://doi.org/10.1086/667621

Beaudry, M. C. and T. G. Parno, eds. 2013. *Archaeologies of Mobility and Movement*. New York: Springer. https://doi.org/10.1007/978-1-4614-6211-8

Bentley, R. A. 2006. "Strontium Isotopes from the Earth to the Archaeological Skeleton: A Review." *Journal of Archaeological Method and Theory* 13 (3): 135–187. https://doi.org/10.1007/s10816-006-9009-x

Ben-Yehoyada, N. 2016. "'Follow Me, and I Will Make You Fishers of Men': The Moral and Political Scales of Migration in the Central Mediterranean." *Journal of the Royal Anthropological Institute* 22 (1): 183–202. https://doi.org/10.1111/1467-9655.12340

_____. 2017. *The Mediterranean Incarnate: Region Formation Between Sicily and Tunisia Since World War II*. Chicago: University of Chicago Press. https://doi.org/10.7208/chicago/9780226451169.001.0001

Buchli, V. and G. Lucas, eds. 2002. *Archaeologies of the Contemporary Past*. London and New York: Routledge.

Burmeister, S. 2000. "Archaeology and Migration: Approaches to an Archaeological Proof of Migration." *Current Anthropology* 41 (4): 539–567. https://doi.org/10.1086/317383

Chang, C. and H. A. Koster. 1986. "Beyond Bones: Toward an Archaeology of Pastoralism." In *Advances in Archaeological Method and Theory, Volume 9*, edited by M. Schiffer, 97–148. New York: Academic Press. https://doi.org/10.1016/B978-0-12-003109-2.50006-4

Chang, C.-S. 2007. *The Rise of the Chinese Empire: Nation, State, & Imperialism in early China, ca. 1600 BC-AD 8*. Vol. 1. Ann Arbor: University of Michigan Press.

Charanis, P. 1961. "The Transfer of Population as a Policy in the Byzantine Empire." *Comparative Studies in Society and History* 3 (2): 140–154. https://doi.org/10.1017/S0010417500012093

Colson, E. 2003. "Forced Migration and the Anthropological Response." *Journal of Refugee Studies* 16 (1): 1–18. https://doi.org/10.1093/jrs/16.1.1

Croucher, S. K. and L. Weiss, eds. 2011. *The Archaeology of Capitalism in Colonial Contexts: Postcolonial Historical Archaeologies*. New York: Springer. https://doi.org/10.1007/978-1-4614-0192-6

Dawdy, S. L. 2010. "Clockpunk Anthropology and the Ruins of Modernity." *Current Anthropology* 51 (6): 761–793. https://doi.org/10.1086/657626

_____. 2016a. *Patina: A Profane Archaeology*. Chicago: University of Chicago Press. https://doi.org/10.7208/chicago/9780226351223.001.0001

_____. 2016b. "Profane Archaeology and the Existential Dialectics of the City." *Journal of Social Archaeology* 16 (1): 32–55. https://doi.org/10.1177/1469605315615054

Foucault, M. 1988 [1981]. "Practicing Criticism." Interview with D. Eribon, translated by A. Sheridan in *Politics, Philosophy, Culture: Interviews and Other Writings 1977-1984*, 154–155. London and New York: Routledge.

Frachetti, M. D. 2012. "Multiregional Emergence of Mobile Pastoralism and Nonuniform Institutional Complexity across Eurasia." *Current Anthropology* 53 (1): 2–38. https://doi.org/10.1086/663692

González-Ruibal, A. 2008. "Time to Destroy: An Archaeology of Supermodernity." *Current Anthropology* 49 (2): 247–279. https://doi.org/10.1086/526099

_____., ed. 2013. *Reclaiming Archaeology: Beyond the Tropes of Modernity*. London and New York: Routledge. https://doi.org/10.4324/9780203068632.ch1

Graves-Brown, P., R. Harrison, and A. Piccini, eds. 2013. *The Oxford Handbook of the Archaeology of the Contemporary World*. Oxford: Oxford University Press. https://doi.org/10.1093/oxfordhb/9780199602001.001.0001

Harrison, R. 2016. "Archaeologies of Emergent Presents and Futures." *Historical Archaeology* 50 (3): 165–180. https://doi.org/10.1007/BF03377340

_____. and E. Breithoff. 2017. "Archaeologies of the Contemporary World." *Annual Review of Anthropology* 46: 203–221. https://doi.org/10.1146/annurev-anthro-102116-041401

_____. and J. Schofield. 2010. *After Modernity: Archaeological Approaches to the Contemporary Past*. Oxford: Oxford University Press.

Honeychurch, W. and C. Amartuvshin. 2008. "States on Horseback: The Rise of Inner Asian

Confederations and Empires. In *The Archaeology of Asia*, edited by M. T. Stark, 255–278. Malden, MA: Blackwell.

Journal of Contemporary Archaeology 2014. "Editorial." *Journal of Contemporary Archaeology* 1 (1): 1–6. https://doi.org/10.1558/jca.v1i1.1

Kelly, R. L. 1983. "Hunter-Gatherer Mobility Strategies." *Journal of Anthropological Research* 39 (3): 277-306. https://doi.org/10.1086/jar.39.3.3629672

Latour, B. 1993. *We Have Never Been Modern*. Translated by C. Porter. Cambridge, MA: Harvard University Press.

Leary, J. 2014. *Past Mobilities: Archaeological Approaches to Movement and Mobility*. London and New York: Routledge.

Lelièvre, M. 2017. *Unsettling Mobility: Mediating Mi'kmaw Sovereignty in Post-Contact Nova Scotia*. Tucson: University of Arizona Press.

_____. and M. E. Marshall. 2015. "'Because Life It Selfe Is but Motion': Toward an Anthropology of Mobility." *Anthropological Theory* 15 (4): 434–471. https://doi.org/10.1177/1463499615605221

Leone, M. P. and J. E. Knauf, eds. 2015. *Historical Archaeologies of Capitalism*. New York: Springer. https://doi.org/10.1007/978-3-319-12760-6

Leone, M.P. and P. B. Potter, eds. 1999. *Historical Archaeologies of Capitalism*. New York: Springer. https://doi.org/10.1007/978-1-4615-4767-9

_____., and P. A. Shackel. 1987. "Toward a Critical Archaeology." *Current Anthropology* 28 (3): 283–302. https://doi.org/10.1086/203531

Lightfoot, K.G. and A. Martinez. 1995. "Frontiers and Boundaries in Archaeological Perspective." *Annual Review of Anthropology*: 24: 471–492.

Lucas, G. 2005. *The Archaeology of Time*. London and New York: Routledge.

Matthews, C. N. 2012. *The Archaeology of American Capitalism*. Gainesville: University Press of Florida.

Morrison, K. D. 2010. "Dharmic Projects, Imperial Reservoirs, and New Temples of India: An Historical Perspective on Dams in India." *Conservation and Society* 8 (3): 182–195. https://doi.org/10.4103/0972-4923.73807

Munn, N. 1986. *The Fame of Gawa: A Symbolic Study of Value Transformation in a Massim (Papua New Guinea) Society*. Cambridge: Cambridge University Press.

Murra, J. V. 1972. "El 'Control Vertical' de un Máximo de Pisos Ecológicos en la Economía de las Sociedades Andinas." In *Visita de la Provincia de León de Huánuco en 1562*, edited by I. Ortiz, 429–476. Huánuco, Peru: Universidad Nacional Hermilio Valdizán.

Oded, B. 1979. *Mass Deportations and Deportees in the Neo-Assyrian Empire*. Wiesbaden: Verlag.

Olivier, L. 2011. *The Dark Abyss of Time: Archaeology and Memory*. Lanham, MD: AltaMira.

Parker, B. J. and L. Rodseth, eds. 2005. *Untaming the Frontier in Anthropology, Archaeology, and History*. Tucson: University of Arizona Press.

Price, T. D., J. H. Burton, and R. A. Bentley. 2002. "The Characterization of Biologically Available Strontium Isotope Ratios for the Study of Prehistoric Migration." *Archaeometry* 44 (1): 117–135. https://doi.org/10.1111/1475-4754.00047

Schiller, N. G. and N. B. Salazar. 2013. "Regimes of Mobility Across the Globe." *Journal of Ethnic and Migration Studies* 39 (2): 183-200. https://doi.org/10.1080/1369183X.2013.723253

Scott, J. C. 2009. *The Art of Not Being Governed : An Anarchist History of Upland Southeast Asia*. New Haven, CT: Yale University Press.

Smith, A. T. 2011. "Archaeologies of Sovereignty." *Annual Review of Anthropology* 40: 415–432. https://doi.org/10.1146/annurev-anthro-081309-145754

_____. 2015. *The Political Machine: Assembling Sovereignty in the Bronze Age Caucasus*. Princeton, NJ: Princeton University Press.

Thomas, J. 2004. *Archaeology and Modernity*. London and New York: Routledge.

Ur, J. A. 2009. "Emergent Landscapes of Movement in Early Bronze Age Northern Mesopotamia." In *Landscapes of Movement: Paths, Trails, and Roads in Anthropological Perspective*, edited by J. E. Snead, C. E. Erickson, and J. A. Darling, 180–203. Philadelphia: University of Pennsylvania Press.

Witmore, C. L. 2007. "Landscape, Time, Topology: An Archaeological Account of the Southern Argolid, Greece." In *Envisioning Landscape: Situations and Standpoints in Archaeology and Heritage*, edited by D. Hicks, L. McAtackney, and G. F. Fairclough, 226–250. Walnut Creek, CA: Left Coast Press.

Wurst, L. A. and S. A. Mrozowski. 2014. "Toward an Archaeology of the Future." *International Journal of Historical Archaeology* 18 (2): 210–223. https://doi.org/10.1007/s10761-014-0253-6

Parker VanValkenburgh is Assistant Professor of Anthropology at Brown University in Providence, USA and director of the Proyecto Arqueológico Zaña Colonial and the Proyecto Paisajes Arqueológicos de Chachapoyas, both based in Peru. Address for correspondence: Department of Anthropology, Brown University, 128 Hope Street, Box 1921, Providence, RI 02912, USA. Email: parker_vanvalkenburgh@brown.edu

Index

Prepared by Jody Ineson

CPSIA information can be obtained
at www.ICGtesting.com
Printed in the USA
LVHW072006211222
735703LV00007B/148

9 781781 797112